T0070202

THE SPEEDICUT PAPERS
Book 9 (1900–1915)

Also by Christopher Joll

Uniquely British: A Year in the Life of the Household Cavalry

The Speedicut Papers Book 1 (1821-1848): Flashman's Secret
The Speedicut Papers Book 2 (1848-1857): Love & Other Blood Sports
The Speedicut Papers Book 3 (1857-1865): Uncivil Wars
The Speedicut Papers Book 4 (1865-1871): Where Eagles Dare
The Speedicut Papers Book 5 (1871-1879): Suffering Bertie
The Speedicut Papers Book 6 (1879-1884): Vitai Lampada
The Speedicut Papers Book 7 (1884-1895): Royal Scandals
The Speedicut Papers Book 8 (1895-1900): At War with Churchill
The Speedicut Papers Book 9 (1900-1915): Boxing Icebergs

THE SPEEDICUT PAPERS
The Memoirs of Jasper Speedicut
Book 9 (1900–1915)
Boxing Icebergs

Christopher Joll

authorHOUSE®

AuthorHouse™ UK
1663 Liberty Drive
Bloomington, IN 47403 USA
www.authorhouse.co.uk
Phone: 0800.197.4150

© 2017 Christopher Joll. All rights reserved.

No part of this book may be reproduced, stored in a retrieval system, or
transmitted by any means without the written permission of the author.

Published by AuthorHouse 07/25/2017

ISBN: 978-1-5462-8022-4 (sc)
ISBN: 978-1-5462-8023-1 (hc)
ISBN: 978-1-5462-8031-6 (e)

Print information available on the last page.

Any people depicted in stock imagery provided by Thinkstock are models,
and such images are being used for illustrative purposes only.
Certain stock imagery © Thinkstock.

This book is printed on acid-free paper.

Because of the dynamic nature of the Internet, any web addresses or links contained in
this book may have changed since publication and may no longer be valid. The views
expressed in this work are solely those of the author and do not necessarily reflect the views
of the publisher, and the publisher hereby disclaims any responsibility for them.

For

EWC

A great supporter

CONTENTS

NOTES ON THE EDITOR

After serving time at Oxford University and the Royal Military Academy Sandhurst, Christopher Joll spent his formative years as an officer in The Life Guards, an experience from which he has never really recovered.

On leaving the Army, Joll worked first in investment banking, but the boredom of City life led him to switch careers and become an arms salesman. After ten years of dealing with tin pot dictators in faraway countries, he moved - perhaps appropriately - into public relations where, in this new incarnation, he had to deal with dictators of an altogether different type.

From his earliest days, Joll has written articles, features, short stories and reportage. One such piece of writing led to an early brush with notoriety when an article he had penned anonymously in 1974 for a political journal ended up as front page national news and resulted in a Ministerial inquiry. In 2012 Joll wrote the text for *Uniquely British: A Year in the Life of the Household Cavalry*, an illustrated account of the Household Cavalry from the Royal Wedding to the Diamond Jubilee. His yet to be published memoires, *Anecdotal Evidence*, promises to cause considerable consternation in certain quarters should it ever appear in print.

Since leaving the Army in 1975, Joll has been involved in devising and managing charity fund-raising events. This interest started in 1977 with The Silver Jubilee Royal Gifts Exhibition at St James's Palace and The Royal Cartoons Exhibition at the Press Club. In subsequent years, he co-produced 'José Carreras & Friends', a one-night Royal Gala Concert at the Theatre Royal Drury Lane; 'Serenade for a Princess', a Royal Gala Concert at the Banqueting House, Whitehall; and 'Concert for a Prince', a Royal Gala Concert staged at Windsor Castle (the first such event to be held there following the post-fire restoration).

More recently, Joll has focused on devising, writing, directing and sometimes producing events primarily for military charities. These include in various different roles the Household Cavalry Pageant (2007); the Chelsea Pageant (2008); the Diamond Jubilee Parade in the Park (2012); the British Military Tournament (2010-2013); the Gurkha Bicentenary Pageant (2015); the Waterloo Bicentenary National Service of Commemoration & Parade at St Paul's Cathedral (2015); the Shakespeare 400 Memorial Concert (2016); The Patron's Lunch (2016), the official London event to mark The Queen's 90th Birthday and *The Great War Symphony* to be premiered in 2018 at the Royal Albert Hall.

INTRODUCTION

With the first publication of *The Speedicut Papers* in 2013, the reading public was shocked to learn that Brigadier General Sir Harry Flashman VC, one of the greatest heroes of the Victorian age, was nothing more than a Paris-based remittance man and a plagiarising fraud. Almost as shocking was the revelation that, for more than 250 years, there has been a secret organisation at the heart of the British Establishment, called The Brotherhood of the Sons of Thunder, which was ruthlessly interfering in the nation's affairs.

These facts were revealed in a cache of letters written over a lifetime by Colonel Sir Jasper Speedicut, Bart to his friend Harry Flashman, which I discovered in 2010 in the basement of the New Walk Museum in Leicester. Taken together, the letters are a comprehensive record of the life and times of Speedicut: soldier, courtier, bi-sexual and reluctant hero.

In this, the ninth volume of *The Speedicut Papers* and the last written by Jasper Speedicut, the public will once again learn of further previously hidden truths that cast a new light on real historical incidents, set against the major events of the 19th and early 20th centuries.

Although the first seven volumes of *The Speedicut Papers* were originally published in letter format, in response to popular demand I have re-edited the books into a narrative text. As with the previously published work, in the interests of clarity I have also annotated the text with dates and historical or explanatory background material.

CHRISTOPHER JOLL
www.jasperspeedicut.com

PRINCIPAL CHARACTERS IN ORDER OF APPEARANCE

Any similarity to persons now dead is <u>entirely</u> intentional

Jasper Speedicut – an officer and a gentleman, usually known as 'Speed'

Harry Flashman – a remittance man mostly based in Paris, who is a friend of Speedicut and his controller in 'The Brotherhood of the Sons of Thunder', usually known as 'Flashy'

Fahran Khazi – second son of the late Muhamad Khazi and Speedicut's valet

Charles-Ethelred FitzCharles, 8th Duke of Whitehall – brother of Lady Charlotte-Georgina Speedicut and Great Boanerges ('GB') of the Brotherhood of the Sons of Thunder

Colonel Sir Claude MacDonald – British Minister in Peking

Countess Tamara Obolenskya – a Russian aristocrat

The Empress Dowager CiXi – the former Yi Concubine and, since 1861, the *de facto* ruler of China

Lady Charlotte-Georgina Speedicut – Speedicut's second wife, sister of the 8th Duke of Whitehall

Frederick Searcy – Speedicut's semi-retired private secretary, originally a riding instructor in the 2nd Life Guards

Atash Khazi – eldest son of the late Muhamad Khazi and the Speedicuts' coachman-cum-chauffeur

Sibella Holland – the wife of a stockbroker

Ivan Searcy – Speedicut's Russian ex-valet and Frederick Searcy's partner

Robert Ross – a Canadian journalist of independent means

Oscar Wilde – a disgraced playwright and poet, living in Paris

Sir Arthur Bigge – Queen Victoria's Private Secretary

Dr James Reid – Physician-in-Ordinary to Queen Victoria

HM Queen Victoria – the ageing British monarch

HRH The Prince of Wales – Heir Apparent to the British throne, usually known as Bertie

HIM Kaiser Wilhelm II – Emperor of Germany

Prince Phillip zu Eulenberg – a close friend of the Kaiser

Captain Frederick Ponsonby – Assistant Private Secretary to Queen Victoria and later to King Edward VII

Reginald Brett, 2nd Viscount Esher – an unofficial but highly influential courtier and a member of the Brotherhood of the Sons of Thunder

HIM The Empress Frederick – Victoria, Princess Royal of the United Kingdom, widow of Emperor Frederick, eldest daughter of Queen Victoria, elder sister of The Prince of Wales and mother of Kaiser Wilhelm II

Baron Wilhelm von Gloeden – a photographer

Countess Beatrice de Lorraine – a Lady-in-Waiting turned courtesan

Prince Dimitri Lieven – Speedicut's son-in-law

Princess Dorothea Lieven – Speedicut's only daughter

Mrs Rosa Lewis – proprietor of the Cavendish Hotel

Gregory Yefimovich Rasputin – a Siberian peasant and faith healer

Sergei de Diaghilev – a Russian impresario

Second Officer Lightoller – an officer on RMS *Titanic*

Major Ulrich von Stumm – an officer in the Prussian Secret Service

Fraulein Hilda von Einem – a Shanghai 'coaster' turned German spy

Mata Hari – an exotic dancer and double-agent

Nurse Edith Cavell – a British spy

SYNOPSIS OF BOOK 8 (AT WAR WITH CHURCHILL)

Book 8 of *The Speedicut Papers* opens with Speedicut, his wife and personal staff on holiday in the Cape where he is persuaded by Cecil Rhodes, in whose De Beers mining business Speedicut has a substantial investment, to assist in the planning of what becomes known as the Jameson Raid. Although Speedicut refuses to join the Raid itself, he is tricked by Rhodes and finds himself involved by default with the Raiders. This has two unfortunate consequences: Speedicut is captured by the Boers and, in the course of his capture, his loyal coachman, Muhamad Khazi, is killed. Speedicut does not remain long in captivity and is sent back to Cape Town by President Kruger with a copy of the Kaiser's notorious telegram of support for the Boers.

Back in London Speedicut has to break the news of Khazi's death to his long-term secretary and Khazi's close friend, Frederick Searcy. In reaction to the news, Searcy says that he would like to retire and take Speedicut's valet, Ivan, with him to run his eponymous catering business. Speedicut agrees but persuades Searcy to remain in his service part-time whilst promoting Khazi's younger son, Fahran, from second footman into the position of valet.

In the aftermath of the Jameson Raid both the Brotherhood of the Sons of Thunder and the government of Lord Salisbury are worried that Speedicut could be called as a witness in the criminal trial of the Raid's conspirators, thus giving the defence lawyers the opportunity of implicating the British government and the Brotherhood of the Sons of Thunder in the Raid. To avoid being called, Speedicut is sent as an official War Correspondent to the Second Matabele War.

During the conflict in Matabeleland, Speedicut becomes involved with Robert Baden-Powell and the American scout, Frederick Burnham, and is accidentally responsible for the murder of the rebel leader, known as the Umlimo. By September 1896, Speedicut has returned to London but not before he has had a brief ship-board romance with the Countess of Grantham. During Speedicut's absence in Africa, Lady Charlotte-Georgina attends the Coronation of Tsar Nicholas II of Russia, with unfortunate consequences for the new autocrat.

At a dinner party given by the Austro-Hungarian Ambassador for The Prince of Wales during the 1896 London Season, Speedicut finds himself sitting next to the widowed Lady Randolph Churchill with whom he has previously had a brief affair. Lady Churchill is insistent that Speedicut help her son Winston with his ambition to be a journalist. Speedicut demurs with the excuse that young Winston is with his Regiment in India. The Prince of Wales intervenes to say that Speedicut can meet with Winston in India as he understands that he, Speedicut, will shortly be posted there as War Correspondent-in-Chief of the Malakand Field Force - a punitive expedition against the Pathans that is being assembled on the North-West Frontier by Major General Sir Bindon Blood.

However, in the event, Speedicut manages not to be posted to India, following the news that the Dowager Empress of Russia has agreed to stand as a godparent to the Speedicuts' twin grandchildren, because this honour necessitates his presence in St Petersburg for the christening. It also emerges that the Malakand Expedition has been postponed.

Once more back in London, Speedicut is appointed an Extra Equerry to Queen Victoria and is tasked with organising her Diamond Jubilee State Procession through London, with particular responsibility for the Service of Thanksgiving at St Paul's Cathedral. This duty brings him into direct conflict with the Dean who, against the wishes of The Queen's Private Secretary, is determined that the Service will be held in the Cathedral not at the foot of the West Steps. This is a problem which is only solved when Searcy surreptitiously locks the door of The Queen's carriage thus preventing her leaving it at the Cathedral.

Later in the Diamond Jubilee year Speedicut and his wife attend the Duchess of Devonshire's Costume Ball, during which Speedicut has a 'close encounter' with Lady Randolph Churchill who mistakes him for the Commander-in-Chief, Lord Wolseley. When she discovers her error, she swears revenge on Speedicut. A couple of weeks later, at the Duke of Richmond's house party for Goodwood Races, Speedicut learns from Winston Churchill, who is in the house party whilst on leave from India, that the Malakand Field Force is at last about to commence its campaign. Churchill also informs Speedicut that Lord Wolseley – probably at the instigation of Lady Randolph – has ordered him to take on the role of War Correspondent-in-Chief and that Churchill is also joining the expedition as a War Correspondent. Whilst on their way to India, Speedicut receives a telegram from Sir Bindon Blood in which he is instructed to 'stick to Churchill like glue' and is tasked with censoring his journalistic output.

During the Malakand Expedition, Speedicut is cut-off by tribesmen in the Mamund Valley, along with the Brigade Headquarters to which he has had to be temporarily attached in order to keep an eye on Churchill. Thanks to the gallant action of Fahran, who rides for help, the Brigade Commander, his Staff and Speedicut narrowly avoid annihilation although Speedicut takes a wound to the head, which results in a period of recuperation in Simla. Once recovered, Speedicut with Fahran sets off for England but is intercepted in Bombay, as he is about to board a ship headed for home, and is ordered to join the Tirah Expedition.

Whilst waiting for the Tirah Field Force to march against the Afridis, Speedicut is instrumental in 'killing' a potentially embarrassing letter sent by the Chief of Staff of the TFF to the influential *Fortnightly Review*, refuting an anonymous article (possibly written by Churchill) which is critical of the Field Force's commander. Fortunately for Speedicut, the Afridis reach a peace agreement with the government of India before the TFF is committed to action and, at last, he is able to return to London.

Scarcely has he unpacked when, as a direct result of his successful intervention with the *Fortnightly Review*, he is ordered by Lord Salisbury to join Kitchener's Expedition to defeat the Dervish uprising in the newly created role of Head of Expeditionary Force Propaganda. Although Speedicut is no friend of Kitchener, and so does not welcome the posting, he is relieved to find that the Commander-in-Chief has blocked Winston Churchill's application to join the Expedition as a War Correspondent.

En route to Egypt, Speedicut has a brief affair in Brindisi with Mrs Lionel Holland who is a friend of Lady Charlotte-Georgina's estranged nephew, Charles Hadfield. On his arrival with the Expeditionary Force, Kitchener informs Speedicut that he will be attached to the 21st Lancers and so will be in the front line rather than safe with the Staff. However, thanks to Fahran's involvement in a covert operation against the Dervishes, Kitchener revokes this instruction. Safely embedded with the HQ Staff, Speedicut is dismayed when Churchill appears shortly before the Battle of Omdurman, attached to the 21st Lancers, and is further dismayed when Kitchener orders him not to let Churchill out of his sight. This results in Speedicut taking part in the charge of the 21st Lancers, during which he is unhorsed and only saved from death by the intervention of Fahran.

The day after the battle, Speedicut is told that his services are no longer required and he leaves for London via Geneva and Paris. On his arrival in Geneva he finds that the Empress of Austria, whom he has met and served on several occasions in the past, is staying in the same hotel. She invites him to join her on an outing to Montreux. Consequently, Speedicut is present when the Empress is stabbed by an Italian anarchist. Because of Speedicut's insistence that the Empress's corset is loosened, she dies of an internal haemorrhage and Speedicut is arrested for her murder. Fortunately, the actual assassin confesses to the crime and Speedicut is released. Before he can continue his journey to London, however, Speedicut is Commanded by Emperor Franz-Josef to return with the late Empress's body to Vienna and to take personal charge of her jewels *en route*.

Once in Vienna, and prior to the State funeral, Speedicut takes a room in the Hotel Sacher where he picks up a high-class prostitute who steals the Empress' famous diamond hair brooches. Matters are not improved when, the following morning, Lady Charlotte-Georgina arrives from London with Searcy, who has brought Speedicut's decorations and Dress uniform for him to wear at the funeral. Fortunately, Searcy solves the problem of the missing jewels by substituting readily available copies made for the tourist market.

Back in London, Speedicut is able to enjoy the London Season of 1899, has a betting coup and buys his first motor car with the proceeds. He is also invited to stand as godfather to Sibella Holland's first child, Charles Lionel Jasper Holland, but declines the invitation. To Speedicut's dismay his peace is rudely interrupted by the outbreak of the Second Boer War and his appointment as Head of Propaganda to General Buller's Natal Field Force. Buller is concerned for his reputation because Winston Churchill, the scourge of Field Force commanders, is once again acting as a War Correspondent; Buller orders Speedicut to keep a close watch on the journalist.

In pursuit of this instruction, Speedicut finds himself on an armoured train which is ambushed by the Boers resulting in him and Churchill being captured and imprisoned in Pretoria. Thanks, inadvertently, to Churchill, Speedicut manages to escape and is given sanctuary by the mining magnate, Solly Joel, who arranges for him to be returned to Cape Town. From there, Speedicut travels to London where his first action is to resign his commission.

Book 8 closes with Speedicut's decision to become a racehorse owner. However, scarcely has he settled down to this retirement pursuit than, thanks to an intimate encounter forty years previously with the Empress Dowager of China, he is ordered by the Great Boanerges to travel immediately to Peking on business of mutual interest to the Brotherhood and the British government...

CHAPTER ONE: CHOP SUEY

Those of my readers who are still alive since the last volume of my reminiscences were published, may recall that I'd just returned to my house in Stratton Street, London, from the bloodstock sales at Newmarket when, on 1st March 1900, I received instructions to get my sagging arse to Peking *aussi vite que possible*. Needless to say, this most unwelcome news had come from the Great Boanarges, otherwise known as my brother-in-law His Grace the Duke of Whitehall who was also my boss in the Brotherhood of the Sons of Thunder, an influential secret society sometimes mistakenly identified by the turds in the sewers of Fleet Street as 'the Establishment'. And what was the purpose of this trip to the aptly named Forbidden City? If only it had been, at least as far as I was concerned. The answer was to use my former contact with the Empress Dowager of China to safeguard the Brotherhood's and Britannia's commercial interests behind the Great Wall.[1]

Quite why anyone thought that I could pull this off was a mystery to me, particularly as none of them knew that I was only 'known to the Empress Dowager' because, in 1860, I'd been shagged silly by the slit-eyed slut. That said, it was extremely unlikely that she would remember me as, since that time, she'd doubtless been rogered by half the male population of China – or at least those who hadn't had their cocks and balls chopped off so that they could serve as eunuchs at the Imperial Court.

Given all of that, I can't think what on earth possessed me to agree to leave the comfort of London, and the pleasures of the turf, for an utterly pointless trip back to the dragon's lair that was doomed to failure from the start. Dammit, I thought, unless I could arrange a very quick turnaround, I wouldn't be able to see my new ponies run at Ascot and Goodwood. It wasn't even as though the GB had promised me that I could retire from the Brotherhood if I got back in one piece. No. It was: 'Brother Speedicut, your country needs you, blah, blah, blah…' I must have been mad. But,

---

[1] Dowager Empress CiXi (1835-1908). See *The Speedicut Papers: Book 3 (Uncivil Wars)*.

I suppose, when your nation and the Brotherhood calls and your wife constantly nags you about your lack of a knighthood... Anyway, a few days after I'd received my marching orders, and still grumbling, my valet Fahran Khazi slung my hammock in a First Class state room on one of the Peninsular & Oriental Steam Navigation Company's better tubs berthed in Southampton and bound for Port Said, Aden, Singapore, Hong Kong, Shanghai and Yokahama.

Towards the end of March 1900, we were at the Hotel Crotte d'Azure in Port Said, a fly-ridden dump, infested with beggars and with nothing to see but bloated Levantines, wharves, sand, and a perfectly absurd statue of de Lesseps leering down at the poxed-up tarts plying their trade on the dockside:[2] I banned Fahran from even thinking of consorting with them. That novelist johnnie, Kipling, who I'd met at Pratt's the night before I left London, told me over George's best sausages and mash that,[3] if you sat around long enough in Port Said, you would see everyone you know: it was an asinine remark and well up to his usual standard. At least in the old days, when one went around the Cape of Good Hope, there were decent views, a breeze and the (limited) pleasures of Cape Town. Progress ain't everything it's cracked up to be.

But if Port Said was bad, our next stop, Aden, made the Gyppo hell hole look like Paris; needless to say, I stayed in my state room whilst the tub re-coaled there. Between Aden and Singapore there was nothing to do except swelter in the heat, so I steeled myself to plough through the GB's exceedingly long briefing paper, the covering summary of which – to save having to copy it and pretend it's my own work - I reproduce below.

TOP SECRET

CHINA BRIEFING PAPER FOR BROTHER SPEEDICUT

---

[2] Vicomte Ferdinand de Lesseps GCSI (1805-1894) was the developer of the Suez Canal.

[3] Rudyard Kipling (1865-1936). Pratt's was and is a private club off St James's Street, owned by the Dukes of Devonshire, which serves well-cooked 'nursery food' to its aristocratic members and where all the staff are called George.

1. SUMMARY

1.a. The Empress Dowager

I believe you are familiar with the Empress Dowager CiXi who, according to our records, you last met when she was still the Yi Concubine and poised to seize power in the humiliation that followed the destruction of the Summer Palace in 1860. As one of the very few Englishmen to have met the formidable de facto ruler of the sprawling and dysfunctional Chinese empire, you are probably the sole reliable English source of information about her character. Occupied as you have been on War Office business in South Africa, you may not, however, be fully aware of the current state of China following the outbreak of the Boxer Rebellion two years ago.

1.b. The Boxers & the Boxer Rebellion

The Boxers, so called because its members refer to themselves as 'The Righteous Fists of Harmony', are a populist movement who have tapped into the Chinese peasants' fear that Christian missionaries and their converts will expropriate their land. The rebellion started in northern China in 1898 with the stated aim of crushing Christianity and driving foreigners out of China.

1.c. The Imperial Chinese government's attitude to the Treaty Powers' interests

Even after more than forty years, the Imperial government is still rankling from the presence of foreign missions and Legations in Peking, the trade concessions that have been exacted from it by the Treaty Powers - the United States, Japan, Russia, France, Italy, Germany and Austria-Hungary – and the operation of the Treaty ports of Hong Kong, Canton, Shanghai, Ningpo, Fuchow and Amoy, which are not only gateways into China for the Treaty Powers but are also the route-in for the highly profitable opium trade in which the Brotherhood has a substantial commercial interest.

As a direct consequence of the brutal murder of the German Baron von Ketteler in 1898, and further atrocities against Europeans since then, the Treaty Powers have initiated a build-up of armed force on the coast at Taku. This has further angered the Imperial Chinese government.

1.d. The Imperial government's attitude to the Boxers

In light of the above, the Imperial government has considerable sympathy with the Boxers' aims but, until recently, has been leery of supporting a movement that might challenge its own declining grip on China.

1.e. Objective of the United Kingdom, the other Treaty Powers & the Brotherhood of the Sons of Thunder

The British government's, and the Brotherhood's, objective - along with that of the other Treaty Powers - is <u>not</u> the toppling of the Imperial regime but the restoration of the status quo ante in China in order that trade, the valuable trading concessions and the tax advantages we all enjoy are not disrupted, or reversed, by revolution or a change of government to one that could be less compliant than the decadent rule of the Qing dynasty.

1.f. Current situation

Recently, the Empress Dowager finally stepped off the fence and, despite considerable internal divisions within the Forbidden City, declared the Imperial government's support for the Boxers.

1.g. Your task

This declaration makes it imperative that the Treaty Powers act now and your task is to persuade the Empress Dowager to stop supporting the Boxers.

...

In Singapore we stayed, all too briefly - for it was much improved since I'd last been there - at Raffles Hotel. Sadly, we soon had to re-board the boat for the final leg of the trip, via Hong Kong, to Shanghai, where we were to finally disembark. If Singapore had improved, I found on our arrival there in April that Shanghai was like a new city. Indeed, it looked more like Monaco than China and the main waterfront, known as the Bund, resembled a combination of Piccadilly and Leadenhall Street. As we were travelling at the Brotherhood's expense – I was, after all, on Brotherhood business – I saw no need to economise, so we put up at the Astor House, which claimed to be the best hotel in all of the Orient.[4]

Although my first impression of the political situation in China was coloured by the prosperous normality of Shanghai, I quickly found out at the bar of the Astor, and then at our Consulate where I went to receive a briefing, that the dragon was lulling me into a false sense of security. For, whilst all seems peaceful on the Bund, it was anything but that up-country with Bannermen, Imp troops and Boxers all competing to see who could flay the most missionaries.

Then, just as I'd just settled into Shanghai, the Consul told me to get my ancient arse off the veranda chairs at the Astor and onto a coaster to Taku, where I was to report to some matelot called Seymour,[5] who would give me my next set of instructions.

It was an uneventful journey, so I won't bore my readers with it, except to record that I picked up some interesting tales in the deck saloon about a new 'palace of varieties' that had opened in Shanghai. By all accounts, it offered 'varieties' not of the musical hall type but something altogether more interesting. I silently made myself a promise to pay the establishment a visit once I've completed my mission for the Brotherhood and Brother Salisbury, which I had every intention of doing in double-quick time.

On arrival at Taku I found preparations being made for what looked like an international Expedition-in-Force up river: Eyties jabbering, Frogs hawking, Ruskies looking grumpy, Nips inscrutable, assorted Krauts, *schnitzel*-fanciers and Hungars strutting around, and our own jolly jack tars trading insults with some laid back Yanks.

Seymour, however, was altogether a different matter: he was all business and clearly a knowledgeable old China hand. According to him the

---

[4] The Astor House Hotel, Shanghai was one of the most famous hotels in the Far East. Located on the Bund, it was established in 1846 as Richard's Hotel. It was renamed the Astor House Hotel in 1859.

[5] Vice Admiral (later Admiral of the Fleet) Sir Edward Seymour (1840-1929), was in command of the China Station from 1897-1901.

situation in Peking was a mess, so nothing unusual there then, with my old coupling partner the Empress Dowager juggling the pro- and anti-Western factions within the Forbidden City.

"The pro-Western faction," said Seymour, "is led by Prince Qing and the Imperial Army' commander, General Ronglu.[6] At the helm of the antis is Prince Duan.[7] The Boxers and the Muslim 'Kansu Braves' are under the command of General Dong Fuxiang.[8] However, Colonel, nothing is straightforward."

As I knew only too well from forty years previous, this last remark was a statement of the blindingly obvious. Apparently, so Seymour went on to say, the Imps and other assorted soldiery, Generals and Princes were as likely to switch sides as they were to fart after dinner - and with as much frequency and as little warning.

"The only enemy about whom we can be absolutely certain," Seymour continued, "are the Boxers, who are about as nasty a bunch of cut-throats as ever graced a paddy field." God help me, I thought: this sounded like a re-run of the Tai Ping business in the '50s and '60s. "You are to report to MacDonald at our Legation in Peking,"[9] he finished. If I remembered rightly, MacD was a dry cove with 'tashes about a foot wide who I'd met on the Kassassin caper. "He'll get you an Audience with the Empress Dowager and, as you know, your job is to get her to switch her loyalty back to us and our Treaty partners."

Well, I thought not for the first time, that's about as tall an order as I've ever received and had about as much chance of success as getting Bertie to settle with his tailors. But it didn't pay to say so. Instead, I looked resolute and asked how he proposed getting me from Taku to Peking, given that between the two there were likely to be several thousand Boxers, not to mention Imps, Bannermen and other assorted thugs keen on getting their

---

[6] Yikuang, Prince Qing (1838-1917); General Guwalgiya Ronglu (1836-1903).

[7] Zaiyi, Prince Duan or Tuan (1856-1922).

[8] Dong Fuxiang (1839-1908).

[9] Colonel Sir Claude MacDonald (1852-1915) was a soldier and diplomat. He was the British Minister in Peking 1899-1900.

hands on another westerner to skin. He didn't have an immediate answer to this, but a day or so later he proposed sending me under armed guard and a *laisser passer* issued by Prince Qing, which was probably as much use, if push comes to shove, as a Chinese paper umbrella in a monsoon. That notwithstanding, I was to travel on the next train from Tianjin to the capital, where I would be installed at the Legation.

"The Legation, Colonel, is an utterly charming spot... And you're not to worry, old chap; we'll soon have enough men here to ensure that we can enforce our rights - even if Her Imperial Majesty doesn't succumb to your old pals' act." *Dulce et decorum est*, I thought, was an altogether more likely outcome if I knew the Chinks.

...

Editor's Note: There is a gap in The Speedicut Papers of at least a month and, probably, at least one missing letter. There was, however, one dated June-August 1900, which appeared to have been written episodically, presumably because there was no opportunity to send it out of Peking. Consequently, the appearance of a Russian Countess is unexplained although her relationship with Speedicut becomes clear as the narrative unfolds. Readers of a queasy disposition, or those who have just eaten, should skip to the end of this chapter.

...

Probably for the hundredth time since I'd arrived at the British Legation, on 9th June MacDonald once again tried and yet again failed, to arrange an Audience for me with my former partner in the carnal arts. Consequently, I told him that my mission was a flop and that I had no alternative but to return to London and report as much to Salisbury (and the GB). What I had in mind in this regard was a quick rickshaw ride to Peking Main and a comfortable journey back to civilisation courtesy of the Peninsula & Oriental Steam Navigation Company. MacDonald rather reluctantly agreed and so, two days later and after a few more relaxation sessions (for which read quite exhausting bouts) with La Obolenskya, Fahran packed my traps, preparatory to us both climbing aboard a train headed east.

Over breakfast on 11th, the blessed day of our departure, I received a note from Akira,[10] the Japanese Minister, who offered me a ride to the station, which - by return - I gratefully accepted. At the appointed hour, his carriage was outside waiting for me. With my bags safely stowed behind, Fahran and I joined the jolly little Nip inside and, leaning out to bid goodbye to the Legation staff, I noticed a rather damp looking handkerchief being waved from a top floor window. It seemed that my Russian Countess had grown rather fond of me...

The driver whipped-up, the carriage lurched forward and we were off to the railway station, with my thoughts already fixed on tracking down Shanghai's new 'palace of varieties' once I'd got there. Akira, who was rigged out in undress uniform, jabbered away next to me, but I paid him little heed beyond the odd grunt of acknowledgement, as we sped past assorted coolies and other grumpy looking Chinks.

Suddenly, the coachman reined-up. Looking out of the open window to see what was amiss, I saw that the road was blocked by an angry-looking crowd of what appeared to be machete-wielding apes. This was definitely trouble, I thought, and I shouted at the driver to turn around; but I was too late. In seconds the carriage was surrounded by screaming Boxers,[11] the far door was wrenched open and Akira dragged out. Filthy hands then hauled me and Fahran out after him.

To my utter shock, we were then forced to look-on as the maniacs held the Nip upright and literally ripped the uniform off his struggling form: I could see, plain as day, that it was true what they say about Orientals' courting tackle. Then, as the poor man yelled blue murder, an ugly brute, who towered over the rest, grabbed what passed for Akira's finest features, gave them a vicious twist, sliced them off and tossed them at my feet. It happened in seconds. Utterly horrified, I retched-up my breakfast over the obscene mess. Then, as I raised my head, I saw Akira's spin in the air and land in the dust with a dull thump, followed by his body, with blood pumping from his severed neck all over me and the dusty road.

---

[10] Sugiyama Akira (1862-1900).

[11] Editor's Note: Minister Akira's assailants were actually Kansu Braves.

At this point I must have passed out, which was not surprising as it was odds-on that I was next for the chop. But no: for, whilst I was out cold, Fahran picked me up without the Chinks protesting, slung me in the carriage and told the driver to get the hell away from the place. I came-to as we were being driven lickety-spit back to the Legation Quarter and put out my left hand to steady myself; it slipped on a warm, wet throbbing piece of meat. I looked down: it was Akira's heart, placed in the carriage next to me as a clear message which I was to deliver to the Legations.

The next thing that I remember was being revived on a large sofa in the British Legation's entry hall, with the Countess shoving smelling salts up my nose and Lady MacDonald trying to pour brandy down my throat. When I could finally speak, and it took at least two large glasses of the Legations' best Napoleon before I could even croak, I told them what had happened. The house had been in an uproar when I recovered consciousness, but you could've heard a pin drop when I got to the business end of the story. To do Tamara credit, she didn't even blink, although I could see her knuckles whitening as she gripped the sofa: Russian women were, it seemed, made of stern stuff.

"Well," said MacDonald, who was so cool you'd think he'd just been told the latest score at Lord's not that a fellow diplomat had been emasculated, decapitated and eviscerated by a hoard of screaming barbarians in front of an elderly colleague, "I must send a memo and a letter of condolence over to the Japanese Legation - and a *very* stern Note to the Empress Dowager."

And that was how it all started. But, at first, the Imp government did nothing, although we heard that the pro- and anti-factions were practically tearing each other's skimpy beards off each other as they argued the case in front of the Empress Dowager. However, Seymour's action in bombarding the Dagu forts, as a move preparatory to advancing on Tianjin and Peking, tipped the scales in favour of the war party and Miss CiXi, in what I guess must have been a last-ditch attempt to save the situation and her throne, sent a note to each of the Legations. This informed each of them of Seymour's action and commanded all foreigners to leave Peking in twenty-four hours or face the consequences. I was taking tea with MacDonald when the note arrived. He read it, then handed it to me.

"What do you think?" he asked, as I handed it back to him.

"Frankly, MacDonald, you have no choice but to pack up and leave," I replied, as I remembered a similar situation in Cawnpore.[12]

"I think not," he parried. "After all, it's what they've been wanting us to do for forty years. For that reason alone, we should stay put. Besides which, if we leave now we'll never get back without a fight."

I tried to get the silly bugger to see sense and close the Legation but he wouldn't countenance it. Instead, he sent for the other Ministers and, having politely but firmly asked me to shift my elderly carcass elsewhere, got them to agree that to leave the safety (hah!) of the Legation Quarter would be suicide. For myself, I would have taken my chances in open country. But then, I'd got that sort of thing wrong before, so perhaps MacDonald & Co were right. However, that didn't stop me from being damned unhappy about it.

The first I knew that the Empress Dowager meant what she said was the sound of a salvo of Baron Krupp's best munitions fired, not by Seymour and his bravos, who we supposed to be on their way to bolster our less than adequate forces,[13] but by the bloody, perfidious Imp army. I pulled up my bags, rolled off the sofa, told Tamara to get dressed and, as fast as

---

[12] See *The Speedicut Papers: Book 3 (Uncivil Wars)*.

[13] Editor's Note: With the apparent consent of the Imperial government, Admiral Seymour, at the head of a mixed nationalities force of 2,000, left Taku by train on 10th June. His objective was to bolster the earlier and much smaller force of sailors, which had left Taku on 31st May and made its way through to Peking. Seymour got beyond Tianjin to Langfang, where he was halted by 5,000 Imperial troops on 18th June and by 26th June he was back in Tianjin having suffered significant casualties. Surrounded and greatly outnumbered, Seymour led his remaining troops back to Taku in junks on the Peiho river to join a substantially larger force led by Lieutenant General (later General Sir) Alfred Gaselee (1844-1918). Seymour was known to the defenders of the Peking siege as 'Admiral See-no-more' because of the time it took him to relieve them

my weary joints would permit, I legged it down the stairs to MacDonald's office to find it already besieged by an unsavoury collection of Dagoes, Wops and other 'lesser breeds without the Law', as Dr Arnold, my *alma mater*'s head beak would have said. Barging my way through the outer cordon of garlic eaters, I finally made it into our Minister's inner sanctum where an *indaba* was already in progress with the senior military men from the other Legations. MacDonald, being a former soldier himself and the ranking diplomat, had taken charge and was already issuing a stream of orders for our collective defence when he espied me.

"Ah, Colonel Speedicut, just in time to give us the wisdom of your experience."

Hold on a moment, I thought, if this is going to be the kind of prize cock-up it promises to be, to say nothing of an out-and-out slaughter, the only part of it I want is a one-way ticket out of Peking.

"Minister," I replied, "I may be the senior officer here, but I am now retired and, in any event, you are the rankin' diplomat. Knowin' as I do your former distinguished service with the Colours, I'm more than content to be under your command and to give you whatever support and advice that I can."

Pure mud in his eye of course, for I was already thinking about how to get out of this hellish mess with my hide intact. You didn't have to be a student of military history to tell at one glance that this was a tighter corner by far than Lucknow, Cawnpore, Isandalwana or Khartoum. After those experiences, I was not about to be signed-up for more of the same or worse - and this time there wasn't even a reliable native to negotiate with or so we believed. But MacDonald took my guff at face value and beamed over his ridiculous 'tashes at me.

"Most generous, Colonel. Now, turning to the creation of a defensive line, the Austrians and the Italians need to withdraw immediately from the outlying Legations, which are clearly indefensible. I propose that the Italians join the Japanese, the Austrians and the French, which should keep our numbers balanced, and the European civilians will move in here. Does that suit you, gentlemen?"

He wittered on for what seemed an age, disposing his 'army', which - readers may be interested to know - amounted to four hundred and seventy-three civilians (of whom around one hundred and fifty were fit to hold a rifle), four hundred and nine assorted uniforms of eleven different nations, and two thousand five hundred wailing Christian Chinese converts, who MacDonald conscripted to build barricades and earthworks. To defend ourselves we had small arms, three machine guns and a cannon that should have been in a museum, which had been lashed together from parts found in the armoury. The Yanks nicknamed it 'Betsy', although God-only-knows why.

In accordance with MacDonald's directions, the Japs and the Eyeties set up a defensive line at the Fu Palace at the northern end of the Legation quarter, the Yanks and Kraut Marines held the Tartar Wall on the southern perimeter and the rest piled into the British Legation compound. We had a total of five hundred and fifty assorted military and armed civvies to guard a defensive line over two thousand yards long. Facing us was a horde of screaming Chinks who probably numbered anywhere from ten to a hundred thousand, all armed to the teeth with modern weapons. Nice odds that were calculated to have me looking for the nearest hot air balloon station. But it soon became clear that there was no way out. Once our troops were armed and positioned, I asked MacDonald where he wanted me.

"Choose your own spot," he said.

So, I collected up a brace of rifles, a pistol, a stash of ammunition and Fahran. Then we headed towards the top floor of the Legation to pick a position from where we could take as many of the slit-eyed buggers with us afore going to join the Heavenly Chorus. We were half-way up the stairs when I heard my name being called.

"Jasper, Jasper, don't leave me!"

I looked over the bannister and there in the hall below was my little Countess, her hair astray and a most becoming blush on her cheeks. She was dressed in her best, which – given the circumstances - was boots and breeches, a silk blouse and a leather jerkin that she must have stripped off the back of a randy Yank when I wasn't looking. Well, Fahran and I were going to need a loader and who better than La Obolenskya who, I was sure, would learn this new skill as fast as she had clearly learnt more pleasurable ones. Holding out my hand, I told her to join us.

CHAPTER TWO: PEKING DUCK

As I've already noted, the command of the foreign forces based in the city was assumed by MacDonald, with the American Minister, Herbert Squeirs,[14] as his Chief of Staff. However, in reality, MacDonald was only able to propose and coordinate rather than command the troops and civilians in the rapidly fortified compound. Once he'd disposed his 'army', our chief's next act was to bring within the perimeter as much food and ammunition as could be found in the outlying Legations. Water was not a problem, but most of the regular food was soon consumed, leaving us to subsist on a diet of horsemeat and rice, which was acceptable to the Frogs and the Nips, who'll eat anything that moves, but tested the appetites of the other nationalities. Perhaps from necessity – or perhaps not - MacDonald left the Chinese Christians within the perimeter to fend for themselves; they were practically starving by the time the siege was lifted. But I anticipate.

From a conventional military perspective, the events of the next fifty-five days were inexplicable. Unlike the siege of Rorke's Drift, where an even smaller number of British soldiers were able to beat-off hordes of assegai wielding Zulus, the forces ranged against us in the Legation compound were well-armed and in overwhelming strength. Interestingly, as I found out later, although the assault on the Legations had, in effect, been initiated by the Boxers, they were themselves virtually absent from the besieging forces which, on the west side included the Gansu Muslim troops of Dong Fuxiang, an Imperial Chinese General bitterly opposed to foreigners. To the east, the forces were mostly drawn from the Peking Field Army. Overall control rested in the hands of General Ronglu, who was a prominent member of the pro-western/anti-Boxer faction and, therefore, the best placed man to ensure that the siege was *not* successful, a possibly deliberate appointment by the Empress Dowager.

---

[14] Herbert Squiers (1859-1911).

The assaults on the Legations started with a concerted attack with fire bombs around our Legation, which had the unintended effect of destroying the Hanlin Academy containing China's national library. The resulting conflagration saw the priceless and irreplaceable collection go up in smoke, but failed to dislodge the defenders.

The second assault focussed on the Fu Palace, which was defended by the Nips led by Lieutenant Colonel Shiba.[15] The *sushi*-men were already at fever pitch following the unprovoked mutilation and murder of poor old Akira, which I'd witnessed, and defended their ground like the samurais that they were - and with considerable loss of life.

Next, the Chinks turned their attention to the Frog Legation, which was defended by just seventy-eight assorted garlic-eaters and Franz Josef's Own in uniform and a handful of armed civilians. Here too, with the front lines only fifty feet apart, the defenders suffered a high casualty rate. However, the really critical defensive point was the Tartar Wall at the south of the Legation Quarter held by the Krauts and the Yanks. Loss of the Tartar Wall would mean that the Chinks would be able to sweep with murderous fire the whole of the besieged area.

By 2nd July, the Frog Legation and the Fu Palace were under intense pressure and likely to fall; Chink snipers had accounted for many of our casualties but the Tartar Wall still held, although the Krauts had been dislodged from their position on it on 30th June. However, early on the morning of 3rd July, a small combined force of Tommy Atkins, Ivans and Uncle Sams managed to dislodge the Chink positions in front of the Tartar Wall and never again during the remainder of the siege did the Imps attempt to take it.

What followed was less good news for us defenders. On 13th July, a large mine was detonated under the Frog Legation making it no longer tenable and, to make matters worse, the Fu Palace looked set to fall too. With the casualty figure in excess of fifty per cent, our morale had reached breaking

---

[15] Lieutenant (later General) Shiba Goro (1860-1945).

point and surrender was a real possibility – indeed, I repeatedly urged MacDonald to raise the white flag 'in order to save the women', of course.

I think that MacD was about to cave in to my demands when, to everyone's surprise, the Imperial Chink government made a peace overture which MacDonald shared with me and the rest of the Legation heads. The upshot of this extraordinary turn of events was that I was selected to act as the negotiator. Well, I was having none of that.

"You must think I'm completely mad, MacDonald," I spluttered, when he proposed the suicide mission. "This is nothin' but another trick by the Imps. Remember you're talkin' to a man who was at Cawnpore. We were damned fool enough then to trust Tantia Tope and look where that got us![16] I'll be damned if I'm goin' to make the same mistake again."

"But be reasonable, Colonel. We know from the deserters that there is discord in the Imperial government and the feebleness of the attacks on our eastern defences by the Imperial Army, when you compare it to the ferocity of the Muslim attacks elsewhere, would seem to bear out the stories of division. Now they have offered us a parley and who could be better placed than yourself, who came here for just this purpose, to meet with the Empress Dowager and her advisers?"

In my view, that was a damned fool question from MacDonald, but I could see the way the land lay and the nodding from the other men - those that still had the energy to nod - showed me which way the wind was blowing me. Once more into the dragon's lair, I thought. Well, perhaps it was preferable to a Chink bullet in the back or watching as a demented Bannerman carried off my wedding tackle on the point of a spear before cutting up the rest of me.

---

[16] Tantia (or Tatya) Tope (1814-1859) was responsible for the treacherous massacre of the British civilians and military who had survived the siege of Cawnpore during the Indian Mutiny. They were gunned down by Tope's troops whilst embarking at the Satichaura ghat under a safe passage arrangement. He was executed by the British in 1859.

"Alright, MacDonald," I said, "I've given you my view - but I know where my duty lies," this said with an attempt at a gallant smile, "and I will do as you request. If I don't return, and you survive, I would be most obliged if you would give this to my wife." I slipped off my signet ring and handed it to the old fool. I swear that half the men were blubbing by this stage, but I – frankly – wouldn't have cared if they'd shat their breeches, those that still had them. "I will be ready to meet Prince Qing's representative in half-an-hour. Meanwhile, I have a small duty to perform."

I turned on my heel, left the room and made for the bedroom at the top of the stairs where Fahran was standing guard and within which I knew Tamara would be waiting for me. If MacDonald and the other asses thought that I was off to make my peace with the Almighty, which they almost certainly did, well - in a way - they were right, for my firm intention was to have one final grapple with a woman who was unlikely to tear out my heart afore meeting with one who probably would. Readers may think that, at my age, I should have had other things on my mind but, as I think I've remarked before, danger has always had a most stimulating effect on me and the Legation siege was no different to other tight spots I'd encountered in my younger days.

"Don't let anyone in," I said to Fahran, as I marched past him.

"Certainly not, huzoor," he grinned in reply as he took post outside the door.

I'm glad to say that Tamara shared my view when it came to preparing for Eternity and I gave her, briefly, of my best on a boarded floor scattered with broken glass and spent cartridge cases. In fact, I may still have a piece of that glass in my rump, for Tamara was on top of the situation from the start. The matter in hand completed, I dragged on what was left of my togs, gave Tamara a playful slap on her naked bum, left Fahran to keep an eye on her and – feeling ready to meet my Maker - headed back down the Legation stairs as a Yankee Major of Marines passed me in the opposite direction.

A short while later I presented myself to MacDonald. Standing next to him was a diminutive Chink in a fine silk robe and a buttoned and feathered hat denoting him to be a Noble of the Fifth Rank. How one remembers these things, I don't know, but that's what the little bugger was. After much bowing and scraping, we left the battered building and climbed into an elaborate litter drawn up by the Legation's broken steps. It wasn't more than an hour, perhaps ninety minutes, before I was back at the Legation and pouring myself a large brandy. When I'd suitably composed myself, just under half of the bottle later, I reported to MacDonald. There was a brief silence when I finished.

"Colonel Speedicut, no possible blame can attach to you. You tried your best but, by your own account, the Imperial Court is in a state of chaos and if they don't know their own minds, there is nothing to be done. We know from messages that help is on its way – so we must fight on until we are relieved by Gaselee or God. Oh, and by the way, this has just arrived for you."

Without explanation, he pushed a small box at me. Much good your piety will do you, I thought as, without giving any further consideration to what I'd been sent or by whom, I shoved the box into a coat pocket.

But faith in the relieving force – or it may have been God - was what held MacDonald together. I'll give him this, he never once flinched or showed his doubts to anyone outside his immediate command circle. Two things were clear to me, however: first, we were for the chop, and second, whatever influence I had once had with the Empress Dowager – and I'm not even certain about that – was long gone.

For, you see, the painted and corseted doll with whom I'd been sent to treat never once looked at me, addressing all her remarks either to the ceiling or to her assembled Princes and nobles. That I was a piece of filth that was fouling her silk carpet was made abundantly clear, despite the deep kow-tow I had made to the old bitch; this last was a fact that I'd been careful to omit when I'd reported back to MacDonald. Although she must have known that we'd met before, La CiXi affected not to recollect it. And even if she did, it seemed to make no difference to her: there was no acceptable deal to be had and, even if there had of been, no one on the Imp side (whichever side that was) was capable of delivering it. So, we resigned ourselves to our fate. But then the most extraordinary thing happened: on 14th July, the firing stopped.[17] It didn't resume, excepting a few low-level breaches, until the night of 13th August.

Meanwhile, on 28th July, news was brought to us by a Chink child that the multi-national troops under the command of Fred Gaselee were at Tianjin and were about to fight their way through to Peking. However, by mid-August, there was neither sight, sound nor further news of them.[18] Then, on the night of the 13th August, the Imp Army started shelling the Legation Quarter again, although they did not make a direct infantry assault on the perimeter. Then, at 2 am on 14th, we heard the unmistakeable sound of machine gun fire: Gaselee had at last arrived.

I learned later that each of the nations represented in the relieving force was given a city gate to seize. Nonetheless, the Yanks chose to scale the walls and our British-Indian troops, who were the first to reach the Legation Quarter, did so via the sewers. You may find this hard to believe but, as they emerged into the Legation grounds, they were greeted with trays of fizz, MacDonald in clean tennis flannels and the Legation ladies, led by the redoubtable Lady Mac, in party dresses. Only the British... And where was I at this happy moment? Tucked up in bed with Tamara and a bottle of the Emperor's best: I've never liked garden parties.

When the final Roll Call came to be taken we, the defenders, had suffered fifty-five dead and one hundred and thirty-five wounded. Casualties on the Chink side were unknown. With our brave lads once more in control,

---

[17] Editor's Note: There has never been a satisfactory explanation for the tactics of the besiegers, their failure to press home advantages or the ceasefire on 14th July. Historians have generally accepted that divisions within the Imperial government, and splits within the military command are the explanation. But, whilst this might explain the deliberate or inadvertent failure of the Chinese troops to take the Legation Quarter, it still leaves open the question why, when victory was in sight and the relieving forces still stuck beyond Tianjin, the attack was suspended. The answer may lie in this account.

[18] Editor's Note: This force of 55,000 set out from Taku on 25th June and captured Tianjin on 14th July. Leaving 35,000 troops as a garrison, Gaselee then set off for Peking and reached there, after stiff resistance, on 14th August.

fighting stopped and the Imp Army and the other forces surrounding the Legation Quarter melted away whilst the Imperial Court and the Old Buddha, as our boys called Miss CiXi, fled to Shanxi.

In the immediate aftermath of the relief of the Legation Quarter and the occupation of the Imperial capital, Fred authorised five days of official looting of the new Summer Palace and the Forbidden City, to be followed by a Prize Auction in the garden of the British Legation. What he did *not* authorise was the rape, mutilation and murder of assorted Chink citizens by the Ruskies and the Nips, nor the commandeering of the Catholic North Cathedral by British 'other ranks' as an unofficial saleroom in which to cash-in the stuff they'd not surrendered to the Prize Committee. It's almost superfluous to add that the looting was carried out on an heroic scale and, in consequence, the official Prize Auction lasted for five days (Sunday excepted). Our Yankee Second-in-Command, Squeirs, bought enough porcelain to fill six railroad cars and Lady Mac filled over a hundred packing cases with assorted artefacts which she too, in due course, shipped off back home. And what did I bag? Well, looting isn't really my style, but I'll admit that at one of the Prize Auctions I bought another of Miss CiXi's pink pearl necklaces, with a pink pearl bracelet *en suite*, principally because the necklace matched the one I'd given Charlotte-Georgina when we got married.[19]. In any event, for these two bits of swag I'd paid less than a day's rent roll from my Wrexham estate.

Whilst all this was going on, it took several days of delay and frustration before I was able to obtain a place for Tamara, Fahran and myself on one of the few trains running to the coast, but we eventually made it onto one with a letter of thanks from MacDonald, which I have since lost, and an official report on the siege for the GB, which I in due course sent to Flashy.

On a whim whilst we were on the train to Shanghai, I decided to give Tamara the bracelet as a souvenir. I'm a sentimental old fool, I know, but it was cheaper than yesterday's left-over fish and she seemed happy enough with it. Anyway, when I reached into my (as it turned out wrong) coat pocket to find the trinket to give her, my fingers closed around the small

---

[19] See *Book 3, The Speedicut Papers (Uncivil Wars)*

box that had been delivered to me shortly after my abortive Audience with the Empress Dowager CiXi. In the heat of the ghastly events which had followed, I'd somewhat understandably completely forgotten about it.

As Fahran and Tamara looked on, I opened the box. Inside its yellow silk interior was a rice paper scroll and, beneath that, a small yellow silk bag embroidered with a five-toed Imperial dragon. I took it out, undid the draw string and tipped the contents onto my lap: a pink pearl the size of a pigeon's egg rolled towards my knees. Fahran caught it whilst Tamara let out a low whistle.

"Where did you get that?" she asked. "It certainly wasn't on sale in any of the auctions." So, I told her. "But who sent it to you?"

"I've no idea," I replied truthfully.

"Perhaps the note will provide an explanation," Fahran said, as he handed me back the pearl. I unrolled the scroll, but the writing on it was in Chinese characters. "Can either of you translate this?" I asked my companions. Fahran took one look at it, shook his head and gave it to Tamara. She scanned it and then slowly read aloud:

> *Fanqi. You thought I had not recognised you, but I did. Yi neither forgets nor forgives, as Dong Fuxiang and his dogs will soon find out. Trust in me to ensure a safe outcome for you and the other fanqi in the Legation Quarter. I enclose with this letter a box that contains a token of remembrance of our last meeting. Farewell, we shall not meet again.*

"What's that all about?" Tamara quite reasonably asked, as she gave me back the scroll.

"It's a long story..." I said, whilst replacing the pearl and the note back in the box, which I then tucked into an inside pocket for safety.

On arrival in Shanghai, we managed to get rooms at the Astor, Fahran stashed our loot (including my present from Miss CiXi) in the hotel safe and we settled down to wait for the next steamers home. Plus, of course, a few further bouts with Her Ruskie Ladyship, although I have to confess that the strain of the previous few weeks meant that, more often than not, I dozed off mid-way through our sessions. Well, that's one of the hazards of old age, but at least I could – providing there is a decent interval between bouts - still perform, which was more than could be said for most of my contemporaries, those who were still above the sod or not poxed into impotence like Bertie.

I saw Tamara off - with many a tear and a farewell grope of her well-padded rump - on a Japanese boat to Vladivostok, from where she was going to take the Trans-Siberian back to Moscow and the warm embrace of her elderly husband. You know, looking back, I never did ask her what she had been doing in Peking in the first place or how she came to be able to read Mandarin. Strange, but I suppose that - for most of the time we were together - her mouth was either too full of my weapon, or cartridges for my rifle, to leave much time for talking.

Anyway, with Tamara safely out of the way and after a brief but much needed rest, I decided that before the P&O boat left for Singapore, home and Charlotte-Georgina's bony embrace, I would try and track down the 'palace of varieties' I'd heard about all those months before. It turned out to be no easy task, as most of the men at the hotel's bar were either too bible-and-bedtime-stories-types to ask or had clearly just got into town themselves. Until, that is, Squeirs from the Yankee Legation turned up to see his trainload of loot safely onto a US Navy boat bound for San Fran in the care of a tall, good-looking Major of Marines by the name of Heston Charlton (or it may have been the other way around: with our cousins across the pond anything is possible when it comes to names), who I only knew in passing but who had been with us throughout the siege.

"Sure, Speed, I know the place you mean. It's at the end of the Bund in a go-down," said Squeirs. "Let's all mosey over there after dinner tonight." Fahran said that he wanted to come to but I was firm: my readers should note that I *do* have a care for the morals of my staff.

When we got there, the dive was an absolute eye-opener even for someone with my experience. A cross between a knocking shop and a music hall, it boasted a stage with a horseshoe of curtained private boxes around it on two levels, a bar at the back, more tarts than have ever trotted the pavements of the 'dilly – and a performance on stage that made Ma Watling's burlesque show in Atlanta look like a Sunday school meeting for spinsters.[20]

I watched a few acts, most of which seemed to call for the performers to be not only double-jointed but massively well-endowed, before retiring to a Turkish Bath on the upper level for some relaxation and relief. There wasn't much steam, at least not from the furnace, so my fellow pleasure seekers' antics were very much on view, including those a blonde European bint in a skimpy sarong, who was making great play of being chased around the room by my Yankee Marine Major, who was dressed in nothing but a tattoo, shouting: 'Come back, Lily!' I couldn't help noticing that Charlton's (or was it Heston's?) marital endowments, sadly for him, matched those of the late Minister Akira. Miss Lily, on the other hand, was definitely one to remember if I ever returned to Shanghai, I thought, but the Chink tart who was astride me at the time thought otherwise. I saw no more of Lily, or my ill-equipped Marine, as yellow udders cascaded around my face and I buried my ancient teeth in 'em whilst my mount giggled and wiggled me to a climax.

The following day we took passage on P&O's *Plassy*, an elegant tub with a single funnel, two masts and plenty of cabins above deck, with a starboard state room on the Boat Deck for me and an inside cabin opposite for Fahran. Before leaving the hotel, however, I went to see the Frog manager to collect my loot from his safe and to settle the bill with an English cheque: well, that fucker Fogg used to say that you could circle the globe with nothing but a Lloyd's cheque book.[21]

"Ah, milord, it 'as been such a pleasure 'aving you stay with us – and *la Comtesse charmante en plus*," oozed the Gallic manager. "Which reminds me; when Madame la Comtesse departed she left zis wiz me for you."

---

[20] See *The Speedicut Papers: Book 3 (Uncivil Wars)*.
[21] Editor's Note: Speedicut is in error. The manager at the time was actually an Italian, Signor Louriero. Auguste Vernon (1851-1918), a Frenchman, only acquired and managed the Astor House Hotel from November 1900.

He slid an envelope across the counter. For some reason, this didn't seem to me to be good news, which - in my experience - women usually deliver face-to-face; it's always bad news that arrives by letter. So, fearing I knew not what – a confession she was riddled with pox, perhaps? - without further ado, I ripped it open. Inside was a short note informing me, with many an endearment, that Tamara had switched the pearls I had bought at the auction: '…as I think I deserve the necklace rather more than your dear wife. She may have had to sleep with you for sixty years, but she has never had to load your rifle.'

I was too surprised by this announcement to be cross and, to be fair, she had a point. Anyway, as I found when the manager opened the safe, she had left the bracelet for Charlotte-Georgina. So, I shrugged, balled up the letter, threw it into the nearest spittoon, gave the manager a cheque drawn on my London account, tucked the Empress Dowager's box into one coat pocket and the pearl bracelet into the other. Then I re-joined Fahran in the lobby and together we left for the boat.

It was only later, once safely aboard and settled in my state room, that I thought it might be wise to check the Empress Dowager's box as well. The scroll was still there, as was the embroidered bag of yellow silk next to it, but when I pulled out the bag to check, instead of a pink pearl the size of a pigeon's egg, this time a smooth pebble from the hotel garden dropped into my lap. Folded up inside the now empty cavity was another note, the contents of which will forever be seared into my memory.

My dear Jasper,

As there is no possible way you can explain this pearl to your wife, I have decided to relieve you of the problem and add it to the pearl necklace you so generously didn't purchase for me. It will look wonderful either as a pendant or set in a tiara that I will encourage Ivan Alexandrovitch to order for me from M. Fabergé as a 'welcome home' present. Don't be too angry, just remember our time together, smile and carry-on as you have always done.

With fond memories,

Tamara

CHAPTER THREE: THE WAGES OF SIN

This time I was speechless with rage. You see, ever since I'd opened the Empress Dowager's parcel on the train to Shanghai, I'd been plotting that - once back in London - I would make my first call on a gem dealer I knew in Hatton Garden, who would certainly have given me enough for this pearl of pearls to rebuild the Dower House to a design by young Measures.[22] Now it was gone and with it my hopes of a comfortable, draught-free modern house in which to live out my remaining days. What was worse was that this bag of swag had – for once - been honestly come by. I was wondering whose side God was on, when Fahran entered with a timely B&S.

"What's the matter, huzoor? You look as though you've lost a sovereign and found a farthing."

"In a manner of speakin' I have, Fahran," I said holding up the empty yellow-lined box.

"Ah," he said, "I wondered when you would find out."

"What the devil do you mean, Fahran? And what do you know about this?"

"My father once told me, huzoor, that you were – how can I say this without giving offence? – somewhat careless when it came to ladies and jewellery."

"He didn't?" I exclaimed, feeling exceedingly affronted.

---

[22] Harry Bell Measures CBE MVO (1862-1940) was a fashionable architect who specialised in the Queen Anne Revival style. Measures was the architect of New College, RMA Sandhurst; Redford Barracks, Edinburgh; all the above-ground stations on London's Central Line; the Union Jack Club, several Rowton Houses for rough sleepers and many town houses for the gentry in South Kensington. By a strange co-incidence, Measures was also the Editor's great-grandfather.

"It's just as well that he did, huzoor."

"Well, whatever he thought, I'm afraid that on this occasion he was right. That bitch of a Ruskie Countess has not only switched the necklace that I bought for Lady Charlotte-Georgina with the bracelet that I bought for her, but she's also stolen what is probably one of the most valuable pearls in the world."

"She may have thought she had, huzoor, but – as I never trusted her after she demanded that I allow that American Major into her bedroom - I took some precautions."

"What Major? What precautions?"

"As to the Major, huzoor, he was the one who showed you around the town last night."

"Oh, him," I said dismissively, "Major Tiny Meat."

"I think you mean Major Heston Charlton, huzoor." I ignored this rather Searcy-like correction by my valet.

"But what do you mean by precautions?"

"You remember that you asked me to deposit the pearls in the hotel safe, huzoor?"

"Yes."

"Well, I took the precaution of exchanging the pearls you had bought – and the Empress Dowager's gift – for some artificial pearls that I'd seen in the market.[23] They weren't expensive but they were very convincing and, anyway, I calculated that the Countess would be in a great hurry and wouldn't take a careful look at what she was stealing."

---

[23] Editor's Note: Cultured pearls were first produced in 1893 by Kokichi Mikimoto (1858-1954).

"So where are they now?"

"Here, huzoor."

Fahran dipped his hand into his pocket and brought out the necklace, the bracelet and La CiXi's going-away present. I was so surprised and overjoyed that I damned nearly got up and kissed him. However, the boundaries of a proper master-servant relationship were a stronger instinct than my immediate joy, so I took them, turned them over in my hand and then handed him back the necklace.

"Her Ladyship already has one of these, Fahran, and she will be very happy with the bracelet. Sooner or later you will need some financial security so here it is. Either keep the string or I can arrange for it to be turned into cash and I will get Mr Rothschild to invest the proceeds on your behalf." Fahran was at first dumbstruck. Then he came right up to me and, silently, gave me an enormous bear hug. "But you'd better not tell Atash," I added, once I got my breath back. "Although I have already made a provision for you both in my Will…"

. . .

Editor's Note: The P&O records show that the Plassy docked in Southampton in late October 1900.

. . .

The first call that I made once I was back in London was to see Mr Abraham at 56A Hatton Garden. He gave me a very good price for Miss CiXi's jumbo-sized pearl although I might have done better at Christie's, but then it would have been all over the rags and that was a price I wasn't prepared to pay. I also cashed in Fahran's necklace, which I then invested on his behalf with Brother Rothschild. Whilst I was selling Abraham the pearls, I mentioned the black jade chess set that I still had stashed in Coutts' deepest vault; I thought his eyes would pop out of his head. However, that box of carved rocks was a rainy-day asset and as, thanks to De Beers, the sun was shining on my investments I decided that it could stay in Angie's safe for the time being. Of course, C-G wanted to know where the money for the proposed rebuild of Wrexham had come from.

"It's one of the perks of government business," I said airily.

"But sadly, not of the variety that appear in the Honours List," she shot back, with utter predictability.

Thinking about it afterwards, though, that last statement of Charlotte-Georgina's wasn't correct as Debrett's was full of peerages awarded for being rogered by royalty – including the Whitehall title - or rooking the Ruskies. Anyway, it distracted her into a rant about my lack of recognition, which I silenced by giving her the bracelet.

"Oh, Jasper, it's exquisite. Where did you get it?"

"It don't do to look a gift horse in the mouth, m'dear, but if you must know I bought it at the Prize Auction after the relief of the Legations."

"It must have cost you a great deal, Jasper."

"Enough," I lied, "now let's go in to luncheon."

My readers should know that I had intended to hold the bracelet back for Christmas, but I had to do something to get the old girl off the subject of my lack of a handle. Speaking of whom, old girls that is, it seemed that Vicky was on her last legs.

"The dear Princess," my beloved confided to me on her return from taking tea at Marlborough House, "says that Her Majesty is in very poor health."

"Really?" I said non-committedly. Frankly, I couldn't have cared less if our aged monarch was alive or dead.

"Yes. The Princess says that Her Majesty's arthritis is now so bad that she can't walk and she's almost blind with cataracts."

"That must make it hard for her to read the State papers."

"Apparently they are read to her by Princess Beatrice."[24]

"Isn't that Arthur Bigge's job?"[25]

"You would think so, but the dear Queen has always preferred that her children serve her."

"Poor benighted bastards," I murmured.

"What's that, Jasper?"

"Nothin', m'dear," I said quickly.

"You know," she went on, "when Princess Beatrice married Henry Battenberg it was on condition that the two of them lived with Her Majesty."

"I wouldn't stand for it," I said, with considerable vigour.

"I don't think the Battenbergs had a choice in the matter. But..." C-G then went off on a long ramble about other put-upon members of our dratted Royal Family. Then she suddenly switched back to the subject of the likelihood of Vicky's imminent demise. "When she goes," said C-G, "there will be an enormous additional burden on the Household."

"It's what they're paid to do."

"That's as may be, Jasper, but with a State Funeral and a Coronation to organise they're bound to be short-handed. Besides which, it's more than sixty years since the last one and so no one will know what to do." She paused for a moment and I could almost hear the cogs whirring in her brain. "Yes," she said with a determined set to her jaw.

---

[24] HRH Princess Henry of Battenberg (1857-1944).
[25] Lieutenant Colonel Sir Arthur Bigge KCB CMG, later 1st Baron Stamfordham (1849-1931).

"Yes, what?" I demanded, although I thought that I knew the answer.

"I shall suggest to the Princess that you would be happy to give the Family the benefit of your considerable experience in these matters."

"You'll do *no such thing*!" I exclaimed, as the prospect of being once again 'in Waiting' reared its hideous head.

"You could hardly refuse if you were asked, Jasper."

"But I won't be asked unless you suggest it and that is somethin' I absolutely forbid you to do - even," I added, "if such service were to be rewarded with a Dukedom."

She said nothing but, ominously, her jaw took on an even firmer set. I immediately decided that I would have to organise an impromptu visit to Dorothea in St Petersburg. Dammit, it was not as though my evening dress was by any means bare, thanks to the Austrian, Prussian, Frog and Mexican monarchies. But according to C-G: 'they don't count'.

Turning to happier topics, I can also record for those of my readers interested in the turf that, whilst I was 'on government business' in the Orient, *Mum's the Word* and *Silent as the Grave* both performed respectably in their final outings at Goodwood. As a result, I was able to offset some of their costs and Dickie Marsh told me that he had high hopes of them the following year.[26] Indeed, I decided there and then that if there was any moolah left over from the new house in north Wales, that I would add a colt or two to my existing string.

I also discovered that, in my absence, Atash appeared to have mastered the intricacies of the Daimler to C-G's satisfaction. However, as a result, the mews was half-empty of horse flesh on my return and I had to fork-out for a second motor for myself. Rather than investing in an under coachman, or chauffeur as the drivers were called, I decided to get Fahran trained-up

---

[26] Editor's Note: In March 1900, Speedicut purchased two racehorses and put them in training with Richard Marsh (1851-1933). See *The Speedicut Papers: Book 8 (At War with Churchill)*.

by Atash in the mysteries of the new motor car so that he could double-up as my valet and my driver. Well, the spending had to stop somewhere.

There was, however, amidst all of the above, one slightly worrying cloud on my horizon: Sibella Holland had written asking for a meeting, so I grudgingly agreed to see her. I had no idea what it was about, although C-G was full of the news that her late sister's boy, who readers will recall was a chum of La Holland's, had proposed to the widow of one of C-G's young cousins who'd blown himself up in his own potting shed: it seemed he was experimenting with the production of illicit whisky. It was a rum business but then, as my beloved reminded me, if the GB didn't produce an heir from the bovine Duchess Maud before he joined the great Brotherhood in the Sky there was only the ghastly Sapphic Suffragette, Lady Charlotte-Edwina, and this fellow Hadfield's aged and widowed employer, Lord Charles-Stephen FitzCharles, between Hadfield and the Dukedom. As Duchess Maud was, in my view, already well beyond child-bearing age, Hadfield would almost certainly inherit. C-G would *not* be pleased if he did.[27]

As so often before, it wasn't long – November 1900 to be precise - before there were developments in my life on two fronts: Mrs Holland's and that appalling old pansy, Oscar Wilde.[28] I will start with La Holland, who I'd agreed to meet in a dingy tea shop in Oxford Street.

"Are you aware, Colonel, that Alan's Tea Rooms is an establishment which is much frequented by members of the Women's Suffrage Movement?"[29] asked Searcy, when I gave him instructions for Fahran on the afternoon before the meeting.

"Oh, God," I groaned, "they'll take one look at me and either pour tea down my collar or throw me into the street."

---

[27] Editor's Note: For those readers unfamiliar with previous volumes of *The Speedicut Papers*, or who have skipped the genealogical bits, the FitzCharles' Dukedom had the unique privilege of descending through the female line if the male line failed.
[28] Oscar Wilde (1854-1900).
[29] Alan's Tea Rooms was at 263 Oxford Street, near to Oxford Circus, and was a Suffragette haunt.

"I doubt that, Colonel, but you would be well advised not to ask for a brandy."

"Why ever not?"

"For a start, Alan's doesn't have a license and, in consequence, the rooms are patronised by members of the Temperance Movement."

"So why does Mrs Holland want to meet me in such a God-awful place?"

"The establishment has one virtue, Colonel: it is discreet."

"But so's the Coburg and it's on the right side of the Park."[30]

"Indeed, Colonel, but I doubt that Mr Holland frequents Alan's whereas I'm sure he is an *habitué* of the Coburg."

"Oh, so you think that this is a personal matter?"

I'd never told him but I was damned sure that Searcy, who knew everything about me, was fully informed of my dalliance with Sibella in Brindisi.[31]

"The choice of venue would seem to indicate that, Colonel."

"Whatever can she want?"

"As to that, Colonel, I have no idea."

"Can't you find out for me through the Nehemiah?"

"Under normal circumstances, Colonel, I could do that with ease. But the Hollands no longer employ a butler nor does Mr Holland have a gentleman's gentleman." Searcy made this last statement with an air of considerable disapproval.

---

[30] The Coburg Hotel was founded in 1815. In 1917, in reaction to anti-German feeling, it changed its name to the Connaught.

[31] See *The Speedicut Papers: Book 8 (At War with Churchill)*.

"So, I have to go to this meetin' in a tea shop full of lesbians and low church teetotallers completely unprepared?"

"It would seem so, Colonel."

"But she might want…"

What? A resumption of our brief affair? Permission to resume it with Fahran? A loan? To advise me that she was leaving her husband? My mind was completely boggled. Maybe it was about her chum Hadfield, who I was sure had been and probably was still one of her mounts, and his engagement to the widowed FitzCharles woman. Then I remembered that Sibella had asked me to be a godparent to her blob. Perhaps she was going to ask me again: some women never take no for an answer, particularly if they can see financial gain for themselves or their offspring. You don't believe me? Then take that bloody woman, Jenny Churchill:[32] she'd have done anything to advance the cause and the career of her dratted brat, Winston.

Speaking of whom, Jenny that is, Searcy told me that she'd got remarried whilst I was in foreign parts. Given what I've just written, my readers would be forgiven for thinking that she would have snared an ageing Marquis with fifty-thousand acres. But, no, her new husband was a Jock Woodentop called Cornwallis-West, who was younger than Winston and probably had an enormous *schwanzstucker*.[33] He was, so Searcy said, a complete nobody although his sisters were good looking gold-diggers: one was married to a Prussian millionaire and the other had snagged Bendor.[34] As I'd told my secretary when he gave me the news, I gave George C-W six months before La Churchill had shagged him to death. Well, at least he would die with a smile on his face.

---

[32] Jenny Jerome, Lady Randolph Churchill (1854-1921).

[33] George Cornwallis-West (1874-1951) was at the time a Captain in the Scots Guards.

[34] Countess Mary "Daisy" von Hochburg (1873-1943) was married to Count Hans Heinrich XV von Hochburg (1861-1938); they became Prince & Princess of Pless in 1907. Constance Cornwallis-West (1876-1970) married Hugh "Bendor" Grosvenor, 2nd Duke of Westminster (1879-1953) in February 1901.

Searcy let out a low cough and I returned to the present.

"Leave it with me, Colonel. Now will you be taking the brougham or the new Daimler?"

"Is Fahran yet ready to drive the motor?"

"He assured me this morning that he was, Colonel, although he has had only two outings in the Park with Atash."

"Hmm. Well, I'll have to risk my neck with him sooner or later and there's no point in leaving the machine to gather rust in the mews."

"Indeed not, Colonel."

"Have you got anythin' else for me, Searcy?"

"There was just one thing, Colonel. Do you recall that Ivan and I are friendly with the Reverend Headlam?"[35]

"Headlam? No, I don't think so. Who is he?"

"He was the gentleman who stood bail for Mr Wilde and then gave him sanctuary when he left prison. You may remember that we took dinner with Mr Headlam and Mr Wilde on the first night of his release from captivity."

I thought for a moment.

"I seem to have a vague recollection." I replied.

"Well, the Reverend Headlam has asked if you would be willing to meet with a friend of Mr Wilde's, a Canadian gentleman called Mr Ross."[36]

"To what end?"

---

[35] The Reverend Stewart Headlam (1847-1924).

[36] Robert Ross (1869-1918).

"It seems that he wants to talk to you about Mr Wilde."

"Why on earth would I want to waste my time doin' that, Searcy?" he didn't answer me but, instead, looked at the carpet. "I read the other day," I continued in order to cover Searcy's obvious embarrassment, "that Wilde is on his beam-end in Paris and living off the kindness of strangers – beggin', to put it bluntly."

"I understand that it's not quite like that, Colonel," Searcy said, whilst continuing to inspect the pile of the Persian rug beneath his feet.

"Hmm. I suppose this Ross fellow wants to touch me for money."

"Something of the sort, Colonel," Searcy replied.

"Why should I be interested in helpin' the bugger?"

"I'm not entirely sure I know the answer to that, Colonel," which meant that he knew exactly why, "I think you will only find that out by receiving Mr Ross."

"Hmm," I said again, "well, I wouldn't do it for Wilde – but I would do it for you, if you asked me straight out." Searcy looked up, fixed his still dazzlingly blue eyes on me and did so. "Very well. I'll see him at the club after I get back from my interview with Mrs Holland. I might as well get all the horrors over and done with in one day."

"Thank you, Colonel," said Searcy, who then turned and left my study.

The following morning, I told C-G that I would take luncheon at the Verulam, probably have a snooze there afterwards and not to expect to see me before dinner. I walked the short distance to the club where, with Johnny Dawson, we both had some excellent truffled turtle soup, foie gras-stuffed ortolans wrapped in crinkled Sicilian vine leaves and a brace of Welsh rarebits, all washed down with a magnum of a very decent Chambertain. Feeling fortified against the unknown to come, I retired with a large brandy to a deep chair in front of the fire in the smoking room to await Fahran with the motor at three-thirty.

...

The tea shop at the wrong end of Oxford Street was every bit as awful as I'd feared. Small round tables, covered with wipe-clean oil cloth and surrounded with cheap bentwood furniture, were dotted around the glazed-tile interior which was lit by spluttering, fly-blown gas lamps hanging from the ceiling and enlivened, if that's the right word, with foxed engravings of Lesbos. Most of the tables were occupied either by pious looking young men sipping tea with elderly clerics, or mannish-looking women sporting wing collars, ties and monocles, in the company of pretty little bints in frilly-edged dresses. Unless I was much mistaken, I saw C-G's aunt, Lady Charlotte-Edwina, in a corner with a girl dressed as a sailor. Along the far wall was a counter behind which a beefy woman with no bust and a boy's haircut was dispensing tea and cakes. Scurrying between the customers and the tea urn were a brace of mousey women dressed as parlour maids, balancing a look of considerable harassment with tin trays groaning under the weight of the alcohol-free beverages. It was a combination of the Second and Sixth Circles of Hell.

As I entered the utterly dismal dump, I espied Sibella in a corner deep in conversation with a large man in a cloak and a felt hat who had his back turned to me. His shape was vaguely familiar but no more. For some reason, although I really hadn't a clue who he was, his presence didn't seem at all odd. I hung my tile and Ulster on a hook and made my way over to them. As I approached, Sibella looked up, gave me a little wave and pointed at the spare chair next to her. The man in the cloak rose to leave, at least that's what I presumed, and bent over Sibella's gloved paw in an old-fashioned gesture of farewell. Then he turned towards me, his face in a deep shadow cast by the brim of his hat.

Although I hadn't a clue who he was, it seemed discourteous not to greet him so I stuck out my hand. He extended his and enveloped my fingers in a damp, flaccid grip; with his other hand, he raised his tile and I found myself looking into a moon-shaped face with dark eye sockets and unnaturally white, almost translucent skin disfigured by open sores. He gave me an utterly ghoulish smile revealing the blackened stumps of teeth set in suppurating gums.

"I see you don't remember me, Colonel – my name is Oscar Wilde."

I tried to scream but no sound came out.

"Wake-up, Colonel!" I felt a hand on my shoulder. "Your motor car and driver are outside."

It was Charles the hall porter. With a start, I realised that I'd been dreaming and that I was still in the Verulam. With very considerable relief, I heaved myself to the perpendicular, rubbed the sleep out of my eyes and made my way downstairs where Charles's assistant, Charles the under porter, was kindly holding my coat, hat, cane and gloves. I could see through the glass panes of the club's front door that Fahran was outside, clad in his new chauffeur's livery and ready to help he up in the motor. I'd acquired a four-seater Daimler for C-G – the same model as Bertie had bought - but had decided on a sportier model for myself, so whilst she had to climb into the rear I simply sat next to Fahran. The engine was already running, if that's the right word to describe the burps, farts and bangs that it was emitting, so Fahran didn't have to crank it into life as I'd seen Atash do with C-G's machine. A moment later he clambered nimbly into the driver's seat next to me.

"Hang on, Colonel!"

It was an instruction that I didn't need, for I'm pretty sure that my knuckles were already white under my gloves. Fahran released the hand brake and rather officiously stuck out his right arm to indicate, I supposed, that he was about to set off. Then, with a lurch and the sound of a thousand cogs being stripped, we were headed down St James's Street. Unlike the time when old Khazi crashed the Whitehalls' ancient State coach into the window of Locke's on our way to Dorothea's Presentation,[37] this time his

---

[37] See *The Speedicut Papers: Book 6 (Vitai Lampada)*.

son rounded the corner into Pall Mall without incident. At Waterloo Place, Fahran made a curious gesture with his right arm, steered the vehicle to the left and we chugged up Lower Regent Street to Piccadilly Circus.

Thus far our journey had been without incident but, as the motor struggled up the hill to the Circus, that was about to change. We were approaching the junction with Jermyn Street, steam rising ominously from the bonnet as the engine struggled with the gradient, when a costermonger's cart shot out from the left. Fahran applied the brakes, the engine stalled but the cobbles were slippery and we skidded gently into the wretched thing, which was piled high with fruit and vegetables. Fortunately, we missed the costermonger himself, but the impact bowled over his barrow. Whilst the Cockney vendor cursed us up-hill-and-down-dale, his assorted cabbages, onions, cauliflowers, swedes, apples and turnips bounced playfully off in the direction of the memorial to the Crimean cock-up at the bottom of the hill.

"Bleedin' lunatics," he screamed, "can't you fuckin' butcher's 'ook where you're fuckin' goin'?"

"Huzoor!" exclaimed Fahran in outrage as he half-climbed out of the motor. I put a restraining hand on his arm.

"Leave this to me, Fahran." Then to the costermonger I called back. "We are hardly to blame, my good man. It was you who should have been takin' care at a junction."

"Junction my soddin' arse," he shot back. "I was jest movin' m'barra down the field of wheat, same as I's always dun…" I decided to cut across him with the voice of authority.

"Look here, my man, there can be no doubt the fault was yours, as I'm sure that member of the Constabulary will confirm in a moment," I said, pointing at a Peeler who was making his way towards us. "But I'm in a hurry and I don't want or need to get the authorities involved in this unfortunate upset. Fahran, give the man a half-crown for his damaged goods." Doubtless seeing the opportunity for a quick profit, the costermonger pointed at his fleeing stock.

"'T'aint fair. I've lorst at least a guinea's worth, t'say nuffink of the damage to me bow an' arrer."

"Very well, I'll give you five pounds as compensation. Fahran, please be so kind as to hand the gentleman this note."

Fortunately, the money seemed to do the trick and, whilst Fahran cranked the Daimler back into life, I told the Constable that the matter had been amicably settled.

"Very good, sir," he said officiously, "but tell your coachman to take more care in future. It's been chaos since we lost the red flags…" I wasn't about to argue the toss, as we were already late for my appointment with Sibella and we still had some way to go. Five incident-free minutes later we drew up with a bang at the kerb outside the tea room at 263 Oxford Street.

"Wait here, Fahran, I won't be long," I said, as he helped me down.

I must say that Alan's turned out to be a far cry from the establishment of my earlier dream: it had a cosy, rather chintzy interior and if it was the haunt of Mrs Pankhurst's Sapphic sisters they weren't in evidence.[38] Sibella was seated on a banquette, mercifully alone, and tea-for-two was already laid in front of her. It would have been an idyllic scene had she not been drumming her nails on the lace cloth with a look of considerable impatience on her face.

"Jasper – at last."

"Better late than never," I replied taking the pew opposite but keeping my coat on. "So, what can I do for you, Sibella?"

"Tea?"

"I never drink the muck." Not strictly speaking true, but…

"A glass of selzer?"

---

[38] Emmeline Pankhurst (1858-1928).

"Look here, Sibella, let's not waste any more of our time: why have you summoned me to this place?"

"It's about my son." Ah, ha, I thought, so she still wants me to be the brat's godfather despite my earlier refusal.

"What about him?"

"I think you should make a financial provision for him."

"What! Why the hell should I?" I shot back in surprise at this blatant and unjustified demand.

"Because he's yours."

CHAPTER FOUR: A BROKEN TOY

"Absolute stuff and nonsense," I exclaimed in shock.

Of course, it was perfectly possible that he was, but I wasn't about to admit it and, anyway, I was by no means the blob's only putative papa.

"If I recall rightly we met on your honeymoon and, whilst I don't imagine for one moment that you were a virgin at the altar…"

"Colonel Speedicut, you forget yourself!"

"Do I? If I remember rightly, Mrs Holland, you gave me to understand that you had a considerable *tendresse* for my wife's cousin, that Hadfield chap."

"I absolutely deny your foul innuendo, Colonel."

"Be that as it may, m'dear, two things are certain: first, your husband had far more opportunities for procreation with you than did I and, second, my valet Fahran Khazi shared even more of your favours than me."

She didn't so much as blush at this. Instead, her eyes and lips narrowed.

"You may think what you like, Colonel Speedicut, but back in the nursery in Bayswater is a boy who shares your fair skin and blond hair – characteristics which he does not share with either his father or your manservant," she paused for a moment, "or Mr Hadfield."

"I see."

"I hope you do, Colonel."

Well, it was bound to have happened sooner or later. I'd had sixty years of unbridled rogering and nothing other than Dorothea to show for it: the odds were clearly not in my favour and shortening by the day.

"Assumin' – and I'm not willin' to make any assumption without the evidence of my own eyes - that you are right, what do you expect me to do about it?"

"I expect you to set up a well-endowed trust for the little boy."

"And if I don't?"

"The next time you are away I will invite myself and Charles to tea with your wife, tell her the whole story and let her draw her own conclusions."

"You wouldn't!"

"Be assured that I would – and also be assured that she will have no difficulty in working out the paternity of my son: it's written all over his face."

"That's blackmail."

"Call it what you like, Colonel. But, whatever it is, be under no illusion that it's an idle threat."

"I see."

"I hope you do. Now, when can I expect you to pay me and our son a visit?" I decided, as so often before, to play for time.

"Look, I have a very busy diary in the run-up to Christmas, which we're spending at Wrexham, and I won't be back in London until early February or possibly later. It will have to wait until then."

I could see that she regarded this as sub-optimal, but what choice did she really have? And a lot could happen in two or three months.

"Very well, Colonel, early March. In the meantime, I will lodge with my lawyer a detailed account of your behaviour and the paternity of our son. I will also give him an instruction to send it to your wife – and *The Times* – if we have not resolved this matter to my entire satisfaction by 15th March."

I grunted my acknowledgement and, as there was nothing more to be said, got up and left without giving her the courtesy of a goodbye. It was in a very black mood that I arrived back at the Verulam, a few minutes late for my rendezvous with Ross. He was waiting for me in the hall.

"Mr Ross?" I enquired of a rather podgy young man with receding hair, a well-trimmed moustache and a well-cut suit. He stuck out a damp paw and gave me a limp handshake.

"Colonel Speedicut, it is a pleasure to meet you."

"That remains to be seen," I growled, for I was still in a filthy frame of mind, "Charles," this to the hall porter, "I'm taking Mr Ross to the library. Please send up a bottle of brandy and two glasses." I turned to Ross. "We won't be disturbed there, hardly any of the members here can read."

We climbed the stairs to the second floor and I settled Ross in a chair by the fire whilst I slumped down opposite him. Once a bottle of Hennessy had been delivered safely by Charles (the bar steward) and we were alone I asked him why he wanted to see me.

"You are I believe, Colonel," he opened in his pleasant North American accented voice, "familiar with my friend and mentor, Mr Oscar Wilde."

"In common with every other member of the newspaper readin' public," I replied non-committedly.

"No, Colonel, I meant that you are *personally* acquainted with Mr Wilde."

"It's certainly true that I've met him on a number of occasions," I said guardedly. "If I remember rightly, he came to my daughter's Comin' Out Ball."

"But you have not seen him since he has been out of the public eye."

"You mean after he went to prison?" Ross winced.

"No, Colonel – I was referring to the time since he ended that terrible chapter of his life."

"I have not, although I understand that he's cavortin' on the Continent with that appallin' pansy, Bosie Douglas."[39] Ross winced again.

"No longer, Colonel. Oscar is living in an hotel on the Left Bank in Paris where I, and others, do our best to keep him in funds and out of the gutter."

"So, he's financially afloat, then."

"Unfortunately, not. The fact is, Colonel, that for every ten francs we give Oscar he spends a hundred on alcohol and…" he paused for a moment, "entertainment."

"I suppose you mean by that the boys of the boulevards." For the third time Ross looked pained, but he didn't deny my assertion. "So, what's Wilde's fall from grace to St Germain got to do with me?"

"Everything."

"What the hell do you mean by that?"

"I mean Colonel that, had it not been for you and a certain organisation, Oscar would still be happily married, fêted as the century's greatest playwright with a dozen more triumphs to his name, rich, honoured and respected."

"I doubt that very much," I said, as I wondered if I'd heard him a'right: 'a certain organisation'? Did he mean the Brotherhood? How the devil could he know about it or its part in Wilde's downfall?[40] "The way Wilde was carryin' on with every pretty-faced groom and valet in London, to say nothin' of flauntin' his relationship with Master Bosie, he was headed for an almighty crash without any help from me."

---

[39] 'Bosie' was the nickname of Lord Alfred Douglas (1870-1945).

[40] See *The Speedicut Papers: Book 7 (Royal Scandals)*.

"So, do you deny that the secret society, to which you and the late Lord Queensberry belong, plotted to trick Oscar into suing Lord Queensberry for criminal libel? And that you did so full in the knowledge that, in so doing, he would expose himself to the vengeance of Society and the law?"

Actually, that wasn't my plan at all, which was for Wilde to flee abroad where he and Bosie could gossip to their hearts' content about Nurse Cavell's role in Clarence's demise.[41]

"I know nothin' of which you speak," I blustered. "I've never been a member of any secret society; I'm not even a Mason."

"So, you deny that you are a member of the Brotherhood of the Sons of Thunder?"

"I've never even heard of it," I lied.

"No? Well, let me enlighten you – it is an organisation dedicated to protecting the Royal Succession and, as it sees fit, the interests of England – and you have been a member of it since 1840."

I was too flabbergasted to reply immediately. Whilst I collected my thoughts, Ross stared into the fire. Under normal circumstances I'd have shown the bugger the door and then informed the GB, who'd have known what to do. But I needed first to find out, if I could, what he knew and how he knew it. So, I decided to continue to deny all whilst trying to discover whatever I could.

"Mr Ross," I said, in as level a voice as I could muster at short notice, "I have never heard of this Brotherhood and, if it exists, I am certainly not a member of it. I am also wholly unaware of any plot to, as you put it, trick Mr Wilde into initiatin' his own misfortunes. Unless you can provide me with any evidence to the contrary, I'm afraid that you will have wasted your time in seekin' this meeting."

---

[41] HRH The Duke of Clarence & Avondale (1864-1892); see *The Speedicut Papers: Book 7 (Royal Scandals)*.

It was my turn to pause. Would he fall for the trick and reveal his source? Ross didn't even blink and a deep silence hung between us. Eventually, I could stand it no more: he wasn't going to blab, so I had to get rid of him and inform the GB as fast as my pins (or Fahran) would get me to Whitehall House.

"However," I at last continued, "for the sake of a former slight acquaintance with Mr Wilde, I'm willin' to give you a small sum of money – say fifty pounds - to ease his exile, but I give it with the promise that it will be both the first and the last such gift."

"To be perfectly honest, Colonel, I fully expected you to make the denials you have made and I also expected you to try and buy me off with a paltry gift. Please be aware that I am playing for much higher stakes than a mere fifty pounds. Your *personal* reputation," he said giving me a very knowing look, "and that of your colleagues is worth considerably more than even five *thousand* pounds."

My God, I thought, to be blackmailed once in an afternoon might be considered a misfortune, but twice looked like damned ill-fortune or worse.

"So, what do you want?"

"I want sufficient funds to ensure that Oscar can live for the rest of his life in the manner to which he's entitled."

"And why do you suppose that I would even consider givin' the wretched man such a large sum?"

"You may not be aware of this, Colonel, but Oscar has written a long letter to Lord Alfred Douglas," he looked as though he was about to be sick as the mere thought of the queer peer, "in which he has detailed all his misfortunes *and* their origins. He wrote it whilst he was in Reading Gaol and he has entitled it *De Profundis* – in case you don't know, that's a reference to *Psalm 130*. He's told me that he's going to entrust me with this letter, which I am to copy and then have delivered to Lord Alfred and to a publisher."

"I can't think why you would bother with a publisher, Ross. If you give it to Douglas, he'll relate its entire contents to everyone he knows before you can say boo to a goose."

"Although not for that reason, Colonel, when Oscar gives me the letter I will *not* be delivering it to Bosie."

"I don't give a damn what you do with Wilde's scribbles."

"You should do, Colonel."

"Why? What can a letter from Mr Wilde to his former catamite possibly have to do with me?" I demanded.

"Let me explain. Whilst Oscar was in prison, and somewhat in the manner of Edmond Dantès and the Abbé Faria,[42] he met a fellow prisoner who had been a member of your Brotherhood and had been betrayed by them. Although, thanks to the awful prison regime, communication was extremely difficult between them, over the course of his incarceration this man told Oscar all about the Brotherhood of the Sons of Thunder and their – and your – involvement in his misfortunes."

"Who was this man?" I demanded.

"I'm not at liberty to say – but his identity is revealed in the letter."

"And where is this letter?"

"In Paris, where I am returning tomorrow. I suggest that you think over what I have said and then contact me at this telegraphic address." He pulled out a card and scribbled on the back of it before handing it to me. "Don't delay, Colonel." He then got up, gave me a courteous little bow and walked out of the room.

---

[42] Editor's Note: This is a reference to *The Count of Monte Cristo* (1844) by Alexander Dumas.

As I've said, my initial instinct was to inform the GB. Then, after I'd downed a large glass of Mr Hennessy's best to steady my nerves, I had second thoughts: before lifting the lid on a potentially poisonous can of stinking worms I needed to consult Searcy, who'd bloody well obliged me to meet Ross in the first place. I staggered back to Stratton Street and, once in my study, sent for him.

"I see," said Searcy, after I'd finished my tale of an utterly awful afternoon. "As to Mrs Holland, Colonel, you have gained your objective of obtaining more time so I propose that we put that issue to one side for the moment. The matter of Mr Ross's threat to 'reveal all' is more immediate and, without doubt, infinitely more embarrassing than Mrs Holland's threat to expose you as the father of her child. I had no idea that was what Mr Ross had in mind when he asked to see you."

"But what am I to do? I'm already committed to rebuildin' the Dower House and I'll be damned if I'll beggar m'self to fund the rest of that bugger Wilde's life. How old is he?"

"Forty-six, Colonel."

"My God, he could live for another thirty years or more."

"That, Colonel, is unlikely. Mr Wilde is in very poor health. A recent operation to arrest an ear infection he acquired in prison has not been a success, besides which I doubt that Mr Wilde's liver or his brain will stand more than a year or two more of being subjected to literally gallons of champagne, whisky and – worst of all – absinthe. No, the problem is not one of money but the threat of revelations. If you are to avoid a scandal that will make Mr Wilde's own indiscretions look like petty larceny then you have to secure the evidence. And the only way to do that is to go to Paris."

"Well, I'm not goin' on my own."

"Indeed not, Colonel."

"But not even Fahran's conjurin' skills will be enough to get me the letter."

"Worry not, Colonel. I will accompany you and, by the time we arrive, I will have a plan."

After I'd fobbed off C-G with a story that I'd been summoned at short notice to our Embassy in the City of Sin in connection with a 'royal duty', Searcy and I took the Boat Train the following day and got to the Meurice in time for luncheon on 29th November [1900]. I'd hoped to see Flashy whilst I was in Paris but there was no answer to the message Searcy left with the concierge at the old *roué*'s apartment, which was only a short walk around the corner from Wilde's hotel in the rue des Beaux-Arts. Anyway, I had more important things to think about than getting pissed with Flashman at the Deux Magots.

Searcy had sent Ross a telegram before we left telling him to meet us at the Meurice at three on the first day where we intended to put Searcy's plan, which included a firecracker, into action. Ross arrived promptly and was shown up to my suite.

"So, where's the wretched letter?" I demanded, as soon as he crossed the threshold.

"I don't have it with me."

"Why ever not?"

"Oscar won't let it out of his sight."

"Then tell him to bring it over here."

"I can't."

"Why not?"

"Because he's not very well and can't leave his bedroom."

"How unwell?" asked Searcy, looking concerned.

"He's in considerable pain from an ear infection. The doctor is with him," said Ross, stifling a sob, "and is administering morphine." Shame it's not the Last Rites, I thought to myself. "If you want to see the letter, I'm afraid that you'll have to come to the Hotel d'Alsace."

"Since our sole purpose in travellin' to Paris is to see the evidence of your absurd allegations, I suppose we'll have to make the tedious journey to the Left Bank. Searcy, please arrange for the hotel's motor to convey us there."

"Right away, Colonel." Whilst Searcy used a telephonic machine to speak to reception, Ross and I stood in silence. "If we go down now, Colonel, it will be at the door shortly."

Twenty minutes later the motor pulled up in front of Wilde's hotel. I didn't know the Alsace and was expecting a dingy hostelry of the kind you find in the backstreets of unfashionable seaside towns on the south coast. Instead, it was a handsome building, which Ross informed us had once been part of a palace occupied by Henry's IV's first mount, Maggie Valois; more recently, and rather appropriately given Maggie's morals, it had been a bordello. Ross showed us into the salon and said he'd be back with the manuscript.

"The wallpaper's simply shocking," I remarked to Searcy, as I looked around the spacious and colonnaded room. "If the quack doesn't kill Wilde, it undoubtedly will."

Before Searcy could reply, Ross reappeared with a bulky portfolio under his arm.

"This is it, Colonel. It's a copy." Damn, I thought, bang goes Searcy's plan to distract Ross and destroy the bloody thing, "The manuscript is being kept safe elsewhere. As you can see, it's rather long so I've marked the relevant pages."

Thank God for that, I thought: the document looked to be the size of a novel not a *billet doux* to a former fuck. Searcy and I flicked through page-after-page of Wilde's sloping and rather rounded script. What little I read, before we got to the reason for our visit, was mostly flowery prose that attempted to explain the old poseur's infatuation with Bosie D and his consequent downfall. It was by turns recriminatory, reproachful and resentful, describing Bosie as a wilful and ignorant child who had treated him like a disposable toy: it was only when we got to the passages I'd come to see that it was accusatory.

In silence, Searcy and I read carefully through a dozen paragraphs about the Brotherhood, the private life of Clarence, our plot to silence Wilde and the reasons for it. It was a fizzing powder keg. So explosive was it that, were it to be published, the GB and I would be escorted into a darkened room with a brace of pistols and a bottle of spirits – and Bertie, even though he was guiltless, would have had to flee the country to save the succession. There was only one answer to this damning document: bluff.

"Facinatin' stuff, Mr Ross," I said, when I'd finished the marked passages, "you really should get Mr Wilde to turn it into a novel; it would be an instant best seller. Of course, he'd have to take advice to ensure that he didn't find himself once more in the dock for libel."

"What do you mean, Colonel?"

"I mean, Ross, that this is the most defamatory garbage it's ever been my misfortune to read. You can't plead justification, as Queensberry did, because it contains not a shred of hard evidence nor are you likely to find any."

"I'll get an affidavit from Mr Wilde's informant and he could be called as a witness. As a peer, his word would carry great weight in Court."

"A peer, eh?"

Ross looked as though he'd just fallen head-first into a sewer. Well, that made life a lot easier: there couldn't be that many members of Burke's in the slammer. Given what I'd just read, I was sure that the GB would swiftly identify the leaking and incarcerated aristo and 'arrange' for him to be un-contactable in perpetuity (as, indeed, later happened).

"That's if you can find him," I added.

"But he's in prison."

"Exactly."

"But… you wouldn't… you couldn't."

Before I could reply, a servant hurried in with the news that Wilde had taken a turn for the worse. Now's our chance I thought: if only Ross left the manuscript behind. But he didn't. Instead he scooped up the portfolio, asked us to wait and ran out of the room. He returned about five minutes later, empty handed.

"Colonel, Mr Wilde's physical and spiritual well-being has become my first priority. Could I ask you to return here tomorrow morning, at which time I'm sure we can come to a sensible arrangement?"

"I doubt that," I said, "but you may expect us at nine o'clock. Searcy, we're leavin'."

Over the next twelve hours we batted the problem back and forth. It was essential that we secured the incriminating pages, but neither of could think how. A loaded pistol and a bottle of brandy haunted what little sleep I managed that night.

CHAPTER FIVE: DEATH OF AN OLD QUEEN

The following morning found us back on the steps of the Hotel d'Alsace at nine. An air of gloom seemed to hang over the hotel; the reason was soon explained.

"J'ai un rendezvous avec Monsieur Ross," I said to the concierge.

"Je regret, monsieur, mais Monsieur Ross est occupé."

"Avec quoi?"

"Avec les arrangements funéraires."

"De qui?"

"Le pauvre Monsieur Wilde."

"Wilde's dead?" I exclaimed.

"Précisément, monsieur."

"Alors, s'il vous plaît dire à Monsieur Ross que je veux le voir pour exprimer mes condoléances."

"Certainement, monsieur, Gaston!" he said, as he clicked his fingers for a hall boy. Searcy tugged my sleeve.

"Colonel, let's go into that sitting room. I've had an idea."

A few minutes later Ross appeared. His appearance can only be described as woebegone.

"I've heard your news, Ross," I said, as he entered, "I'm many things, but I'm not a hypocrite, so I can't say that I'm sorry - but you have my condolences for the loss of your friend and a very talented man." Ross wiped a tear from his eye. "However, under these somewhat changed circumstances, I have a proposition for you which I shall leave my secretary to describe."

Ross nodded but said nothing.

"In the light of your tragic news, Robbie, Colonel Speedicut proposes a settlement."

"What settlement?" said Ross, in a dull voice.

"Whilst Oscar, as an un-discharged bankrupt, might have risked the publication of *De Profundis*, you - as a man of not-unlimited means - most assuredly could not. Your evidence may look strong now, but in Court it might be a very different thing. Besides which, your attempt to blackmail Colonel Speedicut for an income for Oscar is now no longer valid. However, by your own admission, Oscar has been a considerable financial burden on you and your friends for the past two-and-a-half years." Ross nodded again. "He is now dead, but there are bound to be unpaid debts, funeral expenses, a monument and so on. Am I right?"

"You are," he replied.

"Colonel Speedicut is willing to cover all those costs in return for the pages of the *De Profundis* manuscript - and any copies of it which are in existence - which you marked for our attention yesterday."

"If I agree, how do I know he will not renege on the arrangement as soon as he has the passages?"

"I will hold one thousand pounds to cover the sundry expenses and I will act as your banker."

Ross thought a while as I prayed that he would accept. Eventually he did, but he had a condition which he addressed to me.

"The letter is in Oscar's room along with two typewritten copies. If I am to hand over the sections you demand then you must come with me to get them."

"Why?" I asked.

"Because I want you to leave this place with an image burnt into your brain of the consequences of your actions."

"Very well," I said. "Lead on."

It seemed a small price to pay and, as I'd seen plenty of corpses before, the prospect of seeing the dead pansy held no terrors for me. It should have done. The first inkling I had of what was to come was the appalling stench that hit my nostrils outside Wilde's door. It was even worse when we entered the room, in which a priest and another man were loitering beside the bed on which lay the late Oscar Wilde. The curtains were drawn, but the emaciated body of the playwright was lit from above by a gas lantern and, in its flickering light, it was plain as day that the undertakers had yet to do their work. The body lay on bare sheets that were soaked with blood, puss and excrement, as was the night shirt in which he had died. It was the most disgusting thing I'd ever seen and I was speechless with the shock of it.

"We don't know why but, shortly after he died," said Ross in a flat voice, "every orifice erupted with corruption. Now, if you'll wait there I'll fetch the relevant passages."

Thank God, it didn't take him long. I seized them and ran from the room and I didn't stop running until I'd reached the motor that was waiting for us outside.

"*Les Deux Magots. Vite!*" I ordered the driver as Searcy climbed in next to me.

It was only after I'd consumed the best part of a bottle of the café's finest Armagnac that I felt able to return to the hotel where I noted the name of the peer and then burnt the incriminating pages in the fire place of my sitting room.

"After that I don't feel much like luncheon," I said to my secretary. "I think I'm goin' to take a nap. Book a table for the two of us at Ledoyen tonight, but don't wake me before six. And, once again, thank you."[43]

...

No sooner had I returned from Paris than it was time to pack up and hoof off to Wrexham for Christmas, which was to be the last big event before the builders moved in. It was as well that I was able to snooze in the library through most of the festivities, which were considerably enlivened by our Russian grandchildren, for the New Year brought a letter from the Palace. C-G's eyes lit up at the sight of the heavily embossed coat-of-arms on the back of the cream-coloured envelope. She should have been - but she wasn't - disappointed by its contents, which were not an invitation to bend the knee for a long overdue tap on the shoulder by our ailing monarch, but a Command to wait upon her at her gloomy Italianate mansion on *ultima Thule*.

Quite why the wretched old frump thought that anyone in their right mind would want to spend January by the seaside was (and is) beyond me, but that's a Hanoverian for you: her grandpapa was a certified loony, her uncle the Regent was barking and her father was a sadistic brute or so the Iron

---

[43] Editor's Note: Although *De Profundis* was addressed to Lord Alfred Douglas, he claimed never to have received it. The letter was first published by Ross, who was Wilde's literary executor, in 1905 in an edited edition which made no mention of Queensberry or the Brotherhood of the Sons of Thunder. Subsequent versions were published, but Ross consigned the original manuscript to the British Museum with instructions that it was not to be opened until 1960. In April of that year, the publisher Sir Rupert Hart-Davis (1907-1999) examined the manuscript in the library of the British Museum and produced a new, corrected text from it which was published in *The Letters of Oscar Wilde* in 1962. He wrote: 'I had the excitement of being the first [person] to see the original manuscript of Oscar's longest, best, and most important letter *De Profundis*, which had been given to the British Museum by Robbie Ross with a fifty-year ban on anyone seeing it, so as to make sure Lord Alfred Douglas never saw it. To our delight, we found that the published versions were wildly inaccurate, so [my] version in *The Letters* was the first accurate text in print.' The British Library published a facsimile of the original manuscript in 2000; it also contained no mention of the Brotherhood of the Sons of Thunder.

Duke once told me. Actually, thinking about it, why should Vicky have been any saner than her forebears? As evidence of this, and besides the fact of her obsession with freezing fresh air, I had it on good authority that she'd spent sixty-plus years throwing her toys out of the bassinet whenever she couldn't get her own way. Apparently, when she heard that Bertie had acted as a pall bearer at Gladstone's funeral *and* kissed the widow Gladstone's hand by the coffin,[44] the old girl practically had to be put into the family's straight jacket.

But to be fair, barking or not, she'd always been moderately charming to me whenever our paths had crossed in the past and I even think there was a time when she fancied my cavalry whiskers. That's not to say that I was ever in the running to be a candidate to fill the gap in her over-heated affections left when her Saxe-Coburg stallion went prematurely to the knacker's yard: that was a job taken-on by the ghastly John Brown, until he joined the Prince Consort. But even worse was to come when Brown's buckled shoes were filled by the Munshi who,[45] my readers may find it hard to believe, Vicky had appointed as her 'Indian Secretary'. Brown, of course, was only her 'Highland servant'. He may have bossed around the courtiers and Bertie, to their fury, but at least he kept his digits out of the till. However, all of that is now water under the bridge and the Munshi was packed off – kit and kaboodle - to India after the old gird popped her clogs. Which brings me to a subject on which I now propose dealing in some detail, for I was there and I witnessed the quite extraordinary, not to say bizarre, circumstances surrounding her demise. If you are curious, dear reader, read on:

It all started when Fahran and I arrived at Osborne on the afternoon of Friday 18th January [1901], where I was greeted by Bigge.

"I'm extraordinarily grateful that you've volunteered to help, Speedicut," were his opening words as I was bundled out of a pony chaise and into the chilly interior of Vicky's villa by the sea. Volunteered? I'd done nothing of the sort, but I didn't need Searcy's brain to guess who had done so on my behalf.

[44] William Ewart Gladstone (1809-1898).
[45] John Brown (1826-1883) & Abdul Karim (1863-1909), known as the Munshi

"Think nothin' of it," I lied. "So, what's the situation?"

"Not good, I'm afraid." As Fahran and a royal footman tackled the bags, Bigge ushered me into a saloon that looked as though its entire contents had been looted from the Great Mooghal's palace in Delhi and probably had been. "Frankly, Her Majesty is not well and it's Reid's and Laking's opinion, both of whom are 'in Waiting', that she has not got long to live."[46]

"What's wrong with her?"

"The ravages of time, mostly. She's been confined to bed virtually since the day she arrived here and, more recently, she's spent much of her time dozing if not actually asleep. On those occasions when she's fully awake I'm not altogether sure that she's in her right mind."

"What makes you think that?"

"Well, for a start, she's stopped giving orders and meekly does everything she's told. And she's lost her appetite."

"Is The Prince of Wales here?" I asked.

"No. I've told His Royal Highness to expect the worst but he maintains that Her Majesty is just 'out of sorts and will soon revive in the sea air'."

"What about Princess Beatrice? Surely, she's told her brother what's goin' on?"

"She hasn't, nor has Princess Helena.[47] Strictly between you and me, Speedicut, I think that the last thing they want is to have The Prince and Princess of Wales getting in their way here."

---

[46] Dr James (later Sir James) Reid (1849-1923) & Dr Sir Francis Laking Kt (1847-1914).
[47] HRH Princess Christian (Helena) of Schleswig-Holstein (1846-1923) shared the ask of looking after her mother, Queen Victoria, with her sister HRH Princess Henry (Beatrice) of Battenberg.

"So, in addition to yourself, Lakin' and Reid, who else knows what's goin' on?"

"Mrs Tuck."[48]

"Who?"

"She's The Queen's principal dresser and has been for the past thirty years; she's going to be a vitally important person when the time comes."

"Why?"

"Because she's been entrusted by The Queen with 'Instructions', which Her Majesty drew up in 1897 and which are to be carried out at her death. The contents of these Instructions are known only to Mrs Tuck. That's where you come in."

"What do you mean?"

"Your job, Speedicut, is to befriend Mrs Tuck and to ensure that - whatever it is that she has been instructed to do - it does not cause, err, *embarrassment*."

"How on earth could these Instructions do that?" I asked in bewilderment at the courtier's obvious concern and my dismay at being made the old besom's keeper.

"I have good reason to believe," said Bigge, "that these Instructions include The Queen's desire to be buried with a number of souvenirs."

"Nothin' unusual or embarrassin' in that, surely?"

"No - unless some of them are not connected with her immediate family, if you follow my meaning..." he replied, arching an eyebrow and looking off into a corner where there was a peculiarly ugly statue of the horrible Highland servant.

---

[48] Mrs Mary Tuck (dates unknown).

"I see," I said, as the light dawned. "So, what do you want me to do? Stop The Queen's wishes bein' carried out?"

"God forbid!" said Bigge, looking genuinely shocked.

"What then?"

"To ensure that the, err, more controversial contents of her casket are kept out of the sight of her family."

"How on earth am I supposed to do that. I'm not a conjuror, y'know."

"Reid may have an idea; I suggest you consult with him."

"Anythin' else?"

"No," said Bigge. "Although if the Kaiser is as good as his word and makes an appearance before the end, I may also need some help with him."[49]

"Why me? Surely that's a job for Fritz?"[50] I replied, as the prospect loomed of not only having to befriend a batty old maid but also to humour the horrendous Hohenzollern.

"As a holder of both the Order of the Black Eagle and the Red Eagle,[51] you are the obvious – and, indeed, the only - choice, my dear Speedicut. I trust that you've brought those decorations with you." Bigge said cracking a most uncourtier-like smile at my obvious discomfiture.

In the event, Mrs Tuck was the least of my worries for the Kraut Kaiser - and the rest of the Saxe-Coburg & Gotha clan - did indeed descend *en masse* on Osborne. But I anticipate. It happened thus:

---

[49] HIM Kaiser Wilhelm II (1859-1941).
[50] Captain (later Colonel Sir) Frederick 'Fritz' Ponsonby, later 1st Baron Sysonby (1867-1935) was, at the time, The Queen's Assistant Private Secretary. On the Accession of King Edward VII he remained in the same job.
[51] See *The Speedicut Papers: Book 4 (Where Eagles Dare)*.

After breakfast on Saturday 18th January, the day following my arrival, I decided without delay to seek out Reid, whom I knew to be a sensible cove, and get a frank assessment of the state-of-play *and* solicit — as Bigge had suggested - some ideas with regard to my funerary duties. Both of The Queen's quacks had been at the meagre Household dinner the night before, but the royal rule of silence at mealtimes still prevailed, despite the fact that the Crown Imperial was confined to quarters. My need for an urgent consultation arose primarily because I'd had a pretty frosty reception from old mother Tuck when I'd tried to charm her the night before. It was so chilly, in fact, that I reckoned the only hope of my getting back to London with my own clean bill of health lay with Reid. He wasn't at breakfast, so I got a footman to direct me to the medico's office. I was *en route* there when Reid himself, all bald head, bushy moustache and *pince nez*, came barrelling around a corner and damned near bowled me over.

"I most dreadfully sorry, Colonel. Are you alright?" I was and I said so. I also explained that he was just the man I wanted to see. "Not problems with your piles?" he asked solicitously.

"Certainly not," I replied, with not a little heat, "I'm in perfect workin' order, thank you. No, it's about your royal mistress that I want to speak."

"Ah, well I'm not sure what I can tell you. I'm on my way to see Bigge. Come along with me and I'll ask him if I can bring you up to speed - as it were." This was not at all what I'd intended, as it might have looked as though I doubted what Bigge had told me, so I followed after Reid to ensure that he didn't blot my copybook with the Private Secretary. Half-a-mile of corridor later we fetched up at an oak on which Reid knocked and then opened without waiting for a reply. Bigge was bent over a telephonic machine into which he was shouting at the top of his voice. I'm sure that the person on the other end could have heard him clearly even without the dratted apparatus.

"No, no, Knollys,"[52] Bigge bawled, "His Royal Highness *must* be made aware of the actual situation... what's that you say?... I don't care what Princess Helena is writing to the Prince, The Queen is *not* getting better... hang on a moment, Reid's just arrived. I'll call you back when I know the latest situation." He slumped back in his desk chair with a profound sigh. "So, what *is* the state of Her Majesty's health, Reid?" But before the royal witch doctor could answer, Bigge spotted me. "I'm not sure you should be here, Speedicut."

"Look here, Bigge," I said, "I don't see how I can do anythin' if I don't know what goin' on. Mrs Tuck has clammed up on me and I was on my way to consult with Reid here."

"Yes, yes, of course – I'm sorry, Speedicut, I'm working under very difficult circumstances. You may stay. So, Reid, what's your prognosis?"

"I've just come from examining Her Majesty and I regret to have to tell you that Laking and I believe she has suffered a slight stroke in the night. In the normal course of events, she is likely to suffer several more before one of them takes her off. I think it is imperative that The Prince of Wales is informed of the true situation and that a public bulletin is published."

"I see," said Bigge, "and how long would you give her?"

"It's impossible to say," he replied. "She could go at any time. In any event, I would be astonished if she was still here this time next week."

"Thank you, Reid. I will inform Knollys accordingly," said Bigge, looking more than usually distraught. "Then I will see Princess Helena." He sighed again. "She must be persuaded that the Heir to the Throne has the absolute right, indeed the duty, to be at the deathbed of his predecessor particularly as the lady in question is his eighty-one-year-old mother. Would you be so good, Reid, as to prepare a draft bulletin for my approval?"

---

[52] Sir Francis (later 1st Viscount) Knollys KCB (1837-1924) was at this time Private Secretary to The Prince of Wales.

Reid gave Bigge a head nod, turned on his heel and I trailed after him. I assumed he was going back to his study but, instead, we arrived at the royal residence's telegraph office where he sent a telegram to Berlin informing the Kaiser of the situation.

"Not a word of this to Bigge, please," he said, when he realised that I had followed him.

"My lips are sealed, Reid," I replied. "But why on earth did you do that?" I asked as we once more set course for his rooms.

"Because I promised His Imperial Majesty that I would."

"And in so doin' you've dropped me right in it," and, doubtless, collared a Kraut Order for yourself, I thought.[53]

"Whatever do you mean?"

"Only that if the Kaiser appears, I've been detailed off to look after him. It's bad enough that I've been appointed Mrs Muck's minder *and* tasked with keepin' the casket clear of unseemly clutter..."

"Here we are," the doctor said, as we arrived at a door with his name on it. "Come in, lie down on that couch and tell me all your troubles."

I rather reluctantly did as he suggested. When I'd finished, he lobbed a wholly unexpected question out of deep cover.

"What did you dream last night?"

"No idea. Why? Does it matter?"

"Dr Freud seems to think so."[54]

---

[53] Dr Reid was awarded the Prussian Order of the Crown (2nd Class) in 1901.
[54] Sigmund Freud (1856-1939).

"Who's he? The Kaiser's quack?" Reid didn't answer this. Instead he asked me if I'd ever wanted to sleep with my mother! "Look here, Reid, she's been dead for years and, if it wasn't for the portrait of her at my house in the country, I don't suppose I'd ever give her a second thought."

"Interesting..."

I'd had enough of this, so I cut across him.

"Dammit, Reid," I said, as I sat up and then struggled to my feet. "I came to consult you about Mrs Kluck and the Kaiser, not for you to use me as a test bed for some damned fool theories you've picked up from readin' *Witchdoctor's Weekly*. Now can you help me or not?"

I thought he might show me the door following my outburst but, instead, he looked contrite.

"I apologise, Colonel. It's just that Dr Freud has such interesting theories that I can't resist any opportunity to try them out."

"Well, I'd rather you experimented on your royal patient than me."

"I fear she is no longer a suitable subject for analysis. It can't be long now, you know."

"Which is why I'm here. As I've just told you, Bigge has tasked me with makin' sure that Mrs Buck doesn't embarrass Bertie and the others by puttin' John Brown's sporran in the coffin. Frankly, I haven't a clue how to stop her."

"You can leave Mrs Tuck to me, Colonel, although I would appreciate it if you could be on hand. As to the Kaiser, I'm afraid I can't help you there."

"Why ever not? You seem to be on his payroll."

"Colonel Speedicut, that is a most improper allegation which I demand that you withdraw immediately!"

It was my turn to be contrite, so – as I needed him to keep me out of the mire - I apologised profusely.

"Yes, well, thank you. But I repeat that I cannot be of assistance where His Imperial Majesty is concerned."

Realising that I'd got as much out of the meeting as I could, I thanked him and bimbled back to my quarters where I found Fahran.

"What's the news in the Servants' Hall?"

It was not only Searcy who knew what was going on well before the rest of us: palace servants made the secret squirrels in the War Office and Scotland Yard look like amateurs. Come to think of it, they are.

"The latest news, huzoor, is that The Prince of Wales will be arriving at five o'clock today."

"Damn! Well, at least he won't be able to bring the Kaiser with him. Not even that *pickelhaube* would be able to make it from Berlin by this afternoon."

"Not this afternoon, huzoor, but rooms are being prepared for the Kaiser and his Staff as they are expected to arrive in a matter of a day or so."

"Bloody hell! My only hope is that the old girl pops her clogs before the bugger gets here."

"Huzoor?"

"I'll tell you later, Fahran, but keep your ear to the ground and keep me informed of developments. Meanwhile, don't stray far as I may need you."

"As you command, huzoor."

Leaving Fahran to sew a black band onto the sleeve of my Shiner's Full Dress tunic, I went off in search of a newspaper and a glass of something stronger than water or tea. I found the former in the library but not the latter. I stowed myself in a corner behind a folding screen and was about half-way through the racing reports when I heard the door open and the unmistakable voices of Reid and Laking.

"Here's what I will propose to Bigge should be published: 'The Queen is suffering from great physical exhaustion accompanied by symptoms that cause concern'. What do you think?" asked Reid.

"I think," replied Laking, "that I'd say 'prostration' rather than 'exhaustion' and 'anxiety' rather than concern. It's stronger."

Good, I thought to myself, it can't be long now: Bertie may get here in time but there's no way that bloody Kaiser Bill can. In that I was wrong, for Vicky rallied that evening, thanks to oxygen, and told Reid that Bertie should be informed. By that time he was already in the house but, as Reid told me later, he didn't ask to see her and left the following morning, Sunday, for London. Although there hadn't been much change in Vicky's condition, Bertie was back by Monday lunchtime with the rest of his family and, as I was informed by Bigge, the Kaiser.

"You'll have your hands full," said the Private Secretary, "even though he's only bringing a small suite: an Equerry, a valet, his personal hairdresser to curl his moustaches," Bigge raised both his eyebrows, "and his two closest councillors."

"Who are they?" I asked. Bigge consulted a file on his desk.

"His Adjutant, General Kuno von Moltke, and Prince zu Eulenberg."[55]

"Not Phillip zu Eulenberg?" Bigge consulted his notes again.

"Yes, that's the chap."

"Oh, my God!" I exclaimed, as I collapsed in a chair.

---

[55] Lieutenant General Count Kuno von Moltke (1847-1923) & Prince Phillip zu Eulenberg und Hertefeld (1847-1921).

"Are you alright, Speedicut?"

"I need a brandy," I gasped.

"Why? Whatever's the matter?"

"A nasty turn. It happens at my age, y'know."

He looked sympathetic but unconvinced. Either way he didn't get me a restorative.

"Do you know Prince zu Eulenberg?" he asked, as the colour returned to my cheeks.

"I do – and Kuno von Moltke," I said as, through my mind, flitted dim, thirty-five year old images of a giggling pair of pansies at the Hotel König von Ungarn in Vienna, then the incident in the Turkish bath in the Sonnenfeldgasse when Searcy had arranged to have them and their master, Baron 'Fruity' Fritz von Einem,[56] arrested for gross indecency – and, finally, the denouement in the Azores when, in self-defence, I'd kicked Master Phillip so hard in the balls that he was probably still struggling to drag 'em down.

"Excellent," said Bigge briskly. "Knowing the two of them should make your job a lot easier."

If he did but know: but, of course, I couldn't explain so I put on my most resolute face and asked when the Imperial party was arriving.

"In time for luncheon. I'll meet them in the hall and then you can settle-in the Kaiser's Staff."

"What about the Kaiser?"

---

[56] Editor's Note: One of Speedicut's earlier Nemesis was Baron Fritz von Einem of the Prussian Secret Service. See: *The Speedicut Papers: Book 2 (Love & Other Blood Sports)* and *Book 4 (Where Eagles Dare)*.

"You'll be 'in Waiting' to him."

"What's that goin' to involve?"

"Keeping him as far away from His Royal Highness as you can… and, when they are together, don't forget that the Kaiser always takes precedence."

As it turned out, my task was easier than I could ever have hoped was possible. Despite the subdued air at Osborne, Wilhelm of the Absurd Tashes was in a mood to please everyone, particularly Bertie, and to say that he was uncharacteristically self-effacing would be a considerable understatement.

"My dear Oncle Bertie," he said over tea on the Monday, "pleaze do not mind about me. I vud love to zee Grandmama, but only ven you zay zat I can. I am yours to command…"

And his Staff? Well, I didn't recognise either von Moltke or zu Eulenberg, who were much changed from the pretty boys I'd once known: both were bald, von M had Kaiser-like upturned 'tashes and zu E a full, greying beard. I didn't think that they had recognised me either and, on both that Monday and the following day, I hardly saw anything of them, although I gave Fahran instructions not to let them out of his sight whenever they left their rooms. As for their Imperial employer, he Commanded that I trail along behind him wherever he went. Listening to his endlessly self-aggrandising prattle, delivered from dawn-to-dusk to whomever he could corner, was a chore but no worse. Here's a taste of it:

Over an utterly dismal luncheon on the Tuesday, the whole Royal Family, along with the Households-in-Waiting, had been told by Reid to prepare for the worst. After coffee, we gathered in the ante-room outside Vicky's bedroom where we waited and waited. It must have been about six and Wilhelm was talking to Randall Whatisface, the Scotch Bishop of Bath & Wells.[57] I, of course, was dutifully lurking and struggling to stay awake.

---

[57] The Right Reverend Randall (later Lord) Davidson (1848-1930), Bishop of Winchester and, from 1903, Archbishop of Canterbury.

"She 'as been a great voman. Just think of it, Bishop: she remembers Georg ze Third *und* now ve are in ze twentieth-zentury. And all zat time vot a life she 'as led. I have nezzer been viz her vizout feeling zat she voz in every zenze *mien grossmutter und* she made me love her az zuch. *Und* yet, ze moment ve began to talk about political zings she made me feel zat ve vere equals and could speak as zovereigns. Nobody 'ad zuch power as she…"

Terrible tosh, but I think he really believed it. On past form, there would have been a lot more of the same thing but, at that moment, Reid entered and had a quiet word with Bertie, who was puffing on a cigar by the window. When the medic had finished, the portly Heir to the Throne stubbed out his Havana and headed over towards our group.

"Willy, the doctorr says that we should go in. Would you carre to join me, Alix and the rrest of the family?"[58]

I thought my temporary employer was going to burst into tears, but he choked back a sob and, along with the rest of the royal mob, entered Vicky's bedchamber. I and the other courtiers trailed in behind. I'm not quite sure what I'd expected, my only other experience of a British royal death being that of Eddy Clarence, which had been an appalling business in a tiny, over-heated room at Sandringham.[59] Of course, I'd been in 'at the death' of LouLou Bonaparte, poor old Ludwig Wittelsbach, Rudi Habsburg and, most recently, his mama, but – as Charlotte-Georgina might have said - foreign royals don't really count.

The curtained and brightly lit bedroom was unexpectedly large, which was just as well given how many we were. The Widow of Windsor was not in the vast mahogany marital bower against the far wall but was lying in a smaller one that had been placed in the middle of the room, surrounded by chairs. Propped semi-upright with pillows, the shrunken figure of the Great White Queen lay there; her white hair was splayed out behind her head, her eyes were closed and a tiny white dog was curled up on the counterpane. She was alternately restless and comatose. Bertie

---

[58] HRH The Princess of Wales ('Alix' - later Queen Alexandra) (1844-1925).

[59] See *The Speedicut Papers: Book 7 (Royal Scandals)*.

took a chair to one side of her by Reid, who was supporting her with his left arm, and Bill the Kraut took one opposite and supported the other side of her with his good right arm. Arthur Connaught and the assorted Princesses – Alix, Helena, Beatrice and Louise - ranged themselves around the foot of the bed.

My readers may have read that Vicky's last word was 'Bertie' and that the porky new King then broke down and blubbed for the United Kingdom at this final gesture of reconciliation. Well, that's not *exactly* what happened. I will now tell you what *really* occurred.

Once the tableau of anticipated death was complete, and as though she'd been waiting for the moment, Vicky stirred and opened her sightless eyes which were milky with cataracts.

"Albert?" she cried out in a small voice. Albert Edward, Prince of Wales, leaned forward and took her hand.

"Kiss me," she croaked.

He lowered his bearded face towards her. She couldn't see him but she must have caught a whiff of his cigars.

"Not *you*, Bertie!"

And with that, as the clock struck six-thirty, she died. Bertie let out a howl like a wounded dog; well you would if your mother had told you at the point-of-death to bugger off, now wouldn't you?

Of course, the tale that Bigge put out to the hacks waiting at the gate was appropriately modified thanks to me: luckily, I'd recounted to him after dinner the night before the story about how Nelson's last words had been altered by the Admiralty.[60] Anyway, who inside the chamber was going

---

[60] Editor's Note: In *The Speedicut Papers: Book 1 (Flashman's Secret)* Speedicut is told that Nelson's last words were 'Kiss *her* for me, Hardy', referring to Lady Hamilton, but that the Admiralty had published an edited version that excluded the reference to Nelson's notorious mistress.

to tell the story otherwise? Besides which, they were all too busy either booing into their hankies or, in between blubs, making their obeisances to the new King who, at Reid's request, had closed the old girl's eyes whilst Bishop Haggis read the Prayers for the Dead. Eventually, we were all shoed gently out of the room by the doctor, who said that he had to 'prepare the body'. I was the last to leave but the quack called me back.

"Mrs Tuck is waiting next door, Colonel. Could you please bring her in?"

I did as he requested and the old crone followed me dutifully back into the death chamber, fell creakily to her knees by the bed and kissed the dead Queen's hands which had been clasped by someone over a crucifix.

"I believe, Mrs Tuck, that you have a list of Instructions entrusted to you by Her late Majesty?" said Reid in a gentle voice.

"I have," she replied quietly.

"May I see it?" Reid held out a hand as the ancient ex-royal dresser struggled to her feet. She reached into her handbag and produced a creased envelope which she handed to him. He opened it, pulled out the black-edged paper and read. "I see. Do you have the items listed here ready to hand?"

"I do, sir," she said, as Reid handed me the Instructions.

"Would you please be so good as to get them?" She gave him a little curtsey and left the room whilst I read the list in growing astonishment.

"You're not goin' to go through with this, are you?" I said, when I'd got to the bottom of the page.

"We have no choice, Colonel."

"But if The King sees some of these items he'll have a fit and we'll be sent to the Tower!"

CHAPTER SIX: BROKEN TRACES

"So, you must ensure that he does not," said Reid.

"How on earth am I goin' to pull that off?" I asked in dismay.

"The first bit is easy. Mrs Tuck, the maids and I will dress The Queen, as instructed, in a white gown with her wedding veil, both of which I'm sure Mrs Tuck will shortly produce. We will then cut and bind her hair for the mourning lockets. Whilst we are doing that, I would be grateful if you could arrange for Her late Majesty's coffin and the pall to be brought up here from the coach house."

"You mean there's already one waiting?" I asked in astonishment.

"Naturally... and, whilst you're about it, ask Bigge to prepare the dining room as we've previously discussed. Then I will ask His Majesty, His Imperial Majesty and His Royal Highness The Duke of Connaught if they would care to lift the body into the coffin. Once they have done that we can complete Her Majesty's other wishes, put the lid on the casket, cover it in the pall and our job will then be done."

And that's what happened. But what, I hear you ask dear reader, were the items to be buried with the Queen which were so shocking that they had to be hidden from her family? I will tell you.

An hour or so after Vicky had gone to her great reward, she was lifted into her coffin as Reid had requested. Then, once the doors were closed behind the royal rumps, Mrs Tuck once more appeared, this time with a large Gladstone bag. As she drew out the various items and laid them in the box she intoned a description of each which Reid asked me to tick off the list.

"The Prince Consort's dressing gown... a plaster cast of the Prince Consort's hand... the Prince Consort's wedding ring, to be placed on her left hand…" The list went on and on – trinkets, photographs, bits of jewellery, keepsakes and mementoes of a long life – and was made even longer when a royal page entered with a posy and instructions from Alix that it was to be placed in the coffin. None of these items were in any way controversial until, that is, we got to the bottom of the list. "… a locket of John Brown's hair, to be placed in her left hand… along with a photograph of John Brown… and his mother's wedding ring to be placed on her finger alongside her own and that of the Prince Consort. There, that's everything."

By the time we'd finished, the contents of the coffin resembled a bric-a-brac stall and the old girl's face and hands, with the ghastly Brown's sepia photograph very much on view, were about the only visible bits of her.

"His Majesty," said Reid, when Mrs Tuck had emptied her bag, "has Commanded me that he wants the Royal Family to pay their respects to Her late Majesty before the lid is screwed on - so I think we'd better do this." He picked up Alix's flowers and placed them over Vicky's dead fingers, thereby concealing the Brown memorabilia.

"Good thinkin', Reid," I said with considerable feeling. "All I have to worry about now is the German grandson and the Guardians of Gomorrah. One down and two to go…" Reid looked mildly shocked but didn't ask me to explain. Instead, he said that I should tell our new King that the late Queen was 'ready for inspection'.

. . .

No sooner had the lid been screwed down, and the heavily embroidered white pall cast over the coffin, than a party of beefy Woodentops marched in and carted the old girl's box off to the dining room where a catafalque, half the contents of the Osborne hothouses and four large candle sticks were already in place under a Union flag. Quite where all the impedimenta of royal mourning had emerged from was a mystery, although I suppose that Bigge and his cohorts had had time enough to be prepared. This rather begged the question as to whether or not these items had been hauled around the kingdom as Victoria progressed between her various homes towards death - or were there, perhaps, identical sets in each location? Whatever the answer, my own duties were now limited to making sure that the Kaiser didn't get under Bertie's boots between Osborne and Vicky's final resting place in the Royal Mausoleum at Frogmore. This journey was to be via the Solent on the *Alberta* (followed by half the Home Fleet), by train from Portsmouth to Victoria, then on a gun carriage across London to Paddington. From there the old bat would go by Royal Train to Windsor, where she was to be loaded once again onto a gun carriage and pulled up the hill to St George's Chapel for the funeral service and two days of Lying-in-State. It was only on 4th February that she would finally be tipped into the crypt at Frogmore next to Albert and my job would be done. In between, there was more than enough time for King Kraut, or his boyfriends, to make life difficult for J Speedicut Esq.

The first inkling I had that all was not well came on the day of our departure from the Isle of Fright, eleven interminably long days since Bertie had shed his Welsh feathers for the Crown Imperial.[61] During that time the family, including my temporary charge, were closeted in the Private Apartments whilst the rest of us kicked our heels and damned nearly joined Vicky out of sheer, bloody boredom. At last, we heard through the window the welcome clip-clop and jingle of a Horse Artillery gun team who were to ferry the white covered box to the jetty.

As the coffin was brought out of the house by the Grenadiers, who had stood guard on it since the 21st, Fahran helped me into my cloak and busby for the long walk behind the hearse to which we had all been condemned. In accordance with my role as Temporary Equerry-in-Waiting to Willy, I was directed to walk four paces behind him ahead of the Brothers zu and von Grimm, whilst Fahran and my kit had the luxury of wheeled transport: not for the first time, I reckoned that I was in the wrong job. Anyway, one way or another I'd managed to stay clear on von and zu

---

[61] Editor's Note: As I was informed by the Norfolk Herald of Arms Extraordinary, Major David Rankin-Hunt CVO MBE KCN TD, The Prince of Wales' 'feathers' is the badge of the Heir Apparent and is assumed at birth. The badge of The Prince of Wales is a Welsh dragon, assumed on appointment to the title. I have not, however, corrected Speedicut's misconception.

whilst we were at Osborne, which was a large house, but once *en route* to and then on the *Alberta* there was no escaping the buggers. The matelots had just cast off when the two of them sidled up to me looking menacing.

"I am conzerned, Herr Colonel," said von, "zat His Imperial Majesty's Standard iz not flying from zis boat's mast."

"Before zis is noticed by His Imperial Majesty," said zu in his curiously high-pitched voice, "I zuggest that you arrange viz ze Herr Admiral to hoist it." He handed me a rolled-up flag. "Unlez, of course, you vant an international incident on your hands."

"You know how sensitive His Imperial Majesty is to any hint of a slight by you British..." said von.

With no choice but to comply, I took the gaudily coloured cloth and made my way aft in search of the Captain of the royal tub. Thanks to a couple of handsome tars, I was directed to him quite easily and I explained my mission.

"I'm not sure that we can do that," said Fullerton.[62] "The Royal Standard was hoisted just as soon as Her Majesty's coffin was brought on board and there's no provision in Naval Regulations to fly two Standards at the same time."

"The Kaiser won't be happy," I said, "and when the Kaiser gets upset there's no tellin' what might happen. The Imperial German Fleet ain't far away at Keil..."

"You have a point, Colonel. Give me a minute or two and I'll consult with Bigge."

"There's no time for that," I pleaded. "Any moment now the King and the Kaiser will emerge from the saloon to take the salute of the Fleet and Wilhelm's sure to notice." Then I had a brainwave. "Besides which,

---

[62] Vice Admiral Sir John Fullerton KCVO (1840-1918).

should you be flyin' a dead monarch's flag? Surely you should have the Union Jack at the masthead? If you do that, my temporary employer can hardly complain – in the absence of The Queen's Standard - that you're not flyin' his dishcloth..."

"My God, you're quite right, Colonel. It's the perfect solution. Bosun!"

Unfortunately for the Admiral it wasn't. The Union flag had only just reached the top of the mast when the Fleet started blasting off their guns in a Salute and the two sovereigns emerged from below deck. Quite why he did it, I don't know, but Bertie immediately look heavenwards.

"Fullerton!" he growled, "why is my Standarrd not flying?"

"Err, Your Majesty" said Fullerton, who clearly was calculating which of the King-Emperors facing him posed the least risk to a comfortable retirement, "as The Queen is dead…"

"But *The King* lives!" snarled Bertie. "Hoist the Rroyal Standarrd without delay."

I thought that the Kaiser would protest but, contrary to von and zu, he didn't. I, in the meantime, still had the Hohenzollern tea towel under my arm. I had a choice: drop it overboard or return it to the Krauts. I decided on the former and sidled over to the rail.

"Vot are you doing viz zat?" asked zu's high pitched voice behind me.

"If you do vot ve zink you are going to do, Colonel," said von, "you can be *zehr* zure zat you vill be joining it before ve reach Ports-muth."

"Actually," I said, with reckless abandon, "I was about to blow m'nose on it."

I turned and handed them the flag whilst they both looked utterly shocked at my brazen *lèse majesté*; they couldn't have looked more so if I'd said that I was going to wipe my arse with it. Then, without a further word, I made my way across the deck to join Bigge and some of the other British courtiers and you'd better believe that I stuck close to them for the rest of the short voyage. You see, I had a nasty feeling that zu had at last recognised me. I had no intention, therefore, of giving him the opportunity to wreak his revenge for my all-too-obvious damage to his family jewels. On the train journey to London I stayed clear of the carriage's doors and windows. However, it was only when we got to Victoria that I started to feel completely safe, for the Krauts would never have tried to damage me in front of thousands of onlookers or so I hoped.

Mercifully, we rode from Victoria to Paddington. It was bitterly cold and I was grateful that Sambo III, fully accoutred in Shiner's horse furniture, was well warmed up when Atash, who'd brought her over from Stratton Street, helped me clamber into the saddle from a mounting block whilst Fahran adjusted my cloak over her back.

"I'm afraid she's just come into season, huzoor," said Atash, "but Flashman is lame and I wouldn't trust Boanerges not to play up."

"I'm sure it won't be a problem, Atash," I said, once I was secure in the saddle, "all the Mews horses are gelded."

I caught zu and von looking enviously at my Shiner's horse furniture – or, knowing them, it may have been at Atash - as they wheeled their own rather frisky Hanoverian nags from their Embassy's stables into line behind me.[63] Whilst this was happening, Vicky's coffin, complete with a white pall surmounted by a purple robe of State, the Garter collar, the Imperial crown, the orb and a brace of sceptres, was manhandled onto another gun carriage, which was surrounded by officers of the Household on foot and pulled by eight Hanoverian creams from the Royal Mews.

---

[63] Editor's Note: Uniquely in the British Army, the horse furniture of the Tenth Hussars comprised patent leather bridles, reins & other harness covered in cowrie shells. The elaborately embroidered scarlet shabraque & a leopard skin saddle cloth was standard for Hussar Regiments but, again uniquely, the Tenth did not use throat plumes.

At last, the enormous military cortege, which had been joined by more mounted crowned heads than you could have shaken a stick at,[64] to the beat of muffled drums, sombre funeral music and Minute guns firing in St James's Park, set off from the station and made its way slowly through the largest crowds I'd ever seen – larger even than for the old girl's Diamond Jubilee – held back by Woodentop street liners shoulder-to-shoulder for the entire route. All the houses along the way had been decked out with purple drapes hung from windows and balconies; these had been secured with white bows, for black had been banished on the late Queen's orders. As we clip-clopped up St James's Street behind Bertie, Willy and the crowned heads, I saw many a friendly face peering out from the first-floor windows of Brooks's, Boodle's and White's; I think I even caught a glimpse of Charlotte-Georgina with Johnny Dawson, who'd arranged for her to view the procession from the Verulam.

I say 'a glimpse' because, as we wheeled left onto the level ground of Piccadilly, there was a loud equine squeal and it felt as though I'd been hit by a steam engine from behind: zu's German stallion, which had been snorting louder and louder ever since we left Victoria, had decided to mount Sambo. The impact almost unsaddled me; if I'd had a drawn sword in my hand I'd have run the brute (horse or man) through. As it was, all I could do was dig in my spurs to disengage and scream blue bloody murder over my shoulder at zu.

"Why the hell aren't your horses gelded like you?" I yelled at him, to the amusement of the crowd. "Get that animal off the parade!"

Meanwhile, spurred on by me, Sambo's nose collided with the croup of the Crown Prince of Siam's mount, who damned near toppled out of the saddle as his horse lunged into the rump of Carlos of Portugal's pony, which in turn surged forward and collided with the Grand Duke Michael's

---

[64] HRH The Duke of York, King George I of the Hellenes, King Carlos of Portugal, King Leopold II of the Belgians (in a carriage); the Crown Princes of Germany, Rumania, Greece, Denmark, Norway & Sweden and Siam; the Archduke Franz Ferdinand (representing the Emperor of Austria), Grand Duke Michael Alexandrovitch (representing the Tsar of Russia) and the Duke of Aosta (representing the King of Italy).

mount. Had Michael been a less experienced horseman and not steadied his nag, he would have collided with Bertie, who's no horseman and who would undoubtedly have bowled into the rear of the gun carriage. It could have ended in carnage. Fortunately, it didn't - but it was a very nasty moment and a damnably close-run thing.

Eventually, shaken but in one piece, we arrived at Brunel's grime-encrusted palace of the locomotive north of the Park. Once Vicky and her Woodentops had been stowed in the luggage van, we all dismounted and boarded the Royal Train that was to take us to Windsor, where a large party of non-royal Heads of State were waiting to join the rest of us. On the journey, I took care to ensure that there were plenty of the Household-in-Waiting between me and the Krauts (zu had appeared on foot just as the train was about to leave), although I twice caught them muttering to each other whilst glancing in my direction.

The old girl's coffin was unloaded at Windsor railway station by the Grenadiers as a shipload of blue jackets, who were formed up as a Guard of Honour, gave her a slovenly salute. The box was then placed on a gun carriage drawn by a team of Horse Gunners. The idea was for them to draw it – as they'd done on the Isle of Shite - through the streets to St George's Chapel with the rest of us puffing along behind on foot.

Unfortunately, the train was late and the horses got stiff waiting around in a very sharp February wind. Well, the upshot was that, when the order to move off was given, one of the leaders reared up, kicked over the traces and snapped a splinter bar. It was a miracle that the gun carriage stayed upright, although the crown did wobble alarmingly. Clearly, at this point, Her late Majesty was going nowhere least of all to St George's. The assorted Kings, Emperors and Princes squabbled over what to do next: they were worse than a pack of chimps fighting over a banana and, in consequence, the serving military dared not interfere.

"It looks as though you have a problem," sneered zu, who had sidled up next to me, "and I thought you English vere zupposed to be zo good at zeremonial."

"It vouldn't happen in Potsdam," chimed in von.

After being physically assaulted on a most solemn occasion by zu's over-sexed horse this was adding insult to injury. Without replying I walked over to Fritz Ponsonby, who was supposed to be in charge of the arrangements and was standing to one side of the squabbling royals.

"Look here, Fritz, if you don't do somethin' we'll have a world war on our hands."

"What," he asked, somewhat tartly, "do *you* suggest, Speedicut?" I wasn't expecting that – but then I had a most Searcy-like inspiration.

"Use the Navy to pull the blessed thing."

"The Navy? How the hell are they going to do that? We're not on the river, y'know."

"Get 'em some rope and tell 'em to use their initiative."

"Ah, I see what you mean - that's a damned good idea, Speed. Your Serene Highness," this to Louis Battenberg, who was in charge of the matelot Guard of Honour, "could your men pull the gun carriage?" Battenberg said 'yes', but the drop-short officers in attendance were furious at my advice and Bigge, a former Gunner himself, actually took it up with Bertie.

"Your Majesty," he said, "I must protest. The honour of the Regiment and all that!"

"Honourr be-damned," growled our new monarch. "If something isn't done my late motherr will neverr be burried. Louis," this to Battenberg, "can your sailors really do it?"

"Certainly, Sir."

"Then please instrruct them accorrdingly."

"But, Sir, it's not right!" protested Bigge.

"Rright or wrrong, Bigge, let the Navy get on with it or we'll never be orrf."

So that's what happened. Rope appeared out of nowhere and was hitched to the gun carriage, whilst the assorted Horse Gunners fumed. Then, on an order from Battenberg, the matelots started off from the station up the hill to the Castle. And to be fair to them they did a damned good job:[65] so good, in fact, that after the short Service I heard Bertie tell Ponsonby that he should use the tars to take the old girl to Frogmore after the Lying-in-State. However, I suspect that Ponsonby valued his relationship with Bigge rather more than he did with Battenberg.

"The Artillery has been deeply mortified at their failure to pull the gun carriage, Sir, and they would be seriously hurt if sailors were to replace them again."

"Very well," snarled Bertie, looking dangerous. "But if anything goes wrong, Ponsonby, I will neverr speak to you again."

Bertie buttonholed me after the Service, thanked me for sorting out the mess and said that there was something he wanted to discuss with me after the interment. I assumed he was in another scrape and wanted me to shovel the dung away for him; probably it was something to do with Agnes Keyser and Alice Keppel,[66] who - so it was said around the

[65] The credit for switching from horses to sailors to pull the gun carriage, a practice which has been followed at every funeral of British monarchs since, is usually ascribed to HSH Captain Prince Louis of Battenberg (1854-1921), later Admiral of the Fleet the Marquess of Milford Haven, father of Earl Mountbatten of Burma and grandfather of the present Duke of Edinburgh.

[66] Agnes Keyser (1852-1941) was a rich spinster who conducted a discreet affair with The Prince of Wales, later King Edward VII. Much given to good works, with her sister she founded King Edward VII Hospital for Officers which still exists today. Alice Keppel (1868-1947), was a socialite and the last mistress of King Edward VII. Alice Keppel was the great-grandmother of the present Duchess of Cornwall, the mistress and later wife of the present Prince of Wales.

clubs – had been fighting like alley cats over what little of Bertie's body still functioned.

. . .

Three days later, during which time we kicked our heels in the Castle and I took good care to keep out of the way of von and zu, on 4th February the coffin was taken from the Albert Chapel in St George's to the Royal Mausoleum at Frogmore followed on foot by the royal mourners, the Households and me. Fortunately for Ponsonby, and the Royal Regiment of Artillery, nothing went wrong with the gun team, although I noted that they were led as well as ridden: clearly the Gunners were taking no chances. At the awful Romanesque royal resting place Brother Regy Esher, as the Constable of the Castle, was in charge of the interment. He fussed around like an old mother hen: Esher may have been married but I was certain that he played for the other side.[67] Anyway, nancy or not, he did a good job, at least so he boasted later, but the whole experience was not without its dramas for him.

"My dear," he lisped to me, as we sipped tea in the Equerries' sitting room after the Funeral Service at St George's on the 2nd, "the most terrible thing has happened."

"What? Has Albert's coffin exploded and plastered the interior of the mausoleum with its reeking remains."

"No, no, no, my dear, nothing like *that*. No."

"Well, what then?"

---

[67] Reginal Brett, 2nd Lord Esher (1852-1930). Esher was an extraordinary man who, whilst never holding public office, was a considerable power in the land through the reigns of Edward VII and George V. Esher was also a practising pederast, as James Lees-Milne reveals in his biography of Esher, *The Enigmatic Edwardian*, and Esher's relationship with his younger son, Maurice, bordered on the incestuous. Prior to the publication of this volume of *The Speedicut Papers* it was not known, although it's not surprising, that Esher belonged to the Brotherhood of the Sons of Thunder

"No one seems to know where Marochetti's effigy of the late Queen has been stored.[68] It was carved at the same time, and from the same block of marble, as that of the Prince Consort but its whereabouts now is a mystery."

"Why does that matter?"

"Because it was made expressly to cover Her late Majesty's tomb and without it…" His voice trailed away as he contemplated, I presumed, having to tell Bertie that he would have to fork out for a new statue of his mama. The limp wristed fellow looked quite woebegone for the next twenty-four hours but, on the morning of the interment, he had brightened considerably.

"We've found it!" he confided to me, as Fahran helped me on with my busby and cloak. As he did so, I couldn't help noticing that Esher gave my valet a very penetrating look.

"Found what?"

"The effigy of the late Queen, my dear. It was in a disused stable, covered in rotting straw and…"

Horse shit, I nearly added then thought better of it.

"So, all's well that ends well, eh?"

"Indeed, my dear," he said giving my arm a squeeze: I'm absolutely sure that, if he could have got away with it, he would rather have been squeezing Fahran's crotch, but I digress.

As the interment was 'family only', I was left to freeze outside with the rest of the Households – and von and zu – whilst Vicky was lowered into the crypt and her disinfected statue was then rolled over her. As for the Brothers Grimm, their master was due to return to Berlin the day following the end of the ceremonies. Once they were gone, there would be

---

[68] Baron (Carlo) Marochetti (1805-1867).

no reason for me ever to see the swines again and I could stop constantly looking over my shoulder. It was, therefore, with considerable relief that I watched the Kaiser and his entourage roll out of the Castle's Quadrangle on the 5th as Esher appeared at my side.

"His Majesty Commands that you attend upon him, Brother Speedicut. If you would care to come with me." I had no choice, so I fell into step beside Esher as he chattered away. "My dear, you really should have seen the final ceremony. It was *most* moving. Young David…"

"Who?" I asked as I puffed up the Grand Staircase.

"The Duke of York's eldest.[69] He's a *very* sweet and *most* handsome boy. Quite a young Adonis…" The simpering pervert's eyes became misty with sentiment or it might have been lust. "After the coffin was lowered into the tomb he was led forward by The King and invited to look down on the late Queen's resting place. I thought he would cry. But afterwards he recovered quickly and remarked that his grandmother would not be at all happy in Heaven."

"Why ever did he say that?"

"Because, he said, 'grandmama will have to walk behind the angels'. *So* enchanting, don't you think?"

It was as much as I could do not to be sick. Fortunately, we arrived at our destination before he could say any more. After the usual outer office nonsense followed by bowing and scraping in the Presence I found myself – to my considerable surprise - alone with Bertie.

"Colonel Speedicut, I was most imprressed by your rresourcefulness at Windsorr Station. I may have had my doubts about you in the past," really? "but that quick thinking on your parrt has convinced me that you arre the rright man to carry out a most imporrtant assignment for me."

---

[69] HRH Prince Edward of Cornwall & York (1894-1972), later Prince of Wales, King Edward VIII & Duke of Windsor.

"Sir," I intoned dutifully, "I am Your Majesty's to Command." Particularly if it meant having to dance attendance upon Agnes, Alice or both.

"At the end of the month I am making a prrivate visit to Gerrmany to see my sister, the Dowager Emprress Frrederick."[70] Ah, so he wanted me to deal with the royal mistresses whilst he was abroad. Sensible. "And you vill come with me." Why? His mounts were in London not Krautland; he wasn't taking them with him, surely?

"Of course, Sir – and did you have anythin' particular in mind for me to do?"

"Yes."

"Sir?"

He paused before answering me. Was he having second thoughts, I wondered, at exposing me (so to speak) to his mistresses-of-the-moment?

"What I am going to tell you now, Speedicut, is Top Secrret and must rremain as such. Do you underrstand?"

I said that I did as I wondered what he was going to reveal about his bitch pack.

"You vill prrobably not know this, but the Dowager Emprress Frrederick is very ill. In fact, she's dying."

Oh, Christ, I thought, so this isn't about his loose-hipped fillies: he wants me to organise his sister's funeral procession. Why the bloody hell couldn't he get Brother Esher or Ponsonby to do it?

"During the course of herr life," he went on, "the Dowager Emprress Frrederick has been in prrivate correspondence with our mother, the late

---

[70] HIM The Empress Frederick of Germany, Princess Royal of the United Kingdom (1840-1901).

Queen. In these letters both my sister and my mother exprresed opinions about Anglo-Gerrman relations."

Well, that was no surprise as both correspondents were relations and close ones at that.

"The Dowager Emprress Frrederick and I are both concerrned that these letterrs should not fall into the wrrong hands when the Dowager Emprress dies. It will be your task to remove them from Frriedrichshof before she does so."

No problems there, I thought, and it might even be worth a tap on the shoulder.

"However, neither I nor any of my Household can in any way be implicated in this task."

Naturally, I mused, menial tasks such as collecting and delivering family letters are only suitable for the likes of J Speedicut Esquire - or would that be Sir Jasper?

"You see, my nephew the Kaiserr would verry much like to have these letterrs." Silly sentimental fool, I thought.

"Consequently, he is keeping a close eye on anything and everything that leaves my sister's house. So extrracting them from Gerrmany is going to be *extrremely* dangerous."

CHAPTER SEVEN: LETTERS

"You must be…" I was about to say 'joking' but managed to swerve at the last second, "absolutely confident, Sir, in my ability to carry out this task for you."

"I am," said Bertie. "Ponsonby is fully aware of your task. He will be making all the arrangements and will be in touch with you: we leave for Frriedrichshof on the 23rd. Good-day, Speedicut."

With my guts churning in a way they hadn't for an age, I reversed out of the room, told Ponsonby where he could find me and then headed straight for my draughty room in one of the further flung reaches of the Castle. There I found Fahran.

"We're off. Let's get out of this damned place and back to Stratton Street as fast as we can." We arrived there shortly before dinner.

"Well?" demanded Charlotte-Georgina, who happened to be coming down the stairs as I entered the house. I knew exactly what she meant but I was not in a mood to give her a straight answer.

"Well what, m'dear?"

"Don't be irritating, Jasper, you know perfectly well what I mean. Have your services been recognised? Whitehall says that you saved the day at Windsor railway station, although after that disgraceful incident in Piccadilly it's a wonder that you weren't sent home from Paddington."

"That business with the horses was hardly my fault – although, I wish that I had been sent back here before we ever got to soddin' Windsor. That way I wouldn't have to go traipsin' off to bloody Germany."

"Language, Jasper! And what do you mean you have to go to Germany?"

"Just that. Instead of bein' honoured, I'm bein' sent on a mission to Friedrichshof, probably as a punishment - although Bertie says it's because of my savin' the day with Vicky's hearse."

"Isn't Friedrichshof the residence of the Dowager Empress Frederick?"

"It is."

"So why are you going there – and why haven't I been invited?" I told her as much as I thought she could keep to herself.

"But that's splendid, Jasper. Once you have returned with the Dowager Empress's 'things', whatever they might be, I'm sure that His Majesty will at long last recognise your years of service to the Royal Family. A blue riband will look most becoming on your tunic."

"I wouldn't bet on it m'dear: I'm not a trans-Atlantic steam ship and I certainly won't get the Garter. Well, I'd better go and change and I very much hope that *you* will change the subject once I'm down."

She didn't, but I won't bore my readers (those that are still awake) with any more of my wife's ludicrous and longstanding aspirations on my behalf.

The next couple of weeks sped by all too quickly and, other than a briefing by Ponsonby at the Palace during which it emerged that he was the Dowager Empress Frederick's godson, I spent most of them at the Verulam. Well, there was bugger-all else to do except – thanks to the new club secretary who had a passion for all things modern - to watch my moment of near-disaster on a cinematograph machine. As ill-fortune would have it, there had been a camera operator positioned just outside the club who captured the moment when zu's horse had tried to rape Sambo. Johnny Dawson kept requesting that it be played in the club's library and, every time that it was, it cost me another round of fizz. The compliments that I garnered for my horsemanship did *not* compensate for the attendant expense.

Fortunately, as Ponsonby had told me, Bertie's visit to see his sister was classed as 'private', which meant that our porky monarch would be taking only a small suite comprising Fritz, an Equerry, Laking (officially as Bertie's Physician-in-Waiting but who's real task was to administer more opium to the Empress than her son would allow) two valets and me. However, because of the Kaiser's obsession with uniforms, which exceeded even that of Bertie, I would be required to take both Undress and Full Dress as well as a trunk-load of civilian wear.

"My God, Ponsonby," I said, "if that's the case I'll need to take my man along with me. I can't possibly be expected to dress m'self and I'm not lettin' any damned Kraut servant lay a finger on me."

Besides which, I'd already decided that I needed Fahran to sneak out the letters in his hose. Well, it had worked with the enormous Koh-i-Noor diamond, so why not with a small packet of Vicky's correspondence?[71]

"I think that will be alright, Speedicut, but I'm afraid it will have to be at your own expense."

"Compared to the advantages of havin' my own man to look after me," and the old trot's letters, I thought, "the cost will be insignificant, Ponsonby."

There was nothing much to report about our journey by Royal Train, Royal Yacht, another Royal Train and then a fleet of carriages to the grotesquely ugly residence of the Empress Frederick, which was located near Frankfurt-am-Maine in Hesse. As I knew from previous experience, Bertie always travelled en *Prince* and his Household, in consequence, reaped the benefits of 'First Class all the way'. Very occasionally, so Fritz P told me, in recent years they'd even got to enjoy their employer's rejects and cast-offs. Apparently, on a trip to take the waters at Bad Homburg before Vicky popped her clogs, Charlie Suffield,[72] who had been with me on Bertie's trip to India back in '75, was 'in Waiting'. One day, he

[71] See *The Speedicut Papers: Book 1 (Flashman's Secret)*.
[72] 5th Baron Suffield KCB (1830-1914) was a Lord of the Bedchamber to The Prince of Wales.

was lounging around in the hotel lobby waiting for Bertie when he was approached by a pretty young chit with a bulging top hamper and a wasp waist.

"She told Charlie, bold as brass, that she had come to Bad Homburg expressly to sleep with His Royal Highness," said Fritz.

"What on earth did he say?"

"Charlie told her that would be quite impossible."

"How did she react to that?"

"She said that, in that case, *he* would have to do! And Charlie's over seventy, you know…"

I assumed, correctly as it turned out, that the likelihood of anything like that happening *chez* Frau Frederick was remote in the extreme. Frostbite, however, was almost guaranteed at the dismal *schloss*: its granite eves were hung about with lachrymose icicles and it was set in a funereal, snow encrusted pine forest. Why was it that the Saxe-Coburgs always built their palaces on land more suited for a cemetery? Anyway, this deeply negative initial impression was further reinforced when we drew up in front of the main entrance to be confronted by a Guard of Honour found by a Company of Prussian Guardees, all of 'em about ten feet tall, with Willy on hand, decked out in the white and gold uniform of a Kraut Tinbelly, complete with jackboots, an elaborate cuirass and a helmet on which a golden shite hawk was apparently having a crap. Bertie, by contrast, was uniformed - inappropriately given his enormous girth - as a Prussian *light* cavalryman, with a Death's Head encrusted busby perched precariously on his bald pate.[73] To further deepen the gloom, I spotted the bearded figure of zu Eulenberg mincing slightly to port of the Kaiser's withered left arm. It was not a good start.

---

[73] Editor's Note: King Edward VII held various honorary Imperial German military and naval appointments – including a Prussian Hussar regiment - but, as far I can tell, these did not include the Prussian Death's Head Hussars. I can only assume that Speedicut was using dramatic license in this description.

The stiffness of the German Court had, if anything, increased since I'd last had the misfortune to be involved with the Hohenzollerns and, despite the younger Vicky's well-known dislike of Prussian formalities, rigid protocol had crept into Friedrichshof - along with her appalling son - when the Dowager Empress retired to her bed of pain. Life at Friedrichshof made the drill square at Wellington Barracks looked positively relaxed and in no way enhanced the opportunity I needed to relieve the Dowager Empress of her correspondence. After three days, I was no closer to even seeing the stash than I had been in London, so I decided to take the matter up with Fritz.

That afternoon, we were trudging through the snow-covered grounds of the *schloss*, wrapped in tweeds – his overcoat was a peculiar ginger-coloured garment that I wouldn't have been seen dead wearing - in a desperate attempt to digest the brown Windsor soup, boiled beef, pickled cabbage and spotted dick with lumpy custard, which seemed to be the standard home-sick fare preferred by the Dowager Empress and imposed on her Household.

"Look here, Fritz," I said, when at last we were out of earshot of the constantly lurking Kraut courtiers, "I haven't so much as seen the Dowager Empress, let alone had the opportunity to take delivery of her 'things'. At this rate, I'll return empty handed when we leave the day after tomorrow."

"Patience, Speedicut. It's been very difficult to arrange an Audience with Her Imperial Majesty without the Kaiser being made aware of it. However, there may be a chance after luncheon tomorrow. The King and the Emperor have been invited to pay a call on the Grand Duke Ernst,[74] so they will be away for the afternoon and won't be back until late. I have provisionally arranged for you to see the Dowager Empress at four pm. Assuming I can get the nurses out of the way, I will collect you from your room five minutes before the hour. There won't be much time, so please be ready; I suggest you wear a frock coat as it will be less conspicuous than uniform."

---

[74] Grand Duke Ernst Louis of Hesse and by Rhine (1868-1913) was a nephew of King Edward VII.

At three forty-five the next day I was Under Starter's Orders, complete with a small attaché case in which to secrete the royal scribblings. Fritz arrived on the dot and took me to the Empress's chamber. How he'd arranged it, I don't know, but there were no guards, servants or nurses anywhere to be seen *en route*. He tapped a couple of times on the elaborately carved oak and a rather feeble voice called back that he should enter.

The room was furnished with dark blue brocade on every surface and fake-medieval tapestries on the walls; the curtains were drawn and the only light came from a small electric standard lamp. The Dowager Empress was propped up on a *chaise longue*, of a gothic design that even Mr Maple would have jibbed at stocking, and her lower body was covered in a fur rug. The room reeked of chloroform and the woman herself looked simply dreadful, as though she'd just been taken off the rack. I'd seen photographs of her in happier days, when she'd borne a close resemblance to Vicky after whom she had been named, but now her cheeks were sunken with pain and her face was grey with the pallor of the tomb.

"Fritz" she queried, "have you brought the courier?"

"I have Your Imperial Majesty: may I present Colonel Speedicut?"

"Bring him forward."

Fritz gave me a gentle push towards his godmother. I wasn't expecting that and damned nearly tripped over a bearskin rug; but I managed to steady m'self before I could tumble onto her lap.

"He seems rather old," she warbled at Ponsonby, as she stuck out her hand to me: whether it was to keep me from collapsing onto her or for it to be kissed was not clear. "Are you sure he's up to the task?"

"I may have the odd grey hair or two, Your Imperial Majesty," I said as I took her paw and brushed it with my 'tashes, whilst Fritz backed out of the room, "but I'm more than capable of the carryin' a few letters back to England for you."

"A few, Colonel? I think you will find that is a *wholly* inadequate description of my forty-year correspondence with the late Queen. For not only does the archive include all her letters to me, but I also have all those that I wrote to her. In total there are, I believe, some eight thousand letters."

"Eight *thousand*, Ma'am? But they'll weigh a ton and probably fill a large steamer trunk," I said, as I stared down in horror at my puny attaché case.

"Two, actually, Colonel. They are concealed behind that tapestry," she said pointing at a scene of King Arthur embracing Guinevere whilst Lancelot looked on in disgust. I bimbled over, pulled back the arras and there, as she'd said, were a brace of leather, iron bound trunks of the type usually labelled 'Not Wanted On Voyage' although these ones were labelled 'China With Care' and 'Books'.

"I'll do my best, Ma'am," I said, as I turned back to face her, "but really I've no idea how I'm goin' to do it." Fahran's underwear was clearly a non-starter, but I didn't say so.

"I've been thinking about that," she replied. "It seems to me that the simplest thing would be to add the valises to your own luggage, Colonel. My son is hardly likely to order a search of the belongings of my brother's Suite, now is he?" I hoped to God not, I thought, but I didn't say so.

"But, Ma'am, how do you propose that these trunks are removed from here to my own quarters?"

"I've thought about that too. His Imperial Majesty does not return from Darmstadt until this evening and I still have two servants who are loyal to me. As soon as it is dark, they will remove the portmanteaus from here and take them, via the servants' stairs, to your room. Before you leave tomorrow have them labelled with your own address and all should be well."

My God, the woman should have been a smuggler or in the Secret Service. It was a simple plan, but fraught with opportunities for it all to go horribly wrong. However, as I couldn't think of a better one, I meekly agreed and the trunks duly appeared in my room later that evening.

"What are these, huzoor?" queried Fahran, as they were delivered whilst he pinned the last of the German tin ware to my tail coat.

"Letters," I replied. "Thousands of them between Queen Victoria and her daughter."

"So why have they been delivered to you, huzoor?"

"Because I've been entrusted with sneakin' 'em out of here and gettin' 'em back to England."

"But why the secrecy, huzoor?"

"Search me," I said. "I can only assume that they contain some fairly fruity comments on the character of the Kaiser and his inability to shit whilst squattin' on the Imperial German potty. Anyway, the damned fellow wants to get his mitts on them and his mama is equally determined that he won't. Hence this most unwelcome job."

"I see, huzoor, but if you were found to be carrying these letters it could go badly for you."

"That, my dear Fahran, is a *very* considerable understatement." Fahran looked troubled but said no more and he didn't raise the subject again when he helped me to undress later.

. . .

The following morning after breakfast, a squad of liveried servants collected the luggage, which they piled-up into a great heap in the entrance hall of the *schloss*. I was hovering in the background with Ponsonby, whilst Bertie and the appalling Kraut bade each other farewell.

"My goodness, Oncle Bertie, you zeem to have an awful lot of luggage," cried Willy, as he surveyed the mountain. "It looks like more even than you arrived vith," he said with a gruff laugh. "You English can go nowhere vizout zo many clothes!"

Coming from the most overdressed brute in Europe that was more than a bit rich, but Bertie said something about the requirement to be properly dressed at all times when one was in Germany and the two of them strode out to the waiting carriages. All might still have been well if zu Eulenberg, who I'd hardly seen during our stay, hadn't stepped forward from the shadows.

"I zeem to remember," he lisped, "that you arrived viz three bags, Herr Colonel. Now you zeem to have five, including two vich, onless I'm miztaken, come from Tietz.[75] Please to open them." What choice did I have? To have refused would have been to incriminate myself.

"Help yourself," I said, lobbing the keys at him, as I contemplated the prospect of ending my days in a Potsdam dungeon. He ignored my own cases and made straight for the Dowager Empress's.

---

[75] Tietz was a large department store in Berlin.

CHAPTER EIGHT: DISTANT MEMORIES

In no time at all he had the case labelled 'China With Care' open: inside was a week's worth of soiled linen. He wrinkled his blood-shot nose and moved onto the second trunk labelled 'Books'. From what I could see it contained my uniforms. At that moment one of the Kaiser's Aides-de-Camp came running in from outside and demanded to know why the monarchs were being kept waiting. Zu closed the Empress's trunks, locked them and threw me back the keys.

"Until ze next time, Colonel."

"I firmly intend, you appalin' little Kraut, that there won't be one. Now fuck-off out of my way," I snarled, as I brushed past him.

"I say, Speedicut," said Ponsonby in the carriage, "that was a bit strong."

"Not when you know the circumstances," which I proceeded to tell him.

And what about the letters? Well, once we were safely back at Stratton Street, I decided to supervise the unpacking for, although I was certain that Fahran had switched the contents of my trunks, I wanted to be sure before rewarding him. Somewhat to my surprise, the letters were nowhere to be found. Instead, I seemed to have acquired a wardrobe made for a somewhat larger man. I looked inside the pocket of a particularly revolting tweed overcoat which I thought I recognised. The label read: Frederick Ponsonby.[76]

---

[76] Editor's Note: Prior to my finding this letter, historians have always believed that the correspondence between Queen Victoria and her eldest daughter had been removed from Germany by Frederick Ponsonby, who edited and published the letters in 1928. In a sense this remains true, although it is now clear that Fahran Khazi, in order to protect his master, managed to exchange the contents of Ponsonby's and Speedicut's luggage.

Later that day, we delivered two trunks of clothes to HM's Assistant Private Secretary at Buck House. Once we'd done so, I told Atash to drive Fahran and me to Savile Row where I ordered Mr Huntsman to make Fahran a rather becoming three-piece tweed suit with matching overcoat. He would look very well in it when he next accompanied me to a National Hunt meeting.

...

My readers may recall that Sibella Holland had threatened me with all sorts of dire consequences if I didn't admit to the paternity of her two-year-old blond-headed blob and make a financial provision for the little bastard. In order to settle the issue one way or another, I made the tedious journey to Bayswater shortly after I'd got back from Hesse. To my considerable surprise, I found myself staring at an infant version of me. There was absolutely no doubt about it and, although he lacked my scars – well, he would wouldn't he – it was as though I'd travelled back to the nursery at the Dower House circa 1823. So, I had a son. I admitted as much to Mrs H and said that I would behave responsibly: but what the hell was I to do about it? She gave me a month to decide.

Meanwhile, I had two other bits of bad news with which to contend. The first was that poor old Searcy wasn't very well. It emerged that he'd contracted some sort of chest infection which, so Ivan told me, he was having trouble throwing off. I told Ivan to keep the old boy confined to quarters and I sent instructions for Goodson-Wickes, our aged sawbones, to look-in on him from time-to-time.

The second was that I had been recalled to royal service to help out with the arrangements for Bertie's Coronation the following year. That old fool, Norfolk,[77] as the Earl Marshal was supposed to be in charge but, according to Knollys, who'd taken over from Bigge as Private Secretary, he hadn't a clue. Needless to say, Brother Esher had stepped – or, more likely, barged - into the breach. But even he was finding it anything but straightforward as the two of them told me when I was summoned to St James's Palace:

---

[77] Henry, 15th Duke of Norfolk KG GCVO (1847-1914).

"The problem, Speedicut," said Knollys, "is that it's been so long since the last Coronation that – frankly – no one knows what to do."

"Wasn't it written down?"

"Unfortunately, not," said Esher.

"What about an Order of Service? Surely there's one in the Royal Archives or those of the Dean of Westminster."

"There is, but it only tells us what was sung and said. There are no 'stage directions'," chimed in Esher. "About the only comprehensive account of a Coronation which anyone can find is Pepys's of that of King Charles II."

"And that won't do," said Knollys. "Besides which, the last Coronation was that of a Queen Regnant. This time it's a Coronation of a King and a Queen Consort and there are simply no instructions as to how it's to be done."

"Isn't there a list of those who attended the last one?" I asked. Knollys consulted a small pile of documents before him and pulled out some yellowing bits of paper.

"No," he said, "but there is a list of the royal guests who attended King William IV's Coronation in '31," he said handing me a list of royals, all of whom were bound to be dead.

I was about to hand it back to him when I spotted a name of one whom I was reasonably sure was still in the land of the living: Princess Augusta of Cambridge. The name wouldn't have meant anything to me, if I hadn't heard Charlotte-Georgina witter on about her over luncheon that same day:

"… and the dear Queen, as I must now remember to call her, told me that Augusta Strelitz will be attending the Coronation next year - if she's still alive. It will be her third…"

"Augusta who?" I queried.

"The Grand Duchess of Mecklenburg-Strelitz. She's a granddaughter of George III, a sister of the Duchess of Teck and is The Duchess of Cornwall & York's aunt…"[78]

"Ask the Grand Duchess of Mecklenburg-Strelitz," I said to Knollys and Esher. "Assumin' she hasn't lost her marbles, she'll know all the answers."

"That's a damned good idea, Speedicut," said Knollys, brightening somewhat. "I'll make the arrangements for you to go to go to Neustrelitz as soon as possible so that you can get a thorough briefing from Her Royal Highness."

"Look here, Knollys," I replied, "I've only just got back from Friedrichshof. My horses are running throughout the flat season and if I go hoofin' off to Germany again I'll miss their first outin's."

"I'm afraid that can't be helped," said Esher.

"But if have to go abroad again on a royal excursion without m'wife," I said in desperation, "I'll be in the Divorce Courts before you can say Alice Keppel."

"Speedicut!"

"Well, you know what I mean," I said. "No, I'm afraid it'll have to be an accompanied visit or you'll have to find someone else to run your fact findin' mission for you," I finished as I prayed that there would be no money or precedent for C-G to come with me: the Household was always as mean as weasel shit and absolutely hated setting precedents.

"You'll have to leave it with us," said Knollys. I did.

---

[78] HRH Princess Augusta of Cambridge, Grand Duchess of Mecklenburg-Strelitz (1822-1916); HRH Princess Mary Adelaide of Teck (1833-1897); HRH Princess Mary, Duchess of Cornwall & York, later HRH The Princess of Wales and then HM Queen Mary (1867-1953) was born HSH Princess Victoria Mary (May) of Teck.

Nothing then happened for a few days. Then, one morning whilst I was enjoying a mid-morning brandy, Fahran brought me a pile of letters. On the top was one whose envelope bore the legend: Office of the Earl Marshal. Inside was a letter from Norfolk (the man not the county) informing me that Her Royal Highness The Duchess of Mecklenburg-Strelitz Commanded Colonel Jasper and Lady Charlotte-Georgina Speedicut to attend upon her at our earliest convenience.

"Please take this to Her Ladyship, Fahran," I said, handing him the letter, "and leave the doors open between here and Her Ladyship's boudoir." I then started counting to m'self. I had got to nineteen before I heard an audible gasp from the first floor followed by a patter of feet and a rustle of skirt.

"What is this all about, Jasper?" C-G demanded, as she sailed into my study clutching the Grand Ducal summons. So, I told her. "We are, of course, going to accept."

"I suppose so," I said wearily, although the prospect of spending even twenty-four hours in some gloomy minor German Grand Duchy, holed-up with a deaf old bat whose sole claim to fame was that she was a granddaughter of George III and had been an infant at the Coronation of Sailor Billy, filled me with gloom.

...

Somewhat to my surprise, Großherzogliches Schloss, Neustrelitz, was not another dreary, Scotch baronial-style castle set in a depressing pine forest but a handsome Baroque palace with a domed tower at its centre – not unlike Castle Howard but even larger – beautiful furnishings and charming gardens. It was also very comfortable, the food was the product of a team of French chefs and the resident *chatelaine*, Princess Augusta, was utterly delightful with all the charm of her sister, 'Fat' Mary, but none of her *embonpoint*. Far from been a senile old crone with the memory of a fruit fly, Augusta was, in fact, an elegant little lady with an apparently encyclopaedic and rather romanticised memory. Her recollections of the Coronations of William and Victoria were as fresh as if they had happened yesterday.

"Now come and sit here," she told C-G and me on our first afternoon in Neustrelitz. She pointed us to two Louis Quinze gilded arm chairs, covered in exquisite needlepoint, ranged either side of a blazing fire in her porcelain-lined *kabinett*. "You will find writing materials on that table, next to my copy of *Le Morte d'Arthur*,[79] as I'm sure you'll want to take notes. You know I really do find it quite extraordinary," she said, as she plonked herself onto a matching settee, "that I seem to be the only person alive who knows anything about all this. Now where shall we start?"

"With the Coronation of King William IV and Queen Adelaide, Ma'am?"[80] I asked tentatively.

"Well, you know, there very nearly wasn't one. Dear Uncle William wanted to abolish the ceremony?"

"Really, Ma'am?" gasped C-G in shocked amazement.

"Oh, yes," said the tiny Grand Duchess, "and he very nearly succeeded - and he did manage to get rid of most of the pre-Coronation ceremonies."

"Why was that, Ma'am?" I asked.

"The problem was my Uncle George,[81] the Prince Regent as was. He demanded and got from Parliament a grant of one hundred thousand pounds to stage his enthronement. That was a fortune in those days and, as you can imagine, it was, in consequence, extremely lavish. But his brother, Uncle William, had no such pretensions. He was crowned with King George the First's State crown, which he didn't even bother to have re-sized; instead, he packed the brim with newspaper. He also insisted that the anthems were only accompanied by a single fiddler, the Peers wore their Parliamentary robes and the ushers had to pay for their own livery. The result was that the press called it the 'Penny Coronation'."

[79] *Le Morte d'Arthur* by Sir Thomas Mallory (d. 1471) established the Arthurian legend.
[80] HM King William IV (1765-1837) & HM Queen Adelaide (1792-1849), born HSH Princess Adelaide of Saxe-Meiningen.
[81] HM King George IV (1762-1830).

"You mentioned, Ma'am," said C-G, "that King William abolished all the pre-ceremonial. What did that entail?"

"Well, as my niece didn't have it re-instated I'm not sure that I really know in any great detail, but I think it included roles for The King's Champion, the Almoner and all the other Great Officers of State, since abolished, who used to preside at the Coronation Banquet. That's rather a pity, I think, as the ceremony may have been archaic but it was said to have been rather colourful..." She looked wistfully into the middle distance or it may have been the early part of the last century.

"The greatest gap in the Earl Marshal's knowledge, Ma'am, is the ceremonial relatin' to the crowning of The Queen Consort. Do you remember how it was done for Queen Adelaide?" I asked.

"Dear Aunt Adelaide Saxe-Meiningen. Such a superior person and dear Uncle William did so rely on her common sense. So *very* different to Bertie's Alix, who seems only to be interested in Society, jewels and fashion. Of course, she comes from a *very* minor royal family: the Schleswig-Holstein-Sondeburg-Glücksbergs are only a junior branch of the Oldenburgs and really aren't much more than provincial aristocrats." She allowed herself a small sniff. "Their Duchy is even smaller than dear Mecklenburg-Strelitz. You know, Christian was as poor as a church mouse before he was handed the Danish crown and his girls had to make all their own clothes. It's a wonder how those children have done so well for themselves... But you are interested in how Alix is to be crowned, not in her upbringing."

An hour later she drew breath, by which time I had more than enough information for twenty Coronations. But once Augusta Strelitz had got into her stride there was no stopping her. Over the course of the next three days we met with her before and after luncheon and after dinner. I think that, between us, C-G and I filled several folios with our notes and I was starting to wonder how long it was going to take us to distil them into a brief that would be short enough to hold the attention of Bertie, Ponsonby, Norfolk and Esher. I consoled myself with the thought that I could use the two-day long journey home to come up with a plan for Bertie's enthronement. However, I was also starting to be slightly worried that Augusta Strelitz had somewhat embellished and romanticised her accounts. Could it really be true that

. . .

Editor's Note: The rest of this section of The Speedicut Papers is missing.

. . .

We got back to the real world in early June to find Searcy much recovered, thank goodness. However, I don't think that I've mentioned that I'd written to Flashy, before we set off for Strelitz, asking for his advice about the problem as to how I was to fund my new-found son. His reply was waiting for me when we returned.

Working on the principle that there's no point in taking advice if you then ignore it – and as C-G had never known of its existence - I sold the black jade chess set through the good offices of Mr Abraham in Hatton Garden. I then placed the not-inconsiderable proceeds into a trust for Master Charles to provide for his education and his future; I called it – appropriately - the Black Jade Trust. This satisfied the dratted Mrs Holland. Brother Rothschild agreed to manage the funds - so the little bugger would at the very least be comfortable for the rest of his life - and Ernie Cassel and Eddy Sassoon agreed to be trustees.[82] By the time the trust matured, on my death or the boy's seventeenth birthday (I gained my independence at that age, so it seemed appropriate)[83] whichever was the later date, this chip off the old block (or should that be cock?) might even be stinking rich, providing that the Chosen Race – and I wouldn't have chosen any others - performed as expected. And, in case she tried to use her 'charms' on the two old Semites, there was no way, thanks to some clever trust drafting by Charles Russell,[84] that Sibella could lay her grasping mitts on the capital. Instead, during the life of the trust, she'd

---

[82] Sir Ernest Cassel GCB GCMG GCVO (1852-1921) & Sir Edward Sassoon Bart (1856-1912).

[83] Editor's Note: Speedicut is in error – he was actually eighteen when he left Rugby. See *The Speedicut Papers: Book 1 (Flashman's Secret)*.

[84] The Rt Hon Sir Charles Russell (1863-1928).

get a stipend for herself and an education allowance for the boy and that was it. So far, so good. However, after Sibella had satisfied herself with the trust document, I instructed Russell to insert a codicil of which she had no knowledge. This additional clause stipulated that, for the funds to pass to Master Charles when the trust vested, he had to change his name to Speedicut.

Whilst all this was going on, I delivered my report entitled 'How to Stage a Coronation' to Norfolk and the rest of them at St James's Palace. Their initial reaction to its contents was astonishment and incredulity, as became clear when I was summoned to the bottom end of St James's Street for a cross-examination.

"Do you seriously mean to tell us, Speedicut, that His Majesty must be subjected to the *Sedes Stercoraria*," asked Brother Esher in amazement. "I don't think we even have one. Besides, the idea that His Majesty would consent to having his genitals touched simply to prove what we already know is not even worth considering."

"Popes have to submit themselves to the *Sedes* before their Coronations," vouchsafed Norfolk who was, of course, a left-footer.

"Yes, I know," said Knollys, who wasn't. "But all *true* Englishmen have not been subject to Rome since the Reformation."

"Gentlemen, gentlemen," said Esher soothingly before inter-sectarian warfare erupted, "I think we can forget about the *Sedes Stercoraria*. But that still leaves the ritual purification and the divestment of robes; the very thought of Their Majesties standing in the Abbey before thousands of their subjects clad in nothing but gauzy shifts..."

"Then there's the ritual anointing on the hands, breast, between the shoulders, on the shoulders and on the head, to say nothing of the prostration before the altar: His Majesty will *never* manage that." said Bigge.

"As to His Majesty having to kiss the Bishops… it beggars belief," said Norfolk. "And the music – there may still be some in the Vatican, but I don't think we have any *castrati* in England. I'd have to speak to the Papal Nuncio if we are to get any of them to chant plain song during the enthronement.

"Are you *sure*, Speedicut, that Her Royal Highness hadn't been reading the works of Sir Walter Scott before she met with you?" asked Esher. "Her description of the ceremonies sounds more medieval than nineteenth-century."

"Look here," I said with some irritation, "you ordered me to traipse half-way around Europe to get these instructions and now you are, in effect, sayin' that they are completely unusable. Well, my advice to you is to invent a whole new ceremony." The courtiers looked deeply shocked at this suggestion, but I ploughed on. "You've got damned near a year to dream-up somethin' that won't involve the King's bollocks bein' fondled in public or the clerics havin' to stop tamperin' with the choir boys and kiss their bearded sovereign instead." I thought Esher was going to faint at that. "If you have no further questions for me, gentlemen, I'll bid you a good day." I got up and stumped off out of the office.

The GB told me a couple of days later that Bertie had sacked Norfolk and his Heralds, none of whom – so he said - could be called a gentleman and all of whom were Papists like their boss. Apparently, Bertie hadn't forgiven the tabarded-ones for their inept handling of the Diamond Jubilee and had, instead, appointed Esher to run the whole Coronation show on his own; I was pretty sure that was what Brother Regy, who was an arch-schemer, had been planning all along should happen. God help the Children of the Chapel Royal was all I could think to that: it was a thought that I didn't share with the GB.

So, what else was happening in the Year of Grace 1901?

Somewhat contrary to convention, the day *before* the end of Court Mourning, there was a Court Ball at Buck House. Thanks to twenty years of arse-kissing Alix, C-G wangled us an invitation. Apparently, according to my beloved, Alice Keppel had been bitching and moaning ahead of it that all the women would have to wear black and jet. I knew from C-G, however, that this was all Alix's doing to put La Favorita and the rest of Bertie's bints into the shade. As they might have guessed, but didn't, Alix appeared in a blaze of white brocade and diamonds and, in consequence, outshone the lot of them.

The Court came out of mourning on the 21st July, just in time for Goodwood, where *Mum's the Word* was running with young Hamasa Khazi in the saddle (I had high hopes of another win) and C-G had again arranged for us to stay with her 'cousins' at the big house, which was never a hardship.

Finally, another of C-G's cousins – a genuine one this time, not thirty times removed like the Richmond & Gordons - the Sapphic monster and insufferable Suffragette, Lady Charlotte-Edwina FitzCharles, was released from Holloway as part of a general amnesty to coincide with the real start of the new reign. I mentioned it to Johnny Dawson, who'd just been made Chief Constable of Sussex, and he told me that every police force in the south had been put on alert because they had 'intelligence' from within the movement that she was plotting something big to embarrass Bertie. We didn't have long to find out what had been planned.

Mum's the Word was entered for the Goodwood Cup, a two-miler for three-year-olds for which Marsh thought she was ready. She went down to the start as second favourite, at three-to-one, behind *Fortunatas*. I was on the rails before the race to put a 'pony' each-way on my horse, which was a largish bet for me and more than we used to pay old Mrs Ovenden for a year's worth of cooking. Who should I see amongst the bookies' pitches but Sibella Holland. She was not with the porcine Lionel but with a common-looking fellow in a too-well-cut pearl-grey frock coat who she introduced as C-G's cousin, Charles Hadfield. I was polite, but no more than required, tipped my tile to the pair of them and headed back to the box.

Bertie also had a fancied runner in the race, *Leg Over*, which Marsh had entered as a stable-mate pace-maker for our filly. I'm not sure whether

Bertie knew this, but he joined the house party in the Richmond's box for the race anyway and Commanded that C-G and I stand either side of him.

"You know, Speedicut," he growled, "I was speaking to Esherr the otherr day and he agrreed with me that you should be sent to South Africa to take control of our prropaganda."

"Really, Your Majesty?" I asked in horror.

"Yes. Therre can't be a Corronation until we get some good news out of that damned warr. Ah, they'rre orf…"

Our nag, with Hamasa (the late Khazi's youngest boy) in the saddle, kept tucked-in behind Bertie's runner all the way around the circuit in a small leading group headed by *Fortunatas*. They'd just entered the final furlong, and it looked as though *Leg Over* was starting to slip back, when some bloody woman came running onto the course screaming: 'VOTES FOR WOMEN!'.

I'm not exactly sure what happened next. All I do know is that a man in grey dived under the rails and gave the woman an enormous shove. Whether he meant to push her under the hooves of Bertie's horse or to get her out of its way was unclear.

"My God!" yelled Bertie, clutching my arm hard. But the Suffragette missed Bertie's *Leg Over*, and instead, collided with *Mum's the Word*, who went base over apex.

CHAPTER NINE: GOLF BALLS

I won't prolong the agony: our horse broke a leg and had to be shot, the Suffragette should have been shot but it was unnecessary as the impact had killed her outright, Hamasa was taken to hospital in pretty bad shape (but the quacks said he'd recover) and the man who intervened remained unidentified but was hailed by the hacks as 'the hero in grey who saved The King's horse'. Well, he may have been a hero to Bertie and the great unwashed but, I swore that if I ever found out the identity of the bastard, I'd shoot him on sight.

Besides the injuries and the loss there are two further outcomes of this tragedy. First, with C-G's agreement, I decided that racing was altogether too damned dangerous so we told Marsh that we were selling up. C-G suggested that I take up golf instead.

"The King has made it quite a socially acceptable game, Jasper – and it's a lot let expensive than racing."

"That's as may be, m'dear, but I'm not tempted on either score."

Second, to recover from the shock, we headed off to St Petersburg where we proposed spending the Autumn and Christmas with Dorothea and the grandchildren. It would be peace personified after the events at Goodwood and it would also ensure that I couldn't be called-up on to go and sort out the propaganda for our on-going and thoroughly lacklustre war with the Boers.

Oh, yes, I almost forgot: the Suffragette who killed our horse was none other than the appalling Lady Charlotte-Edwina FitzCharles. C-G and I refused to attend the funeral and we demanded of the GB that the body of the old bitch be barred from the family vault in St Paul's. In that we had the support of what remained of the FitzCharles family and the Dean, who was both a racing man and a militant misogynist.

...

In the event, although the Suffragette FitzCharles didn't make it to St Paul's, we didn't make it to St Petersburg. That was not, however, because I had to traipse after poor old Fritz Ponsonby to the war with the Boers. Instead, and possibly because Bertie felt sorry for me after the beastly business at Goodwood, I was once again back 'in Waiting' as Temporary Unpaid Deputy Assistant Private Secretary, which was only marginally better than camping on the *velt* but (outside the shooting and stalking seasons) without the attendant risk of shot and shell.

Actually, to be more accurate, I had been appointed to Bertie's Household – I suspect as a rest-cure - with a single purpose: to oversee the development of a golf links at Sandringham and then to have a course built for Bertie at Windsor. So, my new title should have been 'Golf Club in Waiting' although, unlike the Colonels of the Tins and the Blues (or the *arriviste republican cavalry*',[85] as C-G calls the Royal Horse Guards) I didn't get a gold-handled niblick to go with the job.

This new task wouldn't have been too bad if it hadn't been for the fact that I couldn't stand even the idea of the bloody game of golf, or 'goff' as it was apparently known, which was invented by the heathen Scotch to aggravate Englishmen. For those of my readers who are as unfamiliar with this pointless pursuit as was I, it involves swinging a whippy, iron-headed pole called a 'club' at a tiny ball and trying to propel it – the ball that is - two hundred yards or more into a miniscule hole. Doing this eighteen times on a laid out 'links' is called a 'round' although, if the links is only nine holes as was to be the case at Sandringham and Windsor, you have to go around twice: logically, it should really be called a 'twice-around'. The game is won by the idiot who takes the least number of 'strokes' to get the dratted ball into the eighteen holes. Unsurprisingly, given its royal endorsement, it had become a hugely popular pursuit for upwardly-mobile suburban stockbrokers with unpleasant accents.

[85] The Royal Horse Guards (The Blues) was originally raised as part of Cromwell's New Model Army and, although greatly favoured by King George III, was only elevated to the status of Household Cavalry by King George IV in 1821.

Quite what our grossly overweight sovereign saw in the game was a mystery to me: the only possible explanation for his newly-found passion was that it gave him a modicum of exercise and the chance to cheat. Whatever the reason, the 1901 Season was scarcely over before I was dispatched, with C-G in tow, to take up residence in Norfolk for the first phase of 'Operation Links': the creation of a nine-hole golf course in the grounds of the ugliest country house in the British Isles. C-G arranged with George Cholmondeley,[86] who can't afford to use the place and whose father tried (unsuccessfully) to sell it to Bertie, to borrow Houghton for us and our staff. It was a great barn of a place, so we shut off the State Rooms and lived in the old private apartments, which were musty but comfortable. C-G was as happy as a lark in this draughty 'stately' in which she could entertain the 'dear Queen' in style; thank God, the rent was negligible.

Anyway, with the help of the Sandringham Land Agent, a certain Frank Beck,[87] and a Regiment's worth of horse-drawn mowers and rollers, the golf course was quickly and easily laid out. In a matter of a few weeks, I was able to inform Bertie that it was ready for his inspection and this took place after luncheon one Friday...

A trap, pulled of necessity by a sturdy pony, conveyed The King, Beck and myself out to the first 'tee', which is the name of the place where you start each hole: if at this point, dear reader, you want to know more about the terminology of the grisly game, look it up in your local library. Meanwhile, Bertie surveyed the well-mown 'fairway', bounded on either side by the un-mown 'rough' and the distant 'green', which had been rolled as flat as a billiard table.

"So wherre are the bunkerrs?"

"Bunkers, Your Majesty?" I burbled in dismay, for nobody had told me that we had to install refuelling dumps on the course.

---

[86] George, 4th Marquess of Cholmondeley (1858-1923).
[87] Frank Beck MVO (1861-1915).

"Yes, Speedicut, bunkerrs. There should be some to either side of the grreen."

"Really, Sir? No one…" But before I could make a complete fool of myself, Beck intervened.

"We haven't yet dug them, Your Majesty, because we wanted your views as to where they should be sited. In the meantime, do you see those hurdles?" he said pointing at some wicker sheep pens that I thought had been left behind when the land was converted from grazing. "They indicate where we thought they *might* be located, subject to your approval."

"Therre's only one way to find out. I will play a rround tomorrow morrning."

'Play around' I thought to myself, surely that's what he did in the bedroom with Alice K.

"We will meet back herre at eleven and see how the courrse plays."

'Coarse play'? The language of the game was barbaric.

As I've already indicated, I'd never played golf. Unfortunately, neither had Beck: so, we were both incapable of playing with our monarch. What the hell were we to do? It was only shortly after breakfast the following day that I discovered that one of the Equerries, Seymour Fortescue,[88] did play. He wasn't 'in Waiting' that day but took pity on my plight and agreed to accompany Bertie whilst Beck and I trailed along behind taking notes and acting as 'caddies': these are the poor unfortunates who have to carry the players' clubs, balls (you can stop tittering) and so on.

We arrived at the first tee, where Beck took sand from a tin box and built a tiny sand hill on which he perched Bertie's ball (I told you to stop tittering: this is a serious story): the old boy was far too rotund to bend

---

[88] Captain the Hon Sir Seymour Fortescue (1856-1942).

down and place it there himself. Our overweight sovereign then swung his club around his waist and attempted to drive the pillock down the fairway.

"Bad luck, Your Majesty," intoned Fortescue, as the ball described a curve to the right – it was apparently known as a 'slice' - and collided with one of the sheep pens.

"Bloody club," said Bertie, hurling the offending stick to the ground. "It always slices my ball… and that damned bunkerr's in the wrrong place. Have it put morre to the rright and away from the grreen. Make a note, Speedicut."

Ten strokes and a great deal of swearing later, Bertie finally pushed his ball into the first hole with an instrument known as a 'putter'. Quite why it is called a putter not a pusher was and still is a mystery to me, but then so too was the reason why the other clubs were called 'woods', 'spoons', 'mashies', 'niblicks' and other ridiculous – and, therefore, presumably Scotch – names.

Very much the same thing happened over the next eight holes with Bertie's complaints at the ineffectiveness of his clubs becoming louder and his denunciations of Beck and myself more violent for our stupidity in the siting of the blasted bunkers. Fortunately, or it may have been deliberately, if Bertie played badly, Fortescue played worse. On the eighth, Bertie managed a reasonable shot onto the green and on the ninth pushed the ball into the hole from about twenty feet.

"Well, I've won and that's enough," announced Bertie, although there were still nine holes to play. "Time for a drink before luncheon, Fortescue." Then he turned to Beck and me. "Make surre that all the hurrdles are moved to wherre I have indicated, Speedicut, and we will see how they play tomorrow."

…

Needless to say, on the following day *and* the one after that, as the air above the Norfolk links assumed a permanently blue tinge, the bloody sheep pens were moved again and again, but all to no avail. Wherever we put them, these conceptual bunkers attracted Bertie's ball like iron filings to a magnet. The crisis point was reached on the third day at the fourth hole with Bertie's fifth stroke, which saw his ball hook sharply to the left and embed itself in the wickerwork.

"Who the bloody hell was so stupid as to put that bunker therre?" he demanded in a voice of thunder. Beck consulted our note book.

"Err, *you* did, Your Majesty."

I thought Bertie would have apoplexy. The colour in his cheeks went from boudoir pink to royal red to imperial purple. This time he didn't throw down his club, instead he snapped it over his knee.

"See that all those damned hurrdles are rremoved immediately, Speedicut and that prroper sand bunkerrs are dug beforre I rreturn next week-end!" Then, without another word, he stomped off in the direction of the house.

"Don't worry, Colonel," said Beck, who was a decent fellow, "I'll get the head gardener to work on it. We'll have the new bunkers in place by the end of the week."

To be fair to Beck, he was as good as his word and it was hardly his fault that Sandringham's chief green-fingers had never been on a links in his life either and hadn't a clue as to what to construct. I'll give him this: the earthworks he created were impressive. Indeed, they would not have looked out of place at Sevastopol, but they were definitely NOT to Bertie's liking.

"What the bloody hell have you done to my golf courrse?" he roared at us as he surveyed the first green the following Friday. "I told you to constrruct bunkerrs, not grreat big forrtifications. Have them dismantled immediately and this time get in the local prrofessional from Hunstanton to advise you." I returned to Houghton with my tail between my legs to be greeted by C-G, who'd just bade farewell to Alix.

"Her Majesty told me that your project is coming along splendidly, Jasper. She and Charlotte Knollys are *so* looking forward to being able to play on the course – and I'm certain,[89] if she enjoys the experience, that Her Majesty will see to it that you are properly rewa... Jasper, whatever is the matter?"

"After today's fiasco, m'dear," I said through gritted teeth, as I slumped onto a threadbare sofa, "the only reward I'm likely to get is the free use of a dungeon in the Tower."

However, thanks to the advice of the local golf club professional, Beck and I managed to have proper bunkers constructed in time for Bertie's next Friday-to-Monday in Norfolk. At first all went well. Bertie contrived to stay out of most of the sand traps for the first eight holes and, thanks to some tactful play by Fortescue, as they went to the ninth they were all-square with one hole to play. Bertie's tee shot was excellent, whilst Fortescue's was lamentable and Bertie had two strokes in hand for a win by the time he lined-up on the green to sink his ball and win the match.

He had just started his swing when we heard female shrieks approaching from behind us. I turned and, to my dismay, saw Alix and the Knollys woman hurtling towards us, clubs in hand, and striking a single ball as though they were playing hockey. Before I could say a word, they'd brushed passed me, Alix clobbered Bertie's ball out of the way and the two women bullied their own ball into the hole.

"I've won! I've won!" cried Alix, as she bounced up and down on her dodgy hips. I thought her husband would explode. As it was, at first he was too angry to speak. At last he got a grip of himself and, in the sort of tone you use to a three-year old, he spoke:

"Alix, it's really *too* bad of you. I was about to win and now you've rruined my game."

---

[89] The Hon Charlotte Knollys (1835-1930) was a long-term Lady-in-Waiting to Queen Alexandra.

"Nonsense, my darling," she gurgled. "I got the ball into the hole first. You're just a bad loser."

"That's not how the game is played…"

But, before he could say another word, she'd taken Charlotte Knollys by the arm and propelled her back towards the house. Needless to say, The Queen was barred from the course for the rest of the Season.

If bunkers had been bear traps at Sandringham, I was determined that I would not fall into them at Windsor. With the Sandringham links finally open for play (to all but Alix), we closed up Houghton in October and moved our entire household to a comfortable (and mercifully smaller) property called The Orangery, located in the village of Sunningdale on the other side of Windsor Great Park from the Castle. The house, in which was installed one of the latest telephonic machines, had been built as a scaled-down copy of the Grand Trianon at Versailles by a dotty Frog émigré who was buried somewhere in the extensive gardens. As the weather was mild, and we had plenty of room, I got Fahran to telephone Stratton Street and arrange for Searcy and Hamasa to come down from Town to complete their recuperation. It was lucky that I did.

Using The Orangery as my base, I organised the building of the Windsor Castle links in the Home Park. Actually, after the problems I'd encountered at Sandringham - and on Searcy's advice - I'd decided that the safest thing to do would be to enlist the services of a talented amateur player and get him to design a nine-hole course; I would then give the design to the Home Farm Bailiff to carry out the works. Johnny Dawson, who played the ghastly game, put me in touch with a fellow called Muir Fergusson, who in due course produced a really excellent plan.

But I'm no fool and, still smarting from the horrors of the links in Norfolk, I decided to take no chances. So, along with the Bailiff and his team of labourers, Fergusson and I walked the entire course and marked out the tees, greens and - most especially - the bloody bunkers with stakes and tape; we positioned the ninth green just below the East Terrace of the

Castle. Then I withdrew to Sunningdale for a well-earned rest whilst the workmen constructed the course.

One afternoon, around about the time that the Bailiff had said the works would be completed, I was having a quiet snooze in the warm, late-Autumn sunshine that was pouring in through the French windows of the drawing room. Suddenly, I was awoken by the shrill ring of the bell on the dratted telephonic device in the hall. Fahran answered it and moments later came to tell me that I was wanted on the line.

"Hello?" I yelled in the manner recommended by the instructions on the base. "HELLO?"

"Is – that – you – Speedicut?" demanded a faint voice.

"This – is – Speedicut," I yelled back.

"Knollys – here – His – Majesty – wishes – to - speak – with - you – hold – the – line." There was a pause.

"Speedicut?" growled a voice I assumed was Bertie's.

"Yes – Your – Majesty?"

"You – have – RRUINED – the Home – Parrk! Get – over – herre – IMMEDIATELY!" And the line went dead.

An hour later I reported to Knollys, who said that Bertie had left for London in a towering rage.

"Have you seen what your men have done?" asked the Private Secretary.

"Well, not recently," I said, "but I left very clear orders."

"Then I suggest you go and have a look, Speedicut. I've already sent instructions to the Bailiff to meet you at the fourth."

He was waiting for me as promised. As far as the eye could see was what I can only describe as a freshly dug graveyard. Where Fergusson and I had placed the posts and tapes for the bunkers were, indeed, bunkers. But instead of shallow, curved sand traps that followed the lie of the land around each green, the damned Bailiff's men had erected a series of identical mounds and ditches which each measured four-foot-high, by four-foot-wide by ten-foot long. The bunker in front of the green at the ninth, *en pleine vue* of the Castle, was the only one not adhering to this funeral design: it was in the shape of the Victoria Cross and planted with flowers!

"D'ye like it, Colonel?"

Not for the first time in my involvement in the ghastly game of golf I was stunned into silence. Eventually, I recovered the power of speech and in a level tone, which I filled with as much menace as I could, I said:

"I'm giving you and those idiots who work for you precisely twenty-four hours to erase those features," I said, pointing at the bunkers, "and when I say 'erase' I mean that no trace of them is to remain. If you do not do so, then I will personally ensure that you and every one of your men involved in this howling cock-up will be placed in those damned ditches *before* they are filled in. Do you understand me?" He started to protest, but I cut him short. "Twenty-four hours." I then walked back to my motor car which was waiting for me by the side of the course. "Home, Atash."

On the journey back to The Orangery, I wrestled with the problem but could find no quick and easy solution. However, sitting outside the front door enjoying the late afternoon sun was Searcy, with a plaid over his knees.

"Just the man!" I cried, as Atash helped me down. "I've got a problem…"

"Not for the first time, Colonel. How may I be of assistance?"

I put the situation to the old boy and he cogitated for several minutes. Finally, he told me what to do. For some reason Atash hadn't parked the motor and was lurking by its bonnet with a polishing cloth.

"To Datchet Golf Club, Atash. As quick as you can," I ordered him.

By the end of the afternoon, I'd agreed with the Secretary of the Club that, in return for a stack of folding money, he would arrange for his groundsmen to construct bunkers in strict accordance with Fergusson's plan and in the accepted style of a commercial links.

"Can you get it done before His Majesty returns to Windsor?" I asked.

"When might that be, Colonel?"

"The end of the week."

"Yes – but it'll cost His Majesty another ten pounds." I fished out my wallet and parted with my last two fivers. At this rate, I thought to myself, golf was proving to be even more expensive than racing.

"Leave it with me, Colonel."

So I did, but I was pretty sure that the whole sorry saga had permanently buggered my chances of 'recognition' – at least recognition of the type for which C-G so longed.

CHAPTER TEN: PUNCTURED & KEBBABED

My unholy, although entirely unintentional, fuck-up of the royal golf links should have ensured my permanent retirement from the Palace. Unfortunately, it didn't. However, for the next few months I was left in peace at Stratton Street whilst Brother Esher whipped the entire Establishment into a complete froth over the Coronation, which he'd based on that of the Regent excluding only, so I hoped, Alix being forced to pound on the doors of the Abbey in order to gain admittance to be crowned.

My retirement from the Royal Household was unexpectedly interrupted by a summons to see Knollys and Ponsonby (recently returned from the war) at the dump at the end of The Mall on 'a matter pertaining to the Coronation'. I assumed it was to be told that I was to be appointed an Extra Equerry-in-Waiting to carry the royal chamber pot at the ceremony scheduled for 26th June 1902 Atash drove me the short distance to Buck House and, after getting through the assorted pansies-in-livery who guard the Privy Purse entrance, Ponsonby swept me off to Knollys's new office. Once seated with a cup of HM's best Darjeeling – a brandy would have been more acceptable, but Vicky was still warm in her box and old habits die hard, I supposed – Francis K unburdened himself.

"His Majesty has not forgotten your quick-witted intervention at Her late Majesty's funeral nor," he cast a warning look at Fritz, "your ingenious rescue of the royal correspondence from Germany. He is even willing to overlook your lamentable, although he acknowledges ultimately successful, management of his goffing facilities."

"Accordingly," said Fritz, "His Majesty has a most important and delicate task for you at his Coronation. It's one that will play to your skills and experience."

Oh, Lord, I thought, what now? Am I to command a Guard of Honour for Esher comprising muscled young matelots, frisky post boys and teenage caddies? Finally, with more hemming and hawing, Fritz got to the point.

"At the Coronation, Speedicut, His Majesty is entrusting into your capable hands the care of his, err, lady friends who are to have a box to themselves."[90]

I damned nearly choked on the tea but carried it off as an old man's coughing fit. So: not Chamber Pot-in-Waiting but Cowherd-in-Chief. Was the old boy having a joke at my expense? Anyway, to Francis's relief I accepted and he then rattled off my duties which, although he didn't phrase it that way, were to prevent the hellcats from scratching each other's eyes out. When I told C-G, I thought she'd have a fit; Searcy nearly died laughing when I told him.

However, two days before the Coronation, Bertie was struck down with appendicitis and wasn't expected to survive. Rather appropriately, given the size of our not-about-to-be-crowned monarch, Laking brought in 'Elephant Man' Treves to perform an experimental operation to remove the offensive appendage: the appendix, that is, not our overweight sovereign.[91] Society held its breath as it awaited the outcome whilst I told Fahran to put my silk smock and specially sharpened pitch fork back in the hall cupboard.

...

In the event, God and Treves saved The King. Treves was awarded a Baronetcy and I was still on the hook for the Coronation, which Knollys told me has been rescheduled for 9th August. Meanwhile, thanks to my idiot wife's royal plotting, I was back 'in Waiting' and Commanded to attend upon Bertie whilst he recuperated on the *Victoria & Albert.*

"It was Her Majesty's idea," said C-G, when I returned from the Palace and told her the fell news. "She wants me to accompany her, not of course

---

[90] This box soon became known amongst Edward VII's racing friends as 'The King's Loose Box', an amusing pun combined with at least one *double entendre.*

[91] Sir Frederick Treves KCVO (1853-1923). In 1886, Treves rescued the grotesquely deformed Joseph Merrick (1862-1890) from a freak show and gave him shelter in the London Hospital, where Treves worked as an abdominal surgeon. In the case of Edward VII's appendicitis, Treves drained rather than removed the appendix.

in an official capacity, and the only way it can be arranged is if you are in His Majesty's Household. As you have given-up both shooting and racing, I thought you would enjoy the cruise."

"I would," I said. "But it's sure to involve more than loungin' around in deck chairs." In that I was not wrong.

...

Bertie was carried on a stretcher from a Mews omnibus onto the Royal Train, which trundled at a snail's pace to Portsmouth with Maud Denmark,[92] 'Toria' Wales,[93] Fritz P, Fred Treves, me, C-G and our personal staff. At the other end, a party of the Navy's finest struggled to get Bertie's stretcher onto the Royal Yacht and into what Fritz told me had previously been (appropriately, as it turned out) the smoking saloon, which had been fitted out at short notice as a sick room. With our esteemed monarch safely parked with a bevy of pretty nurses, Alix took charge and told us that she expected us all to join her for luncheon.

Somewhat to my surprise, it was a really jolly affair. A light breeze blew into the dining room through the open ports, which was as well because it was a hot day, the table was a mass of pink roses and silver-gilt and a Marine Band oompahed away on deck whilst we ate a damned good meal and Alix told joke after joke. I was sat between her and Maud: unfortunately, I had to repeat everything twice to C-G's chum – particularly when the band was playing loudly - and Maud's conversation was as lugubrious as her looks. I had planned earlier that, once the coffee had been cleared, I would hit one of the deck chairs I'd spied earlier on the aft deck. However, my earlier forebodings were correct.

"Speedicut, Treves," said Fritz, as we arose from the table, "I have a message saying that His Majesty has Commanded us to attend upon him."

---

[92] HRH Princess Charles of Denmark (later Queen of Norway) (1869-1938) was the youngest daughter of King Edward VII.
[93] HRH The Princess Victoria (formerly Princess Victoria of Wales) (1868-1935) was the second youngest daughter of King Edward VII.

Bang goes my snooze, I thought, as I followed Ponsonby to the former smoking room where Bertie was lying on top of a bed in the middle of the room, dressed in one of those new-fangled, loose-fitting blue cashmere lounging suits: I wouldn't have been caught dead wearing one. Despite the fact that he was supposed to be convalescing, he had a large Havana clamped between his teeth and his head was wreathed in a cloud of cigar smoke.

"Ah, Speedicut: the last time I saw you I little thought that I should be like this now."

"Indeed not, Your Majesty," I replied sycophantically, "and how are you feelin'?"

"Damnably glad to be out of that sick room at the Palace," he wheezed, "which brrings me to the point. Frritz, am I rright in thinking that the Shah of Perrsia intends paying me a visit before the Corronation?"[94]

"I believe that is correct, Sir."

"Well, Trreves, when will I be fit enough to rrecieve the blighter?

"All being well, Sir, and providing you do not have a relapse," he looked pointedly at Bertie's cigar, "I would have thought a day or two before you have to leave the Yacht and return to London for your Coronation."

"So, around the 3rd August?"

"I think you can rely on that date, Sir."

I was beginning to wonder what all this had to do with me. I didn't have long to find out.

"Speedicut, you know Perrsia don't you?" asked Bertie from behind his Cuban fog bank.

---

[94] HIM Mozaffar ad-Din Shah Qajar (1853-1907).

"It's been a very long time, Sir."[95]

"Yes, yes, but you underrstand these heathens – been to their countrry and all that. And I seem to rremember that you had a Perrsian orderrly who taught my late mother the lingo."[96]

"Actually, he was an Afghan, Sir, but – yes - he did teach Her late Majesty the language, although I believe she thought she was learning Hindoostani…"

"Well, I want you to look after him whilst he's down here: Frritz will tell you what's involved."

Before I could protest, a terrier came bounding into the room followed by Alix. Fritz gave Treves and me the nod and we backed out.

"So, what's that goin' to entail?" I demanded of Ponsonby a few minutes later, whilst helping m'self from the sideboard in the saloon to a large brandy to steady my nerves.

"You know I'm really not sure," said Fritz somewhat unhelpfully. "I'll telegraph Knollys and see what he knows. Treves," he said turning to the monarch's plumber, "do you want to come on a visit I'm organising for Her Majesty to Netley to meet some of our war wounded?"[97]

"Certainly. How very splendid of her," said Treves.

"Well, you know what a close interest she takes in our military medical services. Your wife's going, Speedicut, so you can come too, if you'd like to."

Having nothing better to do, I decided to tag along for the ride as I told Charlotte-Georgina whilst we were undressing after dinner.

[95] See *The Speedicut Papers: Book 1 (Flashman's Secret) & Book 2 (Love & Other Blood Sports)*.
[96] See *The Speedicut Papers: Book 5 (Suffering Bertie)*.
[97] The Royal Victoria Hospital, Netley, near Southampton.

"Netley?" she queried.

"The military hospital near Southampton."

"Oh, yes. Her Majesty asked me to accompany her there whilst she was showing me her cabin – you know it's not like this at all, but large, white panelled, full of comfortable armchairs and it even has a grand piano and a fireplace…" She wittered on for several more minutes until I extinguished the light to silence her.

...

The visit to the hospital proved to be an hilarious interlude before the arrival of the Persian imperial mountebank and the tricky dispatch from Knollys which preceded it. We got to Netley in an elegant little steam pinnace which almost flew across the Solent. Alix had said that, although the Chief Sawbones and the Matron were to be warned of her visit, the patients themselves were not to be told so that they didn't tire themselves trying to spruce-up for the royal visitation. In the event it might have been better if they had been told.

Netley Hospital overlooked the sea and was set back from the shore by only a few hundred yards. We were met on the jetty by the Senior Surgeon, a white-coated fellow with enormous mutton chop whiskers, and a very large woman, Matron Jacques, who nearly pitched off the landing stage when she tried to execute a full Court curtsey. A couple of open carriages took us the short distance to the front door of the hospital from where Alix started to make her tour of the ground floor.

"How are you feeling?" she asked a man with no legs, a missing eye and an arm in a sling.

"As well as can be expected, Miss."

"And how long were you in South Africa?" she asked another who, mercifully, still had both his legs although they were in splints.

"Since the beginning, Miss - two an' 'arf year – an' I've bin in every battle."

"Oh, you poor man," she cried, "at which one were you wounded."

"Actually, I were'nt, Miss."

"Really? So, what are you doing here?"

"I slipped on a wet deck on the bleedin' leave boat when it docked at Southampton and fell down an 'atchway, Miss…"

Hoping, I suppose, that the next recipient of her sympathy would be suffering from a genuine war wound, Alix approached a man with a rather glazed look in his eyes and most of his head bandaged. As she approached he struggled to focus on her.

"'ere, luv," he said, "you'se looks jest like that new Queen we've gort. She's a looker an' all."

"You know," said Alix to the Matron, whose jaw had hit her ample and well-starched top hamper, "I do find that so *very* reassuring."

If that weren't bad enough, it got worse. Alix took it into her head to spend some time in the canteen where she and C-G joined the ladies serving tea and buns to the walking wounded.

"A cuppa' tea an' a firkin, please, Miss," said a rough looking lout in the uniform of a minor county regiment.

"I'm sorry, what did you say, dear?" said Alix, cupping her ear. He repeated his order. Alix looked puzzled and whispered something in C-G's.

"A firkin what?" asked my beloved innocently.

"A firkin great bun, please, Miss" he said, with a grin the width of the Solent whilst his companions howled with laughter.

At this point Matron Jacques intervened and led Alix off to a less bawdy part of the hospital, a ward where every patient was so swathed in bandages that speech was impossible. But by this time the word must have got out as to the true identity of their visitor for, as we left that ward, we were practically mobbed by the wounded. I'll say this for her, Alix took it all in her limping stride and I'm sure that she did no end of good for the standing of the monarchy with the 'brutal and licentious'.

We were about to leave when one last soldier was brought forward to be presented. He was a Corporal of Horse in the Second Battalion and he had five clasps on his Boer War medal – clearly another man who'd served from start to finish.[98]

"It is a privilege to shake your hand, Corporal of Horse Stephens," said Alix when the man was presented. "It's a miracle you survived for so long and relatively unscathed."

"That's was thanks to 'Freddy', Your Majesty."

"Freddy?"

"Me 'orse, Ma'am. 'e carried me from start t' finish and was me lucky mascot. 'fact, Ma'am, 'e woz the only one of the Second Regiment's 'orses 'oo survived the 'ole campaign."

"Where is he now?"

"At Combermere Barracks, Ma'am, with the Musical Ride."

"Well, I hope he has a campaign medal with the same clasps as yours," she said, tapping his chest.

"'fraid not, Ma'am. There's no medals fer 'orses."

---

[98] Editor's Note: As seasoned readers of *The Speedicut Papers* will know the Tenth Hussars, Speedicut's Regiment, and the 2nd Life Guards were very close and usually referred to each other as the 'Second Battalion'.

"We'll see about *that*," said Alix firmly, as we were driven back to the pinnace.[99]

Back on the Royal Yacht there was a coded signal waiting for Fritz. It turned out to be a briefing paper from Knollys about the impending Persian visit; it was not good news. In addition to the fact that the Shah would be arriving with a travelling Suite of forty cut-throats, it appeared that he was expecting to be given the Garter. Indeed, it was his sole reason for braving the briny.

"It seems that the Foreign Secretary has promised it to him,"[100] said Ponsonby.

"So, why's that a problem?" I asked.

"Because, according to Knollys, The King has already stated in no uncertain terms that – despite the fact that the late Queen gave the Garter to two Sultans of Turkey and the Shah's father, Shah Naser – *he* has no intention of bestowing his highest Christian Order of Chivalry on a Mohammedan."[101]

"Oh, dear," I said.

"That, Speedicut, is a very considerable understatement – particularly as the Shah will be here in three weeks and I haven't a clue what's to be done."

"So why don't you bat the problem back at Knollys or better still, Lansdowne. One of them will just have to tell the Shah that he'll have to make do with the Star of India or the Indian Empire or both."

---

[99] Editor's Note: Queen Alexandra did eventually succeed in getting 'Freddy' a Second Boer War campaign medal, complete with the clasps for 'Wittenberg', 'Kimberley', 'Paardeberg', 'Driefontein' and 'Transvaal', although it has previously been thought previously that she first saw and heard about the horse at the Royal Tournament in 1902.

[100] Henry Petty-Fitzmaurice, 5th Marquess of Lansdowne KG GCSI GCMG GCIE (1845-1927).

[101] HIM Shah Naser al-Din Shah Qajar KG (1831-1896).

"I'll try," said Ponsonby, in a resigned sort of tone.

A couple of days later he called me into his cabin after breakfast.

"It seems," said Fritz pointing at a decoded telegram on his desk, "that the Foreign Secretary has told Knollys that he is under the distinct impression that The King told him, a week before he was taken ill, that the Shah was to have the Garter."

"Is there any written evidence?"

"It seems not."

"And no witnesses to the conversation?"

"None."

"Then it looks as though you've got a major problem, Fritz: I suggest you tell Fisher to order the Mediterranean Fleet to get up steam and chug-off to the Persian Gulf."[102]

"Actually, Speed, it's not *my* problem. Knollys says that, as The King has put *you* in charge of the Shah's visit, *you* must come up with a solution."

---

[102] Admiral Sir John (later Admiral of the Fleet the Lord) Fisher KCB (1841-1920) was, until the end of July 1902, C-in-C Mediterranean Fleet.

CHAPTER ELEVEN: HONI SOIT QUI MAL Y PENSE

"My God, Fritz, you're not serious?"

"I'm afraid that I am – or rather Knollys is."

"But what the hell am I to do?"

"As I've already said, I've no idea."

"If only Searcy were here," I said with considerable feeling.

"What's that, Speedicut?"

"Nothin' – but I need time to think about this. Can you get me ashore and out of Waiting for forty-eight hours?"

"Certainly, but why?"

"I need to run up to London."

It will come as no surprise to my readers that my reason for shipping ashore was not – as I told Charlotte-Georgina – the necessity of visiting my barber and my tailor, but the far more important one of consulting Searcy. C-G was, of course, perfectly happy to be left to dance attendance on Alix, whilst I took the train north in search of a solution to the Great Suspender Problem as I had privately labelled it.

"I see," said Searcy, after I'd briefed him in his comfortable sitting room overlooking the mews. "I suspect, Colonel, that, if The King holds to the line that he never consented to the bestowal of the Order on the Shah, the Foreign Secretary will have to resign *and* there'll be a breach in diplomatic relations with the Persians."

"Why does either matter? Lansdowne's almost as useless as the sons of Cyrus."

"Possibly, Colonel, but the resignation of a Foreign Secretary is no small thing and the rest of the government might feel that they had to show solidarity with His Lordship. That would trigger either a constitutional crisis or a General Election. As to the Persians, they are certainly not a Great Power but they are our buffer against any designs which Russia may have on India."

"So, this is a matter of consequence?"

"I'm afraid so, Colonel."

"So, what the hell am I to do about it?"

"Could you give me twenty-four hours to think about it?"

I said that I could and headed for the Verulam in search of a good dinner and a bottle of the Emperor's best. Being late July, the club was mostly populated by refugees from other establishments closed for their summer breaks but, in a corner by the bar, I spotted Johnny Dawson who was jawing away to a broad-shouldered fellow whose outline I was reasonably sure I recognised.

"What ho, Speed! I thought you were boating with Bertie," said the new Chief Constable of Sussex. "Come and join us. I think you know Winston Churchill…"

As fast as my spirits had risen at the sight of Johnny, they fell at the sight of Lady Randy's eldest, who I hadn't since my escape from Pretoria. That said, I'd heard more about him since he'd become an MP than suited my digestion: he may have worn a blue rosette on the Oldham hustings, but he spoke in the House like a damned Liberal.

However, in the event, it was a fortuitous meeting: Churchill may have been a parlour pink, but he was well-informed and had a reasonable grasp of foreign affairs. So, over the cigars and brandy, I told him and Johnny of my dilemma.

"Seems perfectly simple to me," said my old friend, "get Ponsonby to tell Bertie to tell Lansdowne to tell the Persian Minister in London that Bertie's health isn't up to a visit and that it will have to be indefinitely postponed - and certainly too well the other side of the Coronation. That buys you time and, when the old sheep-stealer does eventually show up, you'll no longer be in royal servitude and it will be some other bugger's problem."

"That's a good idea in theory, General, but it won't work in practice," said Churchill.

"Why ever not?" Johnny asked.

"Because I know for a fact that the Shah's visit to His Majesty is only the visible tip of something much bigger."

"What?" I demanded.

"Oil concessions," said Churchill.

"But there aren't any whales in the Persian Gulf," I said quite reasonably.

"Not whale oil, Colonel, but mineral oil: the sort that fuels motor cars and may in the future power the Fleet."

"But there isn't any in the Middle East. The only sizeable source is in North America."

"That's what we all thought," said Churchill, "but it seems that there could be substantial oil fields in Persia."

"Who says so?" I asked.

"A chap called Bill D'Arcy."[103]

"Not 'Arsy-D'Arcy' the racehorse-owning gold-mining millionaire and over-weight poodle-faker?" asked Johnny.

"The same," said Churchill. "He and his partners are convinced that there's oil in Persia and they are willing to invest a lot of their own cash to find it. If they're right and they do find oil, it will be a strategically vital source ideally placed between here and India - and we want it."

"So, what's stoppin' D'Arcy from diggin' in the sand?" I demanded.

"An exploration license from the Shah."

"And I suppose that the old robber won't grant one unless our esteemed sovereign is willin' to strap a velvet suspender below his left knee?" I asked.

"You have it in one, Colonel. Without the Garter, there will be no oil exploration licence and no guarantee of concessions in the future. Meanwhile, the French and the Germans have started to show an interest in the area."

"So, what the hell am I to do?" I asked, as I poured myself another triple shot of Hennessey.

"You'll have to persuade The King to change his mind – or get Mrs Keppel to do so."

---

[103] William D'Arcy (1849-1917). In 1900, D'Arcy agreed to fund a search for oil and minerals in Persia and negotiations with the Shah began in 1901. D'Arcy and his partners eventually paid the Shah £20,000 for a sixty-year concession to explore for oil in Persia across an area covering 480,000 square miles. The concession stipulated that D'Arcy would have the oil rights to the entire country, except for five provinces in Northern Persia, and in return the Shah was given 16% of the oil company's annual profits.

"As to that," I said, "no dice: Alix has banned La Keppel, and the rest of the royal herd, from the Yacht whilst Bertie is recoverin'. I suppose she doesn't want to risk him burstin' his stitches tryin' to straddle one or more of 'em. Any other suggestions?"

"Have you consulted your man, Searcy?" asked Johnny.

"I have," I replied, "and he's goin' to give me an answer tomorrow. But if either of you had any thoughts…" They both shook their heads.

The following morning Searcy appeared in my study after breakfast with a large envelope under his arm.

"I gather you consulted General Dawson and Mr Churchill last evening, Colonel."

"I did: I suppose that half the staff of the Verulam are members of the Nehemiah and told you of our entire conversation."

"Only the Head Steward, Colonel, but – yes – I did get a full report an hour ago. This business of the Garter is even more serious than I thought."

"So it would appear: what's your solution?"

"It seems to me, Colonel, that, in the first instance, The King needs to be persuaded to change his mind."

"That's what Churchill said."

"I know," said Searcy, "and I believe that I have a way to do it. I will speak to Mr Balfour's valet and get him to suggest to the Prime Minister that he should inform His Majesty privately that an early General Election, resulting from a resignation of the government over the issue, would almost certainly result in a victory for the Liberals. That should get The King to back-down: the last thing that His Majesty will want is a new government whose priority will be social reform."

"But that doesn't address Bertie's objection to givin' an overtly Christian decoration to a bloke who thinks that Jesus Christ is a minor Jewish prophet who was nailed up for heresy."

"I've thought of that too, Colonel. The answer is for The King to invest the Shah with a Garter which *doesn't* feature the cross. The Garter strap itself and the Lesser George don't; the breast Star and the badge on the mantle could be re-designed – like this," he said, handing me the envelope. I took it and pulled out from it a stiff piece of paper on which had been painted the new designs.

"Where did you get this?"

"Garter King-at-Arms' gentleman's gentleman is a member of the…"

"Say no more, Searcy. But answer me this: how am I to put this to The King. You know how touchy he is about Orders and decorations; Ponsonby says it's an absolute obsession with him."

"I propose, Colonel, that Lord Lansdowne sends this design to His Majesty just as soon as the Prime Minister has communicated his views to The King."

"And how do you suggest I get him to do that?"

"You don't, Colonel. His valet…"

"… is a member of the Nehemiah."

"Precisely, Colonel."

"Well, let's hope that your plan works."

And it did, at least in part. Balfour sent a coded private message to Bertie, which arrived at the Royal Yacht twenty-four hours before a Foreign Office red box containing the heraldic drawing. I know this because I'd briefed Ponsonby as to what I'd arranged in return for him telling me how matters were proceeding.

One morning, a week after I'd returned to the yacht from London, I was on the After Deck enjoying a smoke before luncheon when Fritz hove into view with the news that I'd been summoned to the Presence. As before, I found Bertie propped up on his bed in his ghastly lounging attire and puffing on a stogie.

"Ah, Speedicut, Ponsonby: come in. It seems that the Shah of Perrsia, his sons and his Suite will be paying me a visit after all. There are far too many of them to fit them all on the *Victoria & Albert* so I plan, Fritz, that Her Majesty and I will entertain the Shah, the Princes and his Ministers here, but you – Speedicut - will have to take the more minor members of his Suite onto the *Osborne*. They won't be any trouble."

Why are monarchs such eternal optimists, I wondered to myself as Bertie went on.

"I will invest the Shah after luncheon with the Garter but…" I noticed that the colour in his cheeks was darkening as he dipped into an open government dispatch box beside him, "… if any damned fool thinks that I'm going to invest him with this trravesty," as his voice rose he held up the drawing I'd last seen at Stratton Street, "HE CAN DAMNED WELL THINK AGAIN!" and with that he scrunched up the paper into a ball and hurled it, with considerable force for a man in his condition, out of the nearest open port hole. "That, gentlemen, will be all."

Ponsonby told me later that the drawing had been caught by a passing stoker who returned it to him in the belief that it was a valuable painting. So far, so good. But I still had the prospect – and the problem – of what to do with Ali Baba's Suite once they arrived, which in due time they did, reeking of garlic and sweat and led by the Robber Chief himself. Bertie, dressed as a Field Marshal, met the Shah, who was followed by five of his six sons, at the top of the companion ladder from where our esteemed Christian monarch invited Sinbad to inspect the Royal Marines Guard of Honour and then presented his own royal brood.

I've seen some ruffians in my time, but I have to say that Mustapha Qoojar [*sic*] took the biscuit. He was swarthy, portly, not very tall and had bloodhound eyes and huge 'tashes like the handlebars of a bicycle. For an oriental, his uniform of a single-breasted black frock coat and overalls was quite sober. The rest of his rig, however, had obviously been looted from Aladdin's cave: a jewel-encrusted scimitar hung from his left hip; ropes of gold chain – in the manner of aiguillettes - were attached from his right shoulder to his top button by a diamond encrusted sapphire of enormous size, which was matched on his left tit by the Star of an Order that put the Lord Mayor's necklace to shame; and his astrakhan fez bore a huge diamond brooch with a giant square-cut sapphire at it centre and a forest of egret feathers protruding above it. We all blinked in the glare of these priceless accoutrements.

With the introductions over, the Shah and his closest chums slouched off after Bertie in the direction of the saloon, accompanied by Fritz, doubtless to talk about oil. This left me with the Second Eleven, a surly crew led by a General with the unintentionally bawdy name of Mustapha Kunt,[104] who looked as though he'd cut my throat at a second's notice. Ponsonby and I had agreed that I would take these brigands to the dining room where I would give them some mid-morning refreshments and then, using the steam pinnace which had collected them from Portsmouth, ferry them across to the *Osborne* for luncheon.

The first part of the plan went off without a hitch and there was a lot of contented nodding and smiling as they wolfed down trays of Madeira cake, lemonade and coffee. Then we encountered a problem. First, stewards came in to clear the table for luncheon. No one moved although some farted in contentment. Then, as the clock on the bulkhead ticked inexorably towards twelve forty-five, the Chief Steward made his way over to me and whispered in my ear that it was time I cleared the room. I politely asked Kunt and his Forty Thieves in English to do so but, not only

---

[104] Editor's Note: I have tried to establish whether or not this oddly-named officer was in the Shah's Suite or if he is a bawdy invention of Speedicut's but have been unable to verify him. However, a Turkish officer of the same name was on the Staff of the Turkish Embassy in Moscow in the 1940s.

did the flatulent buggers show no signs of moving, they actually settled deeper into their chairs.

Of course, I hadn't spoken Persian in years and, anyway, my grasp of it was never complete. Any grasp that they had of English appeared to have escaped them along with their noxious wind. I tried instructing them to join me on the short trip to the *Osborne* by speaking slowly. Then I tried speaking slowly and loudly. No one budged. I was about to give up when I had a stroke of genius, called over a steward and ordered him to fetch Fahran. Moments later he appeared, clad somewhat unexpectedly in his father's oriental finery and with a large dagger in his belt.

"Huzoor?"

"Fahran, your father spoke Persian – do you?"

"I speak a bit of Pharsi, huzoor."

"Good, well, could you please tell these louts in your best and most polite Pharsi to get their saggy arses out of those chairs and to follow me to the pinnace?"

"Certainly, huzoor."

He gave me a little bow, turned to face the Aryan horde and, whilst fingering his dagger, spoke a couple of sentences to them in a low voice. To my amazement, they all sprang to their feet, saluted me and then allowed me to lead them away for luncheon.

"I think you'd better come with me, Fahran, as you seem to know how to control these fellows."

"I am yours to command, huzoor."

It was only later that afternoon, once Darius & Co had departed after a visit which contained no further awkward incidents, that I thought to ask Fahran what he had said that had so galvanised the Persians.

"It was nothing, huzoor."

"No, come on Fahran, it was clearly not nothin'. One moment they were refusin' to shift their bums and the next moment they were treatin' me like Bo Peep. What did you say to them?"

"You won't be angry, huzoor?"

"Of course not, Fahran. Whatever you said saved me from being thrown in chains or worse."

"Well, huzoor, I said that, as His Majesty Grand Vizier, you had the power and the authority to have them all turned into eunuchs and be put to work in The King's harem – and that, if they didn't do as you had ordered immediately, the Royal Marines Guard of Honour were waiting on the quarter deck to hold them whilst I carried out the necessary modifications…"

...

I had hoped that, in the wake of the Shah's visit which resulted in D'Arcy getting his oil permits, there was a chance that I might be excused any further royal duties. No such luck as Fritz Ponsonby informed me.

"You're quite the man of the moment, Speed. His Majesty speaks of you with nothing but praise for your adept handling of the Persian situation. And, of course, he hasn't forgotten your valuable services earlier this year."

"Excellent, Fritz, so am I excused the Coronation?"

"Not a bit of it, old chap. His Majesty is relying on you to look after his, err, lady friends with all the tact and discretion that you used with the Persian Suite."

Little did he know that my secret weapon, Fahran, would be powerless to help me this time. I put on a brave smile and said that it would be 'my pleasure'.

So it was that on 9th August 1902 I found myself in the Abbey, a Temporary Gentleman Usher for the day with a black armband with Bertie's cipher on it tied on my right arm over my Shiners' Levée Dress tunic. Under the circumstances, a cape and a bull whip would have been more appropriate. I was prepared for a stampede: well, you don't corral that many old cows in one small space without expecting trouble as they vied for the best view. But, in the event, Alice Keppel, Agnes de Keyser and Bertie's exes Jennie Churchill, Lillie Langtry, Maggie Greville, Sarah Spencer-Churchill (the war correspondent), Feo Sturt, Minnie Paget (the fabulously rich Yankee), Olga Caracciolo and the rest of them trotted meekly into the box,[105] their jewel encrusted udders swaying delightfully.

All was decorous harmony until Daisy Warwick,[106] who had become a big woman to say the least, pushed her way to the front to get a better view of Bertie being crowned and tripped over La Bernhardt's dicky leg.[107] If I hadn't instantly clapped a gloved hand over Mam'selle B's lips, her yell would have been heard the length of the Abbey; as it was, all that escaped was a muffled yelp, but it was still loud enough to startle that silly old fool Temple,[108] who damned-near jumped a foot in the air and put the crown on Bertie's head arse-about-face.

I won't trouble my readers with even a general account of the lavish ceremony except to tell you – as I did Searcy – that Balfour's bandy legs

[105] Mrs George Cornwallis-West (formerly Lady Randolph Churchill) (1854-1921); Lady Hugo de Bathe (formerly Mrs Edward Langtry) (1853-1929); The Mrs Ronald Greville (1863-1942); Lady Sarah Wilson (1865-1929); Lady Feodorovna Sturt (later Lady Alington); Lady Paget (1853-1919); Olga, Baroness de Meyer (1871-1930).
[106] Daisy, Countess of Warwick (1861-1938).
[107] Sarah Bernhardt injured her left knee on stage. It never mended properly and in 1915, following the onset of gangrene, the leg was amputated. Thereafter Miss Bernhardt wore a wooden leg.
[108] Frederick Temple (1821-1902), Archbishop of Canterbury was 80 years old at the date of the Coronation. In order to ensure that he placed the crown on King Edward's head the right way around, he had a red thread attached to the rear of the crown. Prior to the publication of *The Speedicut Papers*, it has always been assumed that, at some point before the critical moment, the thread fell-off resulting in Temple placing the crown on the King's head back-to-front. Earlier in his career, Temple had succeeded Arnold as headmaster of Rugby School.

looked utterly absurd encased in the saggy silk stockings of his Privy Councillor's uniform and that Alix stole the show. She may have been nearly sixty and was practically stone deaf, lame as anything and heavily reliant on rouge and a wig, but in her Elizabethan-style frock, purple train and with her bodice and neck encrusted with diamonds, she looked like a fairy-tale Princess. After she'd been crowned under a portable cloth-of-gold tent held by, amongst others, my wife, and with the Koh-i-Noor glittering above her forehead, she looked every inch a Queen Empress and put every single one of my herd into the shade.

The next day, I overheard Webb-Carter, one of those young pups in the Grenadiers who litter the Guards Club, say that I should have been given the title Keeper of The King's Cows and issued with a gold-tipped cattle prod. Well, I got a kiss from each of the old girls as they left the Loose Box, which puts me, with Bertie, in probably the most exclusive club in the country – and I will make damned sure that someone applies the black ball to the cheeky little sod if and when Webb-Carter's membership for the Verulam comes up. That will teach him to mock a national treasure.

However, any annoyance that I might have felt was forgotten when I returned home for dinner to find a cream coloured envelope waiting for me in my study. I flipped it over and saw the royal coat-of-arms with, underneath it, the legend: 'Office of the First Lord of the Treasury'.[109] What the bloody hell did Balfour want, I wondered? Didn't the fucker know that I was supposed to be retired... I slit open the envelope and pulled out a single sheet of writing paper, expecting the worst.

---

[109] Arthur Balfour was Prime Minister 1902-1905, First Lord of the Treasury 1895-1905 and Lord Privy Seal 1902-1903. However, the office of Prime Minister did not at this time officially exist hence the title on the envelope.

CHAPTER TWELVE: SARDINES & MONKEYS

10 Downing Street, London SW

Sir

I am instructed by the First Lord of the Treasury to inform you that he has it in mind to recommend to His Majesty The King to appoint you a Baronet of the United Kingdom in recognition of your service to the Crown at His Majesty's Coronation.

Please indicate by return whether or not you are willing to accept this Honour which, if you do so accept, will be published in the Coronation Honours List next week.

I have the Honour to be
Sir
Your Obedient Servant

Hector Tollemache

Private Secretary to the First Lord of the Treasury

You could have knocked me down with a busby plume. After all those years of putting my balls in the vice for Vicky, Bertie, PAV and the rest of them, to say nothing of risking life and limb in the 'service of my country', I was to be elevated to the Baronetage for looking after the Bounder's cast-offs at his enthronement! That put me on a par with Treves, who got one for fixing Bertie's bust inner tube. I didn't know whether to laugh or cry but, of course, I had no intention of doing anything other than accept by return.

I rang for Searcy and told him: he couldn't have been more complimentary. Then I told Fahran and Atash, who immediately insisted on calling me 'Sir huzoor' – until I ordered them not to - whilst the rest of the staff took to genuflecting whenever I appeared. And what did Charlotte-Georgina say when I told her over dinner? You'd have thought, after all those years of nagging and putting me in harm's way, that she would have been pleased. Not a bit of it.

"You know, Jasper, it's really no substitute for the Garter and, anyway, as you don't have a son to inherit the title, a Baronetcy is a bit pointless."

In that she was, of course, only half correct. But, honestly, women - they're enough to make a strong man weep…

…

Since Vicky's funeral, I hadn't been able to decide whether I liked or trusted Brother Esher. The fact was that, once Bertie had parked his enormous arse on the ermine-lined potty, Esher had his finger in every pie and, in particular, anyone with crown a'top it: Alexandra hardly choose a hat without his say-so and Bertie used him as his go-between with Balfour and the Tories. But Fred Cunliffe up at the Hall had told me over Christmas year that his grandson, who was pals at Eton with Esher's boy, Maurice, had been warned by his Dame not to be alone with the pair of them. Which was pretty rum when you came to think about it.

Anyway, like him or not, in February [1903] he sent me a letter to the Dower House where we'd been staying since Christmas, asking if I would meet him at Brooks's for luncheon 'at my earliest convenience'. As the food wasn't bad, although all those badly-dressed Liberals made it a damned uninviting place, I replied that I'd be happy to do so once we were back at Stratton Street at the start of March. Eventually, thanks to an exchange of telegrams - I'd refused to have one of those blasted telephonic machines installed at the Dower House; if I had of done, I'd have got no peace at all - we fixed on Thursday 5th. It was a bloody awful day – blustery, rainy and cold – so I got Atash to drive me in the Daimler the short distance from Stratton Street to Esher's club. Somewhat to my surprise, Brother E had arranged that we lunched privately in the small card room off the hall, which must have irritated some of his fellow members who were deprived of their mid-morning bridge, but that wasn't my affair.

Over the brandy, port (for Esher) and cigars he got down to business, for that was clearly what the meeting was all about: the likes of Esher didn't waste their time with the likes of me without good reason.

"Brother Speedicut, I think you may be aware that His Majesty is proposing a visit to Portugal and Italy next month."

"I had heard somethin' of the sort."

"Although Mr Balfour and Lord Lansdowne are reasonably relaxed about this itinerary, there is a rather tricky situation developing with regards to the Holy See, but let's put that to one side for the moment... A matter of even greater delicacy, which The King has not discussed with his government - so you must keep this entirely to yourself - is His Majesty's intention also to visit France before returning to England."

Was it, by George, I thought. That should be interesting, what with the Frog press still baying for our blood after the Boer business; but I said:

"How's he goin' to pull that off?"

Esher first looked pained at my directness then smug as he answered.

"His Majesty will be travelling on the *Victoria & Albert* and has arranged to be at Gibraltar at the same time as President Loubet is at Algiers to where The King will send the President a personal greeting.[110] This happy and wholly unexpected coincidence is designed to ensure that the President invites His Majesty to call upon him in Paris on his way home."

The crafty old devil; I wonder what he's up to, went through my mind but all I said was:

"I can't imagine Lansdowne's goin' to be very happy about that."

Esher drew on his cigar.

---

[110] Emile Loubet (1838-1929).

"That, my dear Brother Speedicut, is not a matter about which you need to trouble yourself."

"So, what *has* all this got to do with me?"

"It's about the Paris-end of the visit that I wanted to talk to you. His Majesty will be travelling alone – that is to say, without female company – and by the time he reaches Paris his mood may well be, shall we say, a touch tetchy? Now, this would not be helpful with regard to our plans for the French, with whom His Majesty intends to initiate a permanent *rapprochement*."

This was politics at a level way above my head and I wondered what could possibly be coming next, for we were clearly not yet at the point of the luncheon. Esher considered his port, sipped it, leaned forward and continued in positively oleaginous tones.

"We come now to a rather sensitive matter, my dear, with which I believe you may be able to help. Given your most skilled and valuable service to His Majesty at his Coronation, which I am delighted he has so amply rewarded - belated congratulations on your elevation to the Baronetage – we very much hope that you may be able to help him again in a similar vein. He would have spoken to you about this himself, but matters of State and the demands of his timetable in the event could not permit this.

"Anyway, His Majesty would be most, err, *gratified* to meet in Paris with a certain Russian dancer, whose performance His Majesty admired a couple of years ago in St Petersburg and who will be, by another happy coincidence, in Paris at the same time as His Majesty. Do you think you could assist us in this, err, matter…" and he left the rest of the question hanging in the air.

I'll be damned, I thought. I'd done plenty for the Brotherhood and the monarchy but I'd never been asked to procure for either. Well, not exactly. So, not content with getting me to ride shot gun on the infidelity omnibus at the Abbey, Bertie, the Brotherhood or both now wanted me to get him his oats in the City of Sin.

"Brother Esher," I replied, with as much dignity as I could muster, "you must know that I am a man of considerably advanced years. Perhaps, in my younger days, I might have been able to help but I think those days are long gone. Anyway, why me?"

Did Esher, I wondered, who was a relatively new recruit to the Brotherhood, know the extent to which I'd been responsible for potty training PAV? Well, if he did, it might have explained this present proposition. It was more likely he just knew that I was one of the few people about Town who could be trusted to do the business. Hmm. If I was to agree to this disgraceful request I was determined that it was going to cost King Priapus dear – the GCVO,[111] a first class return ticket and a suite at the Meurice would be a good start, I thought.

"Well, as to your age, Brother Speedicut, this will not be a task involving great physical effort. In fact, and I should have mentioned this earlier, you will be invited by His Majesty to join his Household for the entire trip as a supernumerary. So, it will be a holiday, of sorts."

Not if I know anything about the ways of Royal Yachts and Households, I thought.

"As to why you, well His Majesty knows of your Russian connections. All of which we think may come in useful," purred the self-serving courtier, taking another long drag on his cigar as I assumed a truculent look.

"But before you take a final decision, my dear, you should know that His Majesty has been minded for some time to elevate you, shall we say, to an even higher station that the Baronetage."

What was that? A peerage for pimping, surely not? A Grand Cross to add to my Baronetcy and my other assorted tin ware was certainly appropriate and would be a *sine qua non* to my agreeing. But a peerage? Charlotte-Georgina would become quite impossible. Esher must be joking, I thought?

---

[111] Knight Grand Cross of the Royal Victorian Order.

"Well, do let me know, Brother Speedicut, a note to the Lords will find me – as indeed it may, in future, find you." With that he pushed back his chair, thanked me for joining him for luncheon, ushered me to the front door and waved me goodbye.

I tooled over to White's, which I've used as a public lavatory for years and where they think I've been a member or at least they don't have the guts to show me to the door. Once I'd hung up my ulster, I ordered a stiff brandy at the bar. The place was quite empty, so I sat down by the fire and gave myself over to considering Esher's outrageous proposal. I hadn't got to the bottom of the first glass before I'd made up my mind. Lord Speedicut of Acton would look good in the directories and would certainly help with my credit in Savile Row. Without further ado, I dashed off a note of acceptance to Esher and told the porter to get it delivered. Then I bimbled home and told C-G that I would be away for a few weeks.

. . .

Some days after I'd informed Brother Esher that I would act as Pimp-in-Waiting, I received a letter from him giving me my embarkation instructions for the Yacht, confirmation that I would be staying at the Embassy in Paris and the name of the lady I was to coerce into giving Bertie a blow-job: Mathilde Kschessinska.[112]

That name probably won't mean much to my readers, except those who remember reading in an earlier volume that C-G had watched Tsar Nicky's Coronation Procession from Miss K's first floor balcony. For Mam'selle Kschessinska was none other than the ruling star of the Mariinsky Theatre in St Petersburg, a former mistress of the Tsar and a most obliging mattress for most of the rest of the male members of the Russian Royal Family, those at least that didn't prefer their stable boys. So, this was no *ingénue* starlet of the Russian ballet to be bribed into Bertie's bed with a signed photograph: this was a horse (or should that be whore) of an altogether

---

[112] Mathilde Kschessinska (1872-1971) *prima ballerina assoluta* of the St Petersburg Imperial Theatre and, later, Her Serene Highness Princess Romanova-Krasinskya, following her marriage in 1921 to Grand Duke Andrei Vladimirovich of Russia. The other facts as stated by Speedicut are essentially correct.

different colour. You see, Mam'selle Mathilde was the platinum standard when it came to courtesans and she would be sure to be surrounded by great hairy moujiks, placed there as guards by her current Grand Duke of the moment. However, that was a problem which would, of necessity, have to wait until we'd arrived in Paris.

In the meantime, Fahran packed my trunks, I said farewell to Searcy and Charlotte-Georgina, then Atash drove me and my valet to Victoria where we were directed to the Royal Train. On board, in the Household carriage I found Fritz P, Charlie Hardinge from the FO, Stan Clark, Seymour Fortescue, Frank Laking, the Blue Monkey and a greasy Eytie painter called de Martino,[113] whose job it was to record the royal progress. Quite why Bertie hadn't told Alix to lend Fritz her new Kodak Box Brownie for the same purpose was a mystery – unless, according to Fritz when I asked him, Bertie didn't dare to request the loan after the scene Alix had made at not being taken on the Mediterranean jaunt.

Anyway, as Royal Households go, it was a jolly group with de Soveral playing Falstaff and Hardinge in the role of Foreign Office minder. Fritz confided that Bertie had originally intended to travel without the customary Cabinet Minister in the party but, when Balfour cut up rough about it, he'd selected Charlie, who may have been a very junior in the FO but was a fluent linguist, a gent and married to one of Alix's Ladies-in-Waiting. The one fly in our ointment was de Martino, who quickly emerged as the man we all loved to hate; it happened thus.

Most of my readers are probably not aware that courtiers are pricklier than the pushiest mama at school prize giving when it comes to the pecking order, particularly so when foreign royalty are involved. This is not only because courtiers are Presented in strict order of seniority but – much

[113] Sir Frederick Ponsonby, Acting Private Secretary; The Hon Charles (later Lord) Hardinge CB (1858-1944), Minister Plenipotentiary & Assistant Under Secretary for Foreign Affairs; Major General Sir Stanley Clarke KCVO, Acting Master of the Household; Captain the Hon Seymour Fortescue KCVO, Equerry; Sir Francis Laking, Physician-in-Waiting; the 'Blue Monkey' was the nickname of the Marquis de Soveral (1851-1922), Portuguese Ambassador; Eduardo Frederico Chevalier de Martino MVO (1838-1912), official artist.

more importantly – because the foreign tin ware is dished out according to that ranking. So, the most senior member of the Household gets the Grand Cross of the Sacred Cow whilst the most junior is lucky to collect a crappy 4th Class of the Order of the Sweepers. Speaking for myself, over the years I had accumulated so many foreign decorations that there was no space on my tunic or tails for any more and, if it hadn't been for the fact that Bertie loathed the Baronets' neck badge and had forbidden me to wear mine, any additions to my collection would have resulted in my having to set others aside. So, I wasn't at all fussed when Fritz P told me that, as a supernumerary, I wouldn't have to bend the knee (even if I could) or collect a prize. De Martino's reaction on being told that he too was off the list was anything but compliant, as we all witnessed in the Household saloon on the Yacht two days out from Lisbon.

"No, no, Sir Ponsonby," he shrieked, when told of the news. "It is not to be considered. I am taking up the matter with His Majesty."

"You'll do no such thing," snarled Fritz.

"Look here," said Heddy Lambton,[114] trying to pour oil on troubled waters, "de Martino can have my place in the line-up."

"Or mine," said Fortescue.

"Gentlemen," said Fritz, in a more emollient tone, "I will take the problem to His Majesty. He will take a decision that will be binding upon us all."

Ponsonby was as good as his word and Bertie, who found the whole incident 'damnably funny', ruled that de Martino was to be placed at the head of the Equerries. The smug little Chevalier then did his best to lord it over the rest of us. That was a major mistake on his part, as he found out shortly after the Royal Yacht dropped anchor in Lisbon harbour on 3rd April. Fritz had excused me from the formal Presentations on board

---

[114] Rear Admiral (later Admiral of the Fleet) the Hon Hedworth Lambton CVO (1856-1929), Commodore of the Royal Yachts.

but suggested, with a wink, that I might have more fun coming ashore for the State Visit than skulking on the *V&A*.

The day before we dropped anchor, de Soveral had warned us that Portugoose food wasn't up to much, consisting largely of sardines, and that his master, Carlos I,[115] who actually hadn't a drop of Portugoose blood in his veins, was prone to staging rather theatrical ceremonial on those rare occasions when his German, Romanian, British, Italian or Frog relations came calling upon him 'in State'. So, we weren't altogether surprised when a flotilla of brightly painted barges – straight out of a medieval tapestry - approached the *Victoria & Albert*. Bertie was at the head of the gangplank to welcome his cousin, uniformed as a Colonel of a local Lancer Regiment. This was an unhappy, but probably unavoidable choice for our porky sovereign as the very short red cavalry tunic had the effect of magnifying his enormous white-clad arse and made him look like a large scoop of vanilla ice cream topped with a small cherry. Charlie Portugal, by contrast, was rigged out as an Admiral of their non-existent Fleet (unless you counted the barges).

When, eventually, all the Presentations had been made the Chief Sardine ushered Bertie down to his personal barge, a massive green-and-gold affair crewed by eight oarsmen in red uniforms which might have been fashionable in the reign of the Virgin Queen. The rest of the Suite followed on in three rather less ornate boats. Just as de Martino was about to clamber aboard the last of these, Hardinge, who spoke Portugoose, told the bosun to push off. It was only the timely intervention of two of the Royal Yacht's tars that prevented the painter's total immersion in the North Atlantic. As it was, he was soaked from the waist downwards and, as he was wearing white silk Court britches and – as was immediately apparent - no undergarments, his insignificant Eytie assets were clearly visible through the wet cloth. Fortunately for him it was a hot afternoon so, as cannon boomed out from the fortress and bands played on the quayside, he had dried out by the time we landed for the Civic Reception and the Mayoral Address.

---

[115] His Most Faithful Majesty King Carlos I of Portugal & the Algarves (1863-1908) was of the House of Braganza-Coburg.

But if the Italian artist had thought that was the end of it, he couldn't have been more mistaken. After the civic welcome, we were conducted to a fleet of ancient gilded and painted carriages, of the type one sees at the better class of pantomime, drawn by teams of white ponies and with an Escort of scruffy-looking cavalry. Fritz, de Martino and I were assigned to the last of these decrepit vehicles. The floorboards creaked ominously as Fritz and I got in and, when de Martino followed us, gave way completely leaving the Eytie with the top half of his body inside the coach and the rest beneath it.

Before he could extract himself, or ask us to help him do so, the procession set off at a trot. Fritz and I, as required by protocol, waved to the crowds but made no attempt to help the painter – well, we were far too busy waving and smiling, weren't we? - so de Martino had no choice but to trot the entire route. By the time the carriage came to a halt in front of the Ajuda Palace, de Martino was in a muck sweat, the lower half of his body was black with dust, his Court pumps were quite worn through and he was close to his last gasp. Not surprisingly, he begged Fritz to excuse him from being Presented to the Queen Mum, Maria Pia,[116] a stout-looking old baggage who hailed from Savoy and was scheduled to dish-out the gongs.

"Nonsense, Chevalier," said Fritz, "you must be presented to Her Majesty or she'll think that she is being snubbed by one of her own countryman." He pushed de Martino forward.

Now, as my better travelled readers may know, continentals don't wash much but, by the time the artist made his obeisance, he smelt worse than a Guardsman's socks and looked as though he'd just spent a week in the trenches before Sevastopol.

"Your Majesty," intoned Fritz, "may I Present the Chevalier de Martino, His Majesty's Official *Italian* Artist?"

---

[116] Her Most Faithful Majesty Maria Pia, Dowager Queen of Portugal & the Algarves (1847-1911) was the daughter of HM King Victor Emmanuel II of Italy (1820-1878).

Maria Pia took one look at the dishevelled creature bent half-double in front of her, obviously caught a whiff of his armpits and let out a sniff that was so loud Bertie turned around to see what was happening.

"*Disgusto!*" was all she said, as she withdrew her gloved paw from the dauber's grip. She then rather pointedly failed to pick up the Order which a Portugoose Equerry held on a red cushion for her and, instead, pinned it on me when I was brought forward. If de Martino could have got away with it, I'm sure he'd have let out a yell on a par with Sarah B's one that I'd stifled at Bertie's Coronation. As it was, he gave me murderous looks for the next twenty-four hours whilst, in return, I smirked at the thought that it was I who was now an improbable Servant of the Order of the Immaculate Conception of Vila Viçosa, an honour supposedly reserved for Left Footers.

If the carriages had been 'quaintly ancient' our rooms in the palace were 'magnificently ugly', as Fritz later described them, kitted out as they were with furniture that King Arthur would have found familiar and hung all around with fading tapestries and threadbare red plush that made Friedrichshof seem light and airy. And they clearly hadn't been used for years, to judge from the all-pervading smell of mice droppings and bat shit. However, there was a functioning bathroom of sorts on each floor and decanters of Scotch piss by each bed (Fahran emptied mine and refilled it with some of my own cognac).

Over the next three days there followed a series of events and ceremonials, from most of which I was – thank God – excused. However, tipped off by Fritz that there was more trouble in store for de Martino, I did agree to attend, on the second day, a pigeon shoot followed by a State Banquet which preceded a Command Performance at the Teatro Nacional de São Carlos and, on the last day, to go for a drive along the coast with the King's brother, the Duke of Croft & Cockburn.[117]

I had high hopes that Fritz had somehow or other arranged for the painter to be peppered during the pigeon drive or poisoned during the

---

[117] HRH The Infante Alfonso, Duke of Porto (1865-1920).

sardine-themed banquet, but neither happened. I was beginning to think
that I had wasted a full day of lounging about on the Yacht, and was
regretting that I had willingly risked food poisoning from rancid olive oil
and subjected myself to endless hours of grossly overweight divas belting
out ghastly Portugoose *fado* at the opera house, when events took a turn for
the better – at least as far as the 'get de Martino' faction was concerned.

During many years of lurking on the fringes of royalty, one of the things I've
noticed is that the smaller the Royal House (or the more recent its creation)
the greater the amount of flummery imposed and deference demanded:
chez the parvenu Bonapartes during the Second Empire it had verged on
the absurd. So, it was no surprise to me that Charlie Coburg, as I'd privately
renamed His Most Faithful Majesty King Carlos I, insisted that in the Royal
Box only he, the Queen Mother and Bertie could sit during the performance:
the rest of us had to stand. De Martino was, by this time and in a very real
sense, on his last legs. As we all filed into the Box, the painter hung back
presumably so that he could rest his bum on a broad dado rail that ran along
the back wall, a position I'd already marked down for myself. However,
Heddy Lambton pushed him behind Maria Pia's huge gilded throne.

"My dear Chevalier," he murmured, "as an Italian you should stand behind
the aunt of *your* King."

I think we were about an hour-and-a-half into the interminable
performance when there was a pause, the curtain came down and out
from behind it emerged the star of the show to rapturous applause and an
avalanche of flowers from the top boxes. I didn't witness what happened
next but Hardinge told us about it over breakfast the following day:

"De Martino used the brief interlude to limp out of the Box, presumably
in search of a seat on which he could sit-out the rest of the performance.
I watched him from the door. The corridor was bare of chairs, but I saw
him slide behind a tapestry that concealed the Queen Mother's Retiring
Room, where it was certain he would be able to rest his legs. I turned back
into the Box and told one of Maria Pia's Ladies-in-Waiting that I'd seen
a man who looked like an anarchist sneaking into Her Majesty's powder
room with a package under his arms... You won't be surprised to hear

that de Martino spent the night in the cells, from where he has only just been sprung by Fritz."

We all laughed so hard at this story that dust showered down on us from the chandelier above the breakfast table from which we were due to rise and prepare for the motoring trip.

"Gentlemen," said the Blue Monkey as we rose, "a word of warning: His Royal Highness The Infante Alfonso, Duke of Porto, is not only a dangerous driver but a practical joker. I, for one, will *not* be travelling with him."

Half-an-hour later found us all, de Martino included, standing outside the palace in front of a fleet of shiny motor cars with the King's brother beaming at us from the running board of the lead vehicle.

"Who is going to drive with me?" he said in a cheery voice as all of us, except de Martino, held back.

The luckless artist, presumably thinking that he was stealing a march on his tormentors, limped forward and climbed into the passenger seat whilst the Infante took the wheel and the rest of us piled into the vehicles behind. Then, without warning, the Duke's car sped off in a cloud of dust and gravel. During the next hour, we watched from behind it in shocked disbelief as, first, he deliberately ran his motor at a crowd of peasants lining a cliff edge, only jamming on the breaks in time not to hit them but forcing several of them to jump for their lives into the foaming briny fifty feet below. Then he accelerated towards a tunnel, which I certainly judged to be too narrow for his car: it wasn't, but he lost most of the motor's bodywork on its walls. Finally, on the home run, he slowed down and waved to us in the cars behind to catch him up. Our chauffeurs took this as a Royal Command and duly accelerated. As they did so, so too did the Duke. We all rounded a blind corner at about fifty miles an hour to be confronted by a T-junction. The Duke, who must have known it was coming, hauled on the anchors and slewed his car to the left. We had no chance to follow suit. Nor did we have the opportunity to avoid the ditch and wall beyond...

CHAPTER THIRTEEN: AVE MARIA

It was an absolute miracle that none of us was hurt, although two of the cars had to be pulled out of the ditch looking greatly the worse for wear and the third car was so deeply embedded in the wall that it had to be left where it was. Whilst the damned Duke roared with laughter, I was relieved to note that de Martino's hair was on end, his 'tashes were pointing towards his toes and he appeared to have lost the power of speech. However, the fact that the rest of us weren't in a much better state rather took the edge off our pleasure. During the next leg of the trip, which involved a pleasant cruise down the Portugoose coast and through the Straits to Gibraltar, de Martino was subdued to say the least and so we left him alone to nurse his battered body and pride.

I won't bother my readers with the details of our visit to the Rock, except to say that it had few attractions beyond a grand view and the use by the locals of the English language. At Gibraltar our two guard ships, cruisers from the Home Fleet, transferred the *V&A* into the armoured care of an absurdly large escort provided by our boys-in-blue based at Malta and comprising eight battleships, four cruisers, four destroyers and a dispatch vessel. We could have declared war on Italy with less.

Almost immediately, Bertie dispatched four of the battleships to Algiers – as secretly pre-arranged by Esher - to give Loubet, the Frog President, a very noisy greeting which resulted in the anticipated and inevitable invitation to visit the seat of Flashy's exile. Thus far, the Bertie-Esher plan was still firmly on the rails. However, we reached a tricky set of points when we weighed anchor off the coast of Italy.

The intention was to dock first at Naples, where Bertie planned to indulge in some *incognito* sightseeing at Pompeii, Herculaneum and the summit of Vesuvius. This was to be followed by a luncheon at a villa at Posillipo with that deplorable old pervert, Rosebery and several official receptions and dinners. We were then to cruise up the coast to Ostia where we would leave the Yacht to pay visits in Rome on Charlie Coburg's cousin at the

Quirinal Palace and at the Vatican on the Supreme Left-footer, who was so old he made me look like a teenager.[118] From there we were to board a private train to Paris. That at least was the plan.

The wheels started to come off Bertie's carriage almost immediately when he attempted *incognito* tourism: for not only did Bertie have one of the best know mugs in Europe, but the presence of half of the Mediterranean Fleet anchored offshore was a bit of a giveaway to the locals, who formed huge crowds wherever he went. In consequence, he was not a happy man. I had declined to join the royal party for any of these outings or the luncheon with Rosebery, which – according to Fritz - turned out to be a twenty-course affair, each course being more inedible than the one before. Bertie, apparently, was not amused.

Whilst all this was going on, I gave Fahran a few days leave and spent a perfectly delightful time with the notorious Billy von Gloeden in a villa he'd taken on Capri.[119] Readers may remember that, back in '82 I think it was, I had an introduction to von Gloeden from Flashy's utterly depraved neighbour, Robert de Montesquieu, but I never got to meet him because of plague in Palermo or some such.[120] Anyway, before I set off from London I'd sent Billy a letter to his house at Taormina suggesting that we might meet up in Naples or Rome whilst I was in Italy; I found an invitation waiting for me when we docked.

As my readers are well aware, in the past I haven't given many details of my antics on the Uranian side of my life, beyond being honest about its existence. I also seem to remember that I've stated a few pages back that I was reasonably certain that that chapter of my life had closed due to my advancing years. However, the book was flung wide open for me by von Gloeden, a charming if rather effete Kraut with an untrimmed beard and an excellent command of English; he would not have been out of place

---

[118] Archibald Primrose, 5th Earl of Rosebery (1847-1929) the former Liberal Prime Minister; HM King Victor Emmanuel III (1869-1947); Pope Leo XIII (1810-1903).
[119] Baron Wilhelm von Gloeden (1856-1931).
[120] Count Robert de Montesquieu (1855-1921); see *The Speedicut Papers: Book 6 (Vitai Lampada)*.

in the Garrick (if readers get my drift) and, indeed, he looked not unlike the late Fred Leighton.[121]

"I hesitate to raise this with you, Sir Jasper," Billy said, as we sat on the terrace of the Villa Jovis on my first day, sipping a really excellent sweet white wine after a delicious luncheon of white truffles and pasta, "but, as you are an *intimate* friend of dear Robert, I feel able to do so."

"What do you have in mind, Baron?"

"I have a problem and you are the only person who can help me to solve it."

"I'm intrigued, tell me more."

"As I was explaining to you over luncheon, I have set myself the task of recreating the leisure pursuits of the Emperor Tiberius here on Capri - as recounted by Suetonius - and recording them photographically."[122]

"Yes?"

"Well, whilst the young fishermen down at the harbour are equally as compliant as their cousins in Taormina, I would be taking a very serious risk were I to ask any of their grand papas to take on the role of the Emperor."

"So why don't you play the role yourself?"

"I would, although I am considerably younger than was Tiberius at the time I am photographing, but I can't be in front and behind the camera at the same time."

"I see," I said, "but I thought that for the most part Tiberius was a *voyeur?*"

"He was. But he had two practices that involved his active participation. The first

---

[121] Frederick, Lord Leighton (1830-1896).
[122] Emperor Tiberius (BC42-AD37); Gaius Suetonius Tranquillus (AD69-AD122).

...

Editor's Note: The next few lines must have been blanked out by Flashman and the word 'disgusting' had been scribbled in the margin.

...

"I'm sorry, Baron, but I *absolutely* draw the line at your first proposal. In the unlikely event that you were able to procure a suckling babe, I'm afraid that not even I could countenance such a level of depravity. As to the second, that is a rather different matter - although it's been a long time since I've been swimming. Perhaps I should try a few lengths in your bathing pool before dinner. Then, if I find that I'm able to stay afloat after all these years, tomorrow we can see if the locals are up to playing at minnows."

...

I was half-way through drying off after the last session in the pool when von Gloeden reappeared from his dark room with a brown paper package in his hand.

"Thank you so much for all your hard work, Sir Jasper; I do hope you're not too tired – or too sore."

"Not a bit of it," I said, although I think another such frolic inside of a week would have carried me off.

"I hesitate to beg another favour of you, my dear Sir Jasper, but you mentioned earlier that your next stop is Rome."

"It is. But I'm not going to fossick naked for you in the Trevi Fountain, not even if Pasquale, Vincenzo, Peppino and the rest of your fishermen are my companions."

"Of course not, dear Sir Jasper. No, no, what I would like you to do for me is far less, err, strenuous. I wonder if you could be very kind and deliver this," he held up the package he'd been carrying, "to my good friend Monsignor Pacelli at the Vatican?"[123]

"Who's he?" I asked.

"He's rather a dear, you know, terribly good looking and one of my collectors. I've promised him a set of my *Lays of Ancient Rome*."

"Oh, have you illustrated Macaulay?"

"Not *exactly*, Sir Jasper. It's a companion piece to my *Fall of the Roman Empire*. Both are *private* editions, you understand."

"I see," I said, "not illustrated works of literature then; rather more in the way of *art* books?"

"Exactly. Anyway, if - as you tell me - your King is to visit His Holiness you're bound to meet Monsignor Pacelli as he's a member of the Congregation for Extraordinary Ecclesiastical Affairs."

"Christ!" I exclaimed, "that's the Inquisition."

"No, Sir Jasper, calm yourself. It's the section of the Vatican that deals with foreign states, although I have to confess that my friend does have fairly extreme views about the Jews."

"That's not a problem: The King has left his behind in London."

"Anyway, because of his role there, Monsignor Pacelli was sent by the Holy Father to give your King the Pope's condolences on the death of Queen Victoria, so he's certain to be in the Vatican as he is bound to be part of the His Holiness' entourage for your visit."

"I wasn't actually plannin' on attendin' the Audience," I said, "but I'll certainly get my man to deliver it for you, if that alright?"

---

[123] Monsignor Eugenio Pacelli (1876-1958), later Pope Pius XII.

"That would be perfect."

I got back to the Yacht and Fahran before dinner on Bertie's last night in Naples, tired but strangely invigorated, to find Fritz in a terrible state.

"Jasper! Just the man," he cried, when he spotted me indulging in a restorative brandy on the after-deck.

"What's the matter, Fritz?"

"I've got a Papal-sized problem that requires immediate attention and both Hardinge and His Majesty, who are the only people who can deal with it, are ashore at an official dinner and won't return before midnight."

As my readers can easily imagine, after several days of utter decadence with von Gloeden, I was feeling pretty mellow, so I said:

"Sit down and tell me all about it: I probably won't be able to help, but a problem shared and all that."

"You are aware that The King intends to visit the Pope whilst he is in Rome?"

"I can't think why he wants to: the old boy's damned near a hundred and probably deaf, blind and incontinent. I went to an Audience of the present chap's predecessor with the Empress of Mexico: it was nothin' to write home about, just a lot of pansy priests wearing too much lace and reekin' of incense."[124]

Fritz gave me a rather disapproving look.

"The reason that His Majesty wishes to meet the Pontiff is that he is deeply conscious of the fact that several million of his loyal subjects are Roman Catholics and he feels very strongly that the anti-Catholic content of his Accession Oath caused great distress to them."

---

[124] See *The Speedicut Papers: Book 5 (Where Eagles Dare)*.

"So what?" I murmured; Fritz ignored this.

"Encouraged by the Duke of Norfolk,"[125] he ploughed on, "The King believes that the symbolism attendant upon a visit to the Pope could be of great significance to his Catholic subjects and show that he bears no personal animosity to the Catholic Church or its followers."

"So?"

"Against the advice of Lord Esher, His Majesty has taken the unfortunate step of getting Hardinge to officially ask the Cabinet for their consent. Balfour replied this morning telling The King *not* to make the visit."

"Why on earth have the Cabinet taken that line?"

"It would appear that the government is worried that, were it to sanction a visit by The King to the Vatican, it would enrage the Protestant working class voters in a number of highly marginal Tory constituencies."

"In that case, The King should tell the Cabinet to go to hell."

"That is exactly what he has done," said Fritz, fishing a bit of paper out of his breast pocket. "He dictated this telegram to Hardinge just before they left for tonight's dinner and Hardinge instructed me to encipher and send it."

"So, why haven't you?"

"Because, if I did, it would precipitate a constitutional crisis of quite epic proportions."

"Not another one?"

"I fear so," said Fritz, looking as though he was about to disappear under a road roller.

---

[125] Henry Fitzalan-Howard KG, 15th Duke of Norfolk (1847-1914).

"Well then, sit on it until tomorrow when you can discuss it with Bert, I mean His Majesty."

"I can't. I have to confirm the arrangements with the Vatican before then." I thought for a moment or two.

"Can I use your telegraph?"

"Certainly – but why?"

"I need to take some advice before I can give you any."

"But you must not disclose the substance of our conversation to anyone."

"Don't worry, I'll send it in code." I hadn't got one, but I did have a plan.

"Oh, very well – but on your head be it if this ever gets out."

Fifteen minutes later I had sent the following telegram to Searcy:

> *MOST URGENT STOP CHIEF CATTLE BREEDER OFFICIALLY ADVISED BY BANDY LEGGED KEEPER NOT TO ENTER LION CAGE STOP CHIEF CATTLE BREEDER DETERMINED TO PROCEED WITH FEEDING TIME SOONEST STOP HOW IS BLOODSHED TO BE AVOIDED QUERY QUICKSNIP*

I didn't have to wait long for a reply.

> *MOST URGENT STOP REVERSE ADVICE REQUEST STOP TELL KEEPER THAT LION FEEDING IS PRIVATE MATTER STOP IF LION EATS BREEDER THATS HIS AFFAIR STOP CATERING*

I took both telegrams to Fritz, who was in his cabin and looking utterly woebegone.

"There you go, Fritz," I said, as I handed him the flimsies which he read. "I'll wager my entire fortune that you could read these aloud in the House and only the most intelligent members of the damned Cabinet would be any the wiser."

"Who's 'catering'?" he asked after a minute or two.

"None of your business, Fritz. All you need to know is that he's a man who has spent a lifetime gettin' me out of deeper shit holes than the one in which you're currently festerin'."

"So, his guidance is that I send Balfour a telegram from The King stating that he has withdrawn his request for advice because he recognises that, in so doing, he has unintentionally put the Cabinet in an invidious position?"

"More or less. And you should add that if, once The King is in Rome, he determines that a *private* visit to the Pope is appropriate then His Majesty will do so without consultin' 'em and entirely on his own responsibility. They must, however, leave it to him to decide."

"And what will Hardinge say when I tell him that I've completely re-written The King's missive?"

"Don't tell him."

But he did, as I heard through the bulkhead between my cabin and Hardinge's whilst a bell tolled the Midnight Watch.

"You've done *what*, Ponsonby?" shouted the Foreign Office fellow. Fritz told him again and explained why he'd done it. "But you had no authority to alter completely His Majesty's message to his Prime Minister."

"I know," said Ponsonby, "and I wouldn't normally."

"I see," said Hardinge. "It sounded out of character. So, who gave you this rotten counsel?"

Thank God, I could still swim, I thought, as I edged over to the door to my cabin. To my surprise and considerable relief, as I turned the handle I distinctly heard Fritz say 'no one'. So, I slunk back to my bunk and, a short while later, my sleep was filled with images of naked Neapolitan boys frolicking in the Cabinet Room with Esher, Balfour and Bertie whilst I stood taking photographs with Alix's Box Brownie.

As we prepared to disembark the following afternoon at Ostia, Fritz took me to one side.

"Thanks to you, Jasper the crisis has been avoided: Balfour has withdrawn the Cabinet's advice, Hardinge is all smiles and now says that I did the right thing, and, when I told The King, he didn't seem to mind in the least that I had played fast and loose with his text. So, it will be Hail Mary and off to the Vatican, then the visit to the Quirinal before we board the train for Paris."

"I wonder if I could beg a favour, Fritz? After all, you do owe me."

"What's on your mind?"

"I've been tasked by Esher with a private assignment for The King whilst he's in Paris and it may take some organisin'. Would it be alright if I only stayed one night in Rome and then caught an earlier connection to Paris after I've run an errand to the Vatican for a friend? The extra few days there could be absolutely invaluable."

Ponsonby thought for a moment.

"I don't see why not, although - as you know the drill there - I was rather counting on you to help me with the Holy See. Would you hang on for that and then leave for Paris?"

It was my turn to think.

"Very well, but I'll take the night sleeper after Bert, I mean His Majesty, has seen old Leo."

Anyway, I thought, a visit to the Supreme Headquarters of Bells & Smells would mean that, rather than send Fahran to the Vatican with instructions to leave von Gloeden's book with a Swiss Guard on the gate, I could deliver it to the handsome Pacelli in person.

On our arrival in Rome, Bertie and the more senior members of his Household were lodged in the Embassy at the Porta Pia, but there was no room for Laking, de Martino and me so we were packed off to the Hassler at the top of the Spanish Steps, a newish hostelry where we were comfortable enough. The private visit – the word 'Audience' had been banned by Hardinge – was scheduled for the following day and was a very different affair to my last visit to Scent & Sodomy Central. The well-muscled and absurdly uniformed Swiss Guards were as before but, instead of a huge Audience Chamber full of smelly nuns and over-laced priests, Bertie, Fritz and I were led through a series of rooms by a soberly dressed Chamberlain who had met us at the gate. We ended up in a room which, with the exception of the depressing religious pictures hanging on the walls and the pagan artefacts (well, how else can one describe a monstrance?) which littered the tables, was in no way different to those to be found in the Baroque palaces of Munich and Vienna.

Our employer parked his ample, uniformed rump on a gilded and brocaded chair whilst Fritz and I stood behind. We didn't have long to wait. First, the door at the end of the room opened and in strode a dark haired, beaky-nosed priest whose purple buttons, trimmings, stockings and skull cap proclaimed him to be a Monsignor. This I hoped and assumed was von Gloeden's pal and so it was.

"Your Majesty," he oozed ecclesiastically, whilst giving Bertie a deep bow, "I am Monsignor Pacelli. May I welcome you to the Vatican and say what a pleasure it is to see you again." Bertie grunted something non-committal. "His Holiness will be with you shortly. In the meantime, can I offer you some coffee?"

We were just tucking into a pretty decent cup of the local brew when once again the door opened and in came the Pope. Actually, it would be more accurate to say that he was half-carried, half-dragged into the room by two beefy boys in a Dragoon-style uniform. I've already written that Leo XIII was a nonagenarian, the oldest Pope in the history of the Papacy in fact, but what I didn't know before he spoke was that whilst his body was clearly already half-way to the catacombs under St Peter's, his brain most definitely was not. He hardly spoke above a whisper, which was a problem for Bertie whose ears were almost as shot as Alix's with too much shooting, but they leaned towards each other and for thirty minutes or so appeared to get on well across a whole range of subjects with which I won't trouble my readers.

At last it was time to leave, the Pope was dragged out and we were shown by Pacelli to the door and a waiting Chamberlain. In the meantime, I was still clutching von Gloeden's addition to the pornographic canon. As Pacelli straightened up from a farewell bow to Bertie, I seized my chance.

"Monsignor," I said, "I have been asked to deliver this book to you by a German friend of mine who lives for most of the year in Sicily."

I hoped that by saying this he would get the hint, snatch the offending tome and keep it out of harm's way until he got back to his cell to enjoy it. Unfortunately, Bertie overheard me.

"What is that, Speedicut?" he growled, "show it to me."

CHAPTER FOURTEEN: ENTENTE CORDIALE

There have been far too many in times in my life when I've had to pray that the floor would open beneath my feet and this was another one of them. The idea of having to show Bertie a book which, although I hadn't actually had the opportunity to unwrap and scan it, undoubtedly contained page after page of priapic Italian youths laying each other end-to-end, was not an inviting one. But I had no choice so, instead of giving the parcel to Pacelli, who seemed as though he too was invoking the Almighty whilst casting an imploring look at the Chamberlain, I handed it to The King.

"It's a new guide book to ancient Rome, Sir," I said, which was in a way true and would, I prayed, put Bertie off opening it. He fumbled for a moment or two with the string and sealing wax but failed to unwrap the book. Thank God, the man had the patience of a gnat.

"Your carriage is at the door, Your Majesty," intoned the Chamberlain. Bertie harrumphed and handed the book to Pacelli, who looked as though he'd witnessed the Second Coming, whilst I thanked God that for once he'd delivered me from evil.

...

A couple of hours later Fahran and I were heading north on an Italian express train (there's an oxymoron if ever there was one – Italy will only amount to something when they have a King who can make the trains run on time) and I gave myself over to finding a way of getting the Lay of Old Mother Russia between the sheets with our Declined and Fallen Monarch.

I was still wrestling with the problem as the train pulled into the Gare de l'Est where, thanks to Fritz, the Embassy's second-best coach was waiting for me, complete with young Higgins, the Chargé d'Affaires (now there's an appropriate title for me on this trip, I thought). No sooner had the coachman whipped up the horses, than Higgins started wittering on about the difficulties of 'arranging His Majesty's programme at such short notice in a hostile city crawling with anarchists bent on killing The King'.

"You have no idea, Sir Jasper, the trouble this is causing. His Majesty's Private Secretary telegraphed this morning from Rome saying that His Majesty will expect to attend at least one performance at the Opera, but the Sûreté say that will be quite impossible. I am at my wits end…" And then I had a blinding flash of inspiration.

"Look here, Higgins, I may have a solution for you. What are your contacts like with the Ruskies?"

"Well, this year we are talking to them."

"Good. When we get to the Embassy, get your chief to contact his opposite number at the Russian Embassy and get me an appointment with the Ruskie Ambassador at the double. I think I may have a solution to your problems."

And so, the following morning I found myself, this time in our Embassy's best carriage, bowling over to the Boulevard Lannes to see Count Benckendorff,[126] who was Russia's man in London but had come over to Paris to keep an eye on Bertie. I knew Benckendorff from a previous visit to Petersburg, so this was a stroke of good fortune.

"Sir Jasper, this is a great pleasure – how may I help you?" intoned the Count in his best diplomatic manner, once I was safely deposited with an ice-cold glass of vodka – I had politely declined tea - in an elaborate throne-like chair in the gaudy setting of the Russian Embassy's vast salon.

"Well, Count, as you know King Edward is due in Paris next week – but, of course, that is why you are here – and His Majesty has indicated that he would like to visit the theatre one evening whilst in Paris, but the police…"

---

[126] Count Alexander Konstantinovich Benckendorff (1849-1917) was Russian Ambassador to the Court of St James from 1903 to his death in 1917. He was the principal architect of the 1907 Triple Alliance between France, Britain and Russia, which was a development of the *Entente Cordiale*.

I allowed the problem of security to speak for itself, for no one understood better the issues of royal security than a senior Russian diplomat.

"How can I possibly be of assistance to His Majesty in this regard? You know I neither sing nor dance," he said, with what was supposed to be a hearty laugh but sounded more like a bark.

"Nor do I," I laughed back. "But it has come to my attention that the brightest star of the Russian ballet is in Paris and I wondered if she would consider, even for a moment, staging a private performance for the King at our Embassy." I let the thought sink in and prayed to God that he would not put the *correct* interpretation on the word 'performance'.

"I cannot see, Sir Jasper, that your request will be a problem. Mademoiselle Kschessinska is, after all, only a servant of His Imperial Majesty and if you were to tell me that this was a *Command* Performance for His Imperial Majesty's dearest uncle, which of course we will now consider it, how could she refuse? Mademoiselle Kschessinska is, I believe, travelling in the party of His Imperial Majesty's cousin. I will instruct His Imperial Highness's Equerry to contact you at the Embassy to make all the arrangements."

Whether or not Benckendorff suspected that Bertie and I had an ulterior motive, I didn't know. But he was a man of the world and to him a dancer was only a royal plaything, so perhaps he didn't care one way or t'other: as a senior diplomat, his job was to serve his imperial master and, as La Kschessinska was no longer young Nicholas's squeeze since the ice maiden from Hesse had marched him down the aisle, he could take a broad view. At least I hoped so. I returned to the Embassy in high spirits and considerably lifted those of Higgins when I told him the news. Of course, I knew perfectly well that it was one thing to get Kschessinska into the Embassy; it would be quite another to get her into Bertie's bed, but *carpe diem* as the Greeks say.

The following morning, I was about to set out for a stroll up the Faubourg to admire the sights when a liveried footman brought me a note on a silver tray. It was an invitation to dine that evening at Maxim's with someone styling himself 'Chamberlain of the Household of His Imperial Highness the Grand Duke Andrei Vladimirovich of Russia'. There was no name, but that was the Russian way. Had there been I would have been on the first train out of Paris and to hell with Bertie's love life and the promise of a peerage.

So, rather than fleeing the City of Sin *aussi vite que possible*, it was with a considerable bounce in my elderly gait that I walked from the Embassy to Maxim's that evening to settle the arrangements for the first half of the Command Performance. The second half I was still mulling over, although a plan was starting to form in what years of the Emperor's finest had left of my brain. Old Cornuché showed me,[127] with many a bow and a scrape, to a small booth at the back of the restaurant, away from the beauties whom he always positioned by the windows. Seated with his back to me at a table already loaded with champagne and caviar was my host who, at my approach, turned and fixed me with his gotch eye.

I froze: it was Ignatiev,[128] who I'd last seen in '86 by Lake Starnberg. In the interval, he'd become almost unrecognisable having lost his hair and grown rolls of fat under his chin and around his waist. But that bi-coloured eye of his was unique and unmistakeable. His involvement in the affair of the moment put an entirely different complexion on it and, had I had the strength, I would have run straight out of the place. Instead, he extended a cold hand, which I took with some reluctance, and, with a strength that belied his years (for he was surely only ten years younger than me) virtually forced me onto the seat opposite.

"Mr Speedicut - I apologise, *Sir* Jasper - for even in Petersburg I have heard of the honour you have reaped since our last meeting," this said with a sneer and through gritted teeth, whilst I was having the greatest difficulty not swallowing my dentures. "Let us be clear, this meeting gives me no more pleasure than I can see it does you. But we are both ordered to the same end: a Command Performance, no less, by our Kschessinska for your King, who comes here doubtless on a mission to align British and French interests."

---

[127] The manager of Maxim's.
[128] Count Nicholai Pavlovich Ignatiev (1832-1908). Editor's Note: for those readers unfamiliar with earlier volumes of *The Speedicut Papers*, Count Ignatiev had – over many years – been a threat to Speedicut's well-being.

"Correct," I managed to say.

"So why, I wonder, does he choose a Russian not a French ballerina for his entertainment and relaxation?"

Because she's known to sleep with anything close to or on a throne, I thought but did not say. As my readers will note, I was starting to rally, for we were in the finest restaurant in the centre of civilization not a dungeon in the Urals.

"I understand that His Majesty," I replied, "much enjoyed Mam'selle Kschessinska's performance when he was last in Russia and, knowing her to be in Paris, hoped…" I let the request hang between us.

"Of course, but Mademoiselle Kschessinska is in Paris purely on a *personal* visit, and it is her current intention to return next week to Russia with His Imperial Highness."

Well, that's torn it, I thought. Bertie would have to make do with some amateur from the Opera's Corps de Ballet. But, after a short pause and another of his gimlet looks, Ignatiev continued.

"However, His Imperial Highness considers that a gesture of goodwill by Russia might not go un-noticed in the negotiations in which your King and the French President will shortly be engaged, so he has asked Mademoiselle Kschessinska to remain behind for this additional engagement.

"But, Speedicut," he went on, "you should be aware that I am Commanded by His Imperial Highness to attend upon his 'friend' and – let me spell this out for you – *not to let her out of my sight*. I will bring her to your Embassy, she will dance for your King, if he so wishes she will sup with him afterwards and then she will return to her hotel. *And that is all.* Do I make myself clear?" I nodded my agreement. He paused, then went on again.

"You may be old; indeed, we have both survived longer than most of our comrades–in–arms, but I do not trust you a *tochka*. Accordingly, if you, or your King, so much as lay a hair on the sacred body of Kschessinska, your daughter the Princess Lieven - who is at this minute on her way from her husband's country estate to their house in Petersburg - will not live to see your grandchildren grow up." He let that sink in. "And all of London will be informed of your activities in Peking with a certain Countess, who is currently proudly displaying to all her friends in Moscow the trinkets she received from you... Do I make myself *absolutely* clear?"

I nodded, for what else could I do? His information was, as always, on the mark. My sainted daughter and my own precious reputation were to be the hostages for my good behaviour and, presumably, that of Bertie as well; and, if either of us did not comply. Well, it didn't bear thinking about. Ignatiev called over the waiter, threw some notes at him and stood up.

"If you will be kind enough to let me know the date next week for the performance, I will make all the necessary arrangements."

He gave me a curt nod of his head, which I weakly returned, and left me to digest both his remarks and the remains of the caviar, both of which stuck as firmly in my throat as if he had forced them in there with the butt of his *knout*. I didn't linger for any longer at Maxim's than it took to consume some foie gras, a lobster and a scoop of sorbet and, within the hour, I was back in the Faubourg.

...

Of course, I could answer for myself and, whilst I might like to have given the Ruski dancer a warm-up in the collecting ring afore the big race, I had already rejected that as an old man's dream rather than a deliverable reality. No, the problem was Bertie, who quite clearly had only one thing on his mind where Miss K was concerned.

Twelve hours later I was still wrestling with this potentially disastrous situation and was unable to see any way out. Well, my readers know me by now if they've read this far: when faced with disaster I normally run. But this time, I couldn't see the exit. If I abandoned the task and returned to London, the result would be almost as disastrous as if I allowed Bertie to get his podgy paws on the 'sacred' body of the Grand Duke's pirouetting poke.

In a desperate attempt to get my thoughts in order I slunk out of the Embassy and headed for a little café I knew on the edge of the Place Vendôme. As I sat there sipping a glass of the Corsican Corporal's best, with the man himself scowling down on me from his column, I reviewed my options for the hundredth time, but still I could see no way out. Just then a shadow fell across my table.

"Why, Jasper, what brings you to Paris? But, *ma foie*, you look as if you've just been told that you have a week to live. Surely not?"

I looked up from my cognac into the twinkling eyes of Beatrice de Lorraine, the ex-Lady-in-Waiting turned *grande horizontale* who's boss had so nearly married PAV all those years ago. During a brief fling that we'd had at the time, but which I haven't previously recorded, I'd discovered for myself at first hand (and much else besides) that she was one of the best rattles in central Europe. After she'd left royal service, she had set up as one of the grandest (and most expensive) lays on the Continent. Older now, of course, but still - to my sentimental eye - just as beautiful, her athletic figure was clearly outlined by the latest Paris rig whilst she exuded Gallic charm and reassurance.

"Take a seat, m'dear," I mumbled, as I rose with many a cracking joint. "You're a welcome sight for my old eyes. Y'know, I've often meant to look you up, but I heard you'd left royal service and married a Count or some such, so I thought it best to leave well alone."

"The first is certainly true; as for the rest... But tell me, why are you in Paris and why so troubled? No, don't tell me. I think I know one of the answers: your King is soon to meet with our President, *n'est pas*, and you are here in connection with the visit? But as to why you are so miserable, *je n'ai aucune idée.*"

They say that timing is everything and Beatrice had always had the happy knack of turning-up in the nick of time, so without further ado – and I knew she was completely unshockable - I told her everything. She sat there as still and inscrutable as a sphynx. When I had finished she smiled.

"But my dear Jasper, the solution is so simple I am surprised you 'ave not yet thought of it." She then proceeded to outline a plot that was so audacious it fair took my breath away. "....and there is no risk. Your King will simply ascribe it to the fatigue of his Tour. I will send you what you need this afternoon. Now you can buy me lunch at Fouquet's, where we will eat *quenelles de brochet* and talk of old times." And that's exactly what we did.

Later that day, after a tedious conference with Higgins about the arrangements for Bertie's visit during which I found it hard to stay awake thanks to the excellent bottle of Sauternes that Beatrice and I had downed over luncheon, I sent a note to Ignatiev at the Russian Embassy. Would he, I asked in my best diplomatic style, be so kind as to bring La Kschessinska to the Embassy at 6.30pm the following Wednesday, where she would be given a suitable suite in which to change and prepare for the performance? A piano of the appropriate quality would, I told him, be installed in the Embassy ballroom, as would a small stage. Miss Kschessinska's accompanist would – of course - be given prior access to practice on the instrument, should that be required. His Majesty, I went on, had expressed a desire to dine with Miss Kschessinska after her performance and I would set aside a private room in the Embassy for a light supper (well, as light as Bertie was accustomed to, which meant at least seven courses). Ignatiev and I would be the only gentlemen 'in Waiting' but I warned him that the King did not permit his courtiers to dine with him, so there. I received the curtest of curt acknowledgement by return.

Bertie duly arrived in Paris to a deafening wall of silence and hostility, leavened only by the occasional shout from the reeking mob of Paris's bourgeoisie of: 'à bas les Anglais', '*merde à toi*' and other words of heartfelt support and encouragement for our distinctly overweight sovereign, who was trussed-up like a broiler in his Field Marshal's kit.

The first two days of the visit didn't exactly go from bad to worse: they stayed at bad. By the second afternoon, it was clear that Bertie was beginning to wonder if he had made a bad mistake and, from a gruff aside he made to me when he returned to the Embassy after a fraught visit to Les Invalides, he was clearly looking forward to the promised display of La Kschessinska's knickers followed by a bout on the chaise-longue as recompense: for it was looking, otherwise, like a wasted trip.

For myself, I was none too calm: if Beatrice's plan failed, Dorothea and I were doomed. With the Embassy's butler, who wouldn't leave my side for a moment, all afternoon I'd fussed around the ballroom checking the stage, the flowers, the damned piano and the seating. The I checked the supper room, complete with a *chaise-longue*, and the star dressing room that we had created out of a guest bedroom and bathroom by filling it to bursting with bouquets of flowers and oversized mirrors that Fahran had purchased in the market.

At half-past-six La Kschessinska's carriage drew up at the Embassy's main entrance. With a look of loathing at me, Ignatiev escorted her into the building, swept past the Ambassador with barely a word whilst Higgins, who was practically dissolving with diplomatic excitement and ill-concealed lust, took her up the stairs to her dressing room. I scarcely got a glimpse of her, but what I did see explained why our blessed monarch – and half the Russian Court - was so keen to get between her well-muscled thighs. Although she was a tiny she was an absolutely perfect peach, smothered in furs and diamonds and with a swish to her rump that would have made any one of the 2nd Battalion pop the flies off his buckskins.

. . .

An hour later Bertie was ensconced in a large gilt chair in the ballroom, with his Household and all the senior types from the Embassy standing behind him. Ignatiev and I were at the back of the room, keeping a good distance between us. I could tell from the drumming of his fingers on the arm of his chair that Bertie was impatient for the show to start. Suddenly, the newly installed electric lights went out, save for a large glass chandelier over the stage, the pianist struck-up some foreign tune and La Kschessinska wiggled onto the stage, *en pointe*, displaying more of her undercarriage than she'd ever dared to show on the stage of the Mariinsky.

Now, I'm not a great one for the ballet: in my view, I can't see the attraction of glimpsing a girl's knickers when, by paying a sov, you can see and feel what lies beneath. But each to his own. Anyway, once I was certain that every man in the house had his eyes glued on Kschessinska as she swooped and leapt across the stage, I took the opportunity to slide out and check on the supper arrangements.

When I quietly re-entered the room a couple of minutes later I saw Ignatiev give me a very nasty look, but the rest of them were having difficulty keeping their eye balls in their sockets. After what seemed like an eternity, Miss K finished her gymnastics with a deep curtsey to Bertie and swept off the stage. The storm of applause from the randy old goats, who had been ogling her for the past half hour, was so great that she soon swept back in. Bertie clicked his fingers, which brought Higgins running forward with a large bouquet, then heaved himself out of his chair and – at least so it seemed to me – made a lunge for her, practically shoving the bouquet down her heaving cleavage.

"*Milles mercies, ma petite*," he slobbered, dabbing his forehead with a handkerchief. "*Magnifique, absolument magnifique! Et maintenant, du champagne et après à diner...*"

His French was execrable, but it was the only language they had in common. Liveried flunkies appeared as if by magic and the fizz was soon flowing freely, but – as instructed – the assorted hangers-on took their leave after just a glass, reversing out of the room backwards in the approved manner, leaving Bertie, the dancer, Ignatiev and me. With what I hoped was a suitable flourish, I escorted them into the *salon privée* next door and saw them safely to the table, which was already laid with the first course. Fritz had told me that morning that Bertie wanted no waiters or footmen in the room, so the rest of dinner was spread out on a sideboard.

Ignatiev and I left the couple to it and 'took post' on chairs, one each side of the double-doors into the room, which Ignatiev had left slightly ajar as he exited. This lent a whole new meaning to being 'in Waiting', I thought, as I strained my ears for sounds of the lunge or grope which I knew could not be far off. Ignatiev, too, seemed to be straining every fibre for a sound of the type that would start the death knell tolling of *la famille* Speedicut.

CHAPTER FIFTEEN: THE DUCHESS
OF JERMYN STREET

But, to my surprise, Bertie seemed to be on his best behaviour and jabbered away interminably to La Kschessinska, who probably only understood a tenth of what the old boy said between his mouthfuls of food and coughing. The supper dragged on and on. Then, just as I was starting to nod off, I heard the scrape of chairs and Bertie asked Miss K if she would care for a brandy. She declined, but the sound of clinking glass indicated that Bertie was not breaking the habit of a lifetime. There was then the unmistakable sound of the royal rump testing the springs of the *chaise longue* followed by a long silence. I feared the worst.

Suddenly, the doors swung open and there was the star of the Russian ballet, cool as you like and clearly unmolested, whilst from behind her I heard the unmistakable sound of a steam train passing through a tunnel and saw, over her shoulder, that Bertie was fast asleep on the sofa: his left hand was clasped to his top fly button and his right hand still clutched an empty brandy balloon.

With a quick and very shallow curtsey to me, Kschessinska allowed Ignatiev to escort her back to her dressing room and, sometime later, out of the Embassy. I sincerely hoped it would be the last I ever saw of either of them. Meanwhile, I stole back into the dining room and, afore any of the servants could clear away the meal, I quietly poured the rest of the brandy into the overblown flower arrangement on the sideboard. It wouldn't have done for the servants to succumb to the same sleeping draft that I'd slipped into the decanter whilst her ladyship was prancing and pirouetting, now would it?

The next morning, I sent Beatrice a very large bouquet of the most expensive flowers I could find, along with probably the most heartfelt note of thanks I had ever written. As to the peerage? I can say with absolute sincerity that I wouldn't have swapped a Dukedom for the sense of relief I felt for the next few days.

…

Editor's Note: It would seem that, at the conclusion of King Edward VII's 1903 European Tour, Speedicut settled into a well-earned retirement in London and North Wales, interspersed with visits to Paris and St Petersburg. His letters to Flashman did not, however, cease although their contents are mostly fairly banal. Nonetheless, there are a number of anecdotes in the correspondence which I have extracted for their humour or which show that, despite retirement, Speedicut continued in his inimitable way to contribute to world events — usually with disastrous consequences. In the case of these extracts, I have retained their original letter format...

…

Hotel Meurice, Paris, October 1903 [extract]

They say that, if you live long enough, everything comes around twice if not more. I can now prove the truth of this proverb. C-G and I were invited to luncheon at the Embassy last week by Eddie Monson,[129] a grey-bearded old diplomat who's a touch younger that me but looks double my age. It was only a small party and amongst our number was a Frog wordsmith called Sardou,[130] who said he remembered me from a trans-Atlantic trip I made in '67.[131]

"Surely you recollect, Sir Speedicut?" he asked. "You were travelling back from Mexico after *la revolution* and you told my wife the story about the *double-croix* inflicted upon *le pauvre* Emperor Maximilian?"

"Ye-es," I replied rather hesitantly, for whilst I remembered the deceit I couldn't remember the man.

"*Eh bien,* my dear sir, I turned your *histoire* into a play and Monsieur Puccini 'as made an opera from it;[132] a new production in French with, once

---

[129] Sir Edmund Monson GCB GCMG GCVO (1834-1909).
[130] Victorien Sardou (1831-1908).
[131] See *The Speedicut Papers: Book 4 (Where Eagles Dare).*
[132] Giacomo Puccini (1858-1924).

again, *La Divina* in the starring role, opens on Tuesday next at the Opera Comique. You should attend."[133]

"Really? What's it called?" asked C-G who, being an enthusiastic opera *aficionado*, had been ear-wigging our conversation from the other side of the table.

"*La Tosca*, my dear milady."

"Oh, but we should so love to see it, wouldn't we, Jasper?" I groaned inwardly but nodded my assent.

"In which case, milady, I very much 'ope that you will join me in my box for the opening night."

"We should be delighted," said C-G, "won't we, Jasper?" this last said with not a little menace.

"Of course, my dear – and, if you would like to, I can take you backstage afterwards to meet Madame Bernhardt…"

"*That*, Jasper, will *not* be necessary," said my wife, with a loud sniff: C-G thinks that Sarah B is little better than a tart, an opinion which - for once – is pretty much the truth.

So it was that the following Tuesday we traipsed off to the Opera Comique to watch an opera set in Rome around the turn of the last century. It was about a loose-hipped *chanteuse* called Florida Tosca who agrees to be stuffed by the Chief of Police Baron Scarface, in return for him faking the execution of her revolutionary-cum-artist lover, Mr Caravan Dosshouse. The dramatics and the staging were quite good, but I was nearly deafened by the bellowing from the stage and the ear-splitting antics of the orchestra. If only you [Flashman] hadn't been undergoing treatment at the Prieuré de St Samantha you could have taken my place: C-G would never have noticed…

---

[133] Sarah Bernhardt (1844-1923), who made the role of Floria Tosca, sung in French, something of her own.

Anyway, back to the action on stage. Despite having agreed that the Baron could have his wicked way with her in return for the firing squad shooting blanks, Miss Tosca stabs the poor lecher to death the moment he lays a finger on her top hamper. However, the Chief Peeler gets the last laugh for – as with the hapless Max Habsburg – the execution party fire ball, Mr Dosshouse dies and, when she realises that she too has been double-crossed, the silly bitch Tosca throws herself off the top of the Castel San Angelo. This was the only bit of the opera with a laugh in it, albeit an unintentional one. You see La Bernhardt is no fool, and she certainly wasn't going to risk breaking her leg again, so – as I found out later - she demanded and got a large pile of mattresses stacked up behind the scenery to cushion her landing. Unfortunately for her, Tosca-like she'd earlier rebuffed the Stage Manager, who'd quite reasonably proposed a light rogering session after the performance. As revenge was very much in the air, he got his by substituting a well-sprung bedstead for the heaped-up paillasses with the result that, as the curtain was deliberately lowered slowly, the Divine Miss B flung herself from the ramparts and then kept re-appearing over the castellation… It literally brought the house down.

...

Palais Lieven, St Petersburg, November 1904 [extract]

I've been told the most extraordinary story. It seems that the new Imperial blob, the much longed for Tsarevich, Heir to the Throne of Russia, is a bleeder.[134] No, not a 'little bleeder' in the sense of being a pesky nuisance, although that may be his future role in life, but a haemophiliac like Vicky's son Leopold.[135] Given that the hated Alicky, otherwise known as Her Imperial Majesty The Empress Alexandra Feodorovna,[136] is formerly Miss Alix of Hesse & by Rhine and the granddaughter of the late Widow of Windsor, it would seem that the dread disease is an unintentional gift from the House of Hanover. Actually, it's bloody bad luck (if you'll forgive the pun) not only for the boy but for the future of the Romanov dynasty.

---

[134] HIH Tsarevich Alexei Nikolaevich (1904-1918).

[135] HRH Prince Leopold, Duke of Albany (1853-1884).

[136] HIM The Express Alexandra Feodorovna (1872-1918).

Why, I hear you ask? Because, as my son-in-law told me, the so-called 1797 Pauline Law of Succession bars from the throne any Romanov who marries out of the blood-royal. As all those male Romanovs who might be eligible to succeed are either married to a woman of 'Unequal Rank', living with their mistresses in Paris or being buggered senseless by their grooms, the outlook is bleak if the Tsarevich dies before fathering a male heir or Alicky produces no further sons. Of course, there are always the Tsar's four girls,[137] who if they marry unsullied royalty would not be barred, but this is considered to be a sub-optimal solution in a land which is virtually ungovernable even by a tyrant such as the present Tsar's late father.[138]

So, what's to be done? The answer is that those in the know, who are few in number, haven't a clue. I forecast that an endless procession of learned sawbones will be summoned from the four corners of Europe and will all declare that the Tsarevich's condition is incurable, untreatable, unpleasant and will inevitably lead to much pain and an early demise: a bit like being married to C-G. Actually, for once, I jest as the old girl's been on good form and excellent company. She's even managed to part her arthritic hips for a frolic or two when I'm in the mood, which isn't often these days. She's also got a solution to the Imperial problem: a faith healer. She's said as much to Minnie,[139] who she's known at a distance for some years but is now C-G's new best friend thanks to another gushing letter from the old trot's sister, Alix. I'm not entirely sure that C-G has convinced the Dowager, who's no fool, but as C-G's also imparted her wisdom to sundry Ladies-in-Waiting – and this is Russia - it can't be long before some evil-smelling *starets* is dragged from interfering with his goats and the local peasant girls, given a quick wash and told to make miracles.

To add to the Tsar's woes, it looks as though his war with the yellow horde, which he started last year, continues to be an absolute disaster with the Russian Far East Fleet, already reduced to a couple of row boats, blockaded in Port Arthur by the Nips and a Relief Force still trying to

---

[137] HIM Tsar Nicholas II (1868-118); TIH The Grand Duchesses Olga (1895-1918), Tatiana (1897-1918), Maria (1899-1918) & Anastasia (1901-1918).
[138] HIM Tsar Alexander III (1845-1894).
[139] HIM The Dowager Empress of Russia (1847-1928).

make its way overland via the much vaunted but actually incomplete Trans-Siberian Railway. Some while ago I was cornered by the Tsar at a reception at the Winter Palace. He wanted to know what we would do if caught in a similar situation. Frankly, I hadn't got a clue and I'm not a matelot, but I hazarded the idea that one solution would be a surprise attack on the Jap Fleet.

"But our Far East Fleet is bottled up in Port Arthur, Sir Jasper."

"Indeed, Sir, but your Baltic Fleet isn't."

"But it can hardly force a passage through the Artic: it's impassable."

"I know, Sir, but what's to stop it goin' the long way around via the Suez Canal and takin' the Japs by surprise in the rear?"

"That is an interesting idea, Sir Jasper, which we will discuss with our Naval High Command."

It was hardly my fault that Rozhestvensky said '*pas de problem*',[140] then damned near caused a war with us last month by blowing half of our North Sea fishing fleet out of the water on the Dogger Bank. And why did the stupid prick do that, I hear you ask? The answer is because he thought that the herring fishers were a Flotilla of Japanese torpedo boats! It's not for nothing that the idiot Admiral is known as 'Mad Dog': if I was the Tsar, I'd treat him like one and have the bugger shot. Bertie and Balfour were not amused but, instead of treating it as act of war, told Nicky that his armoured tubs would not be permitted through the Egyptian drain. As a result of all this, and the attendant publicity, the Nips are forewarned and by the time the Ruskie Fleet has steamed around the Cape of Good Hope you can be damned sure that our slitty-eyed allies will be waiting for them.

. . .

Palais Lieven, St Petersburg, January 1905 [extract]

---

[140] Admiral Zinovy Rozhestvensky (1848-1909).

Russia is teetering on the brink of revolution and I've told Dimitri and Dorothea to make damned sure they've got plenty of cash and securities stashed in a Swiss bank and know how they'd get out of Russia in a hurry. Dimitri seems to think that I'm being alarmist, but I have to tell you that the situation here is extremely ugly and getting worse by the minute: C-G and I have already booked our passage to Stockholm at the end of the month and I've urged the Lievens to come with us, but to no avail. God only knows if we'll ever see them again.

So why am I so concerned? Events, dear boy, events. For a start, the war with the Nips goes from bad to worse and is now causing real unrest amongst the great unwashed, who are the ones having to fight and die for a lost cause. You [Flashman] may have read in the Parisian rags that the Baltic Fleet, which Nicky stupidly dispatched to the Far East (alright, it was my idea, but…), is stuck in Madagascar where your Froggy hosts, despite their treaty obligations to the Russians, quite sensibly want to prevent it steaming north to its inevitable destruction. Meanwhile, Port Arthur has fallen and the Russian Army of Manchuria is in full retreat.

These military disasters in the Far East have encouraged the Nihilists, the Communists and the Socialists to exploit the situation for their own purposes which are, for the Nihilists, an end to the rule of law; for the Communists, an end to Tsarist rule; and, for the Socialists, improved conditions for the factory workers and the introduction of democracy. The result: strikes, the virtual paralysis of St Petersburg and the country slipping from Nicky's control, despite the best and very brutal efforts of the Okhrana. Of course, the situation would be perfectly containable if only the pretty but ineffectual Tsar would get a grip, as I told Minnie over tea here.

"What is to be done, Sir Jasper?" she asked, as I passed her a slice of Battenberg cake.

"His Imperial Majesty must take firm action against the strikers and the men behind them, Ma'am."

"But how? They are so many and so diverse."

"He needs to make an example, Ma'am, *pour encourager les autres*. Take, for example, the proposed demonstration this Sunday at which the workers are going to march to the Winter Palace and present a petition demanding better working conditions, more pay, an eight-hour week and an end to the war.

"All that His Imperial Majesty has to do is to have the ring leaders arrested when they present their petition and then have them exiled in Siberia – or, better still, shot – and the country will soon come to heel."

"You know, Sir Jasper, I think you may be right. Firm leadership is what is required. I am dining with my son tonight and I will tell him."

I still maintain that I gave the Dowager Empress good advice: it was hardly my fault that the military commander of St Petersburg panicked and ordered the demonstration to be broken up with charges by the Cossacks and volleys of rifle fire from the Imperial Guard. I'm sorry that so many were killed and injured, but omelettes and eggs come to mind. The pity is that, like the war in the Far East, the eggs have ended up on Nicky's face and not in the pan.

Anyway, Russia is no place to be at present. I just pray that we are able to get out of the country before the doubled-headed shite hawk bites the dust.

...

Cavendish Hotel, Jermyn Street, London SW, March 1905 [extract]

I'm down from Wrexham for a few days to escape C-G and to see Searcy, who's not been well. The Verulam's closed for redecoration so, instead of opening up the house, I decided to stay here. You [Flashman] may remember that we used to have a cook called Mrs Ovenden, who had a pretty daughter called Rosa whom Atash and Fahran were constantly trying to entice into the stables to see the 'horse with the green tail'. When she stopped hanging around our kitchen door, Rosa went on to become a celebrated cook for royalty, Society and – if we have special guests - the Speedicuts.[141] Whether or not the boys ever managed to get her alone in the hay loft I don't know, but it seems that Bertie did and, according to Searcy, when La Keppel told him that 'enough was enough', our porky monarch paid off Rosa by buying her this hotel, which she runs on distinctly louche lines. It was a smart move on Bertie's part, as Rosa keeps a room available for his use should he want to play away from home or Mrs K.

Thinking about it, the Cavendish is really more of a private country house than an hotel. It's decorated in a slightly faded but very comfortable way, and the visitors' book is signed on leaving not on arrival (it is *not* available as evidence in the Divorce Courts, so Rosa assured me, nor are the names of the 'nice clean tarts' who she whistles-up at a moment's notice for her guests *in lieu* of hot water bottles). The hall is piled high with uncollected luggage, discarded bearskins (of the Woodentop variety), old polo sticks (I always said that a game which allowed the hoi polloi to rough-ride royalty would attract the *nouveaux riches* riff-raff) and the large centre table is overflowing with unopened letters. There's no bar, all the rooms are suites and have their own private dining rooms where the food's excellent and no questions are asked. The guests, who Rosa rules with a rod of iron from her Parlour, range for country parsons (perhaps as insurance, she's has got a soft spot for 'the Cloth'), through good-looking, polo-playing Yankee millionaires (my earlier point about polo is, thereby, proved in spades) to dashing and often impoverished aristos and their sons (for both of whom she has a positive mania). Many of the latter have, like Bertie, rooms permanently assigned to them and treat the place as their London home. However, Rosa very sensibly draws the line at Grub Street scribblers (and anyone so identified, including many who aren't but are labelled as such) who she immediately has evicted by Scott the hall porter. Not for nothing has she earned the soubriquet of the 'Duchess of Jermyn Street'; she could have given my late mother-in-law lessons in high-handed behaviour.

Another strange feature of the Cavendish is Rosa's charging regime, which is based on the Robin Hood principal: she has no hesitation in billing the fizz – hardly any other drink is served – to those who can afford to

---

[141] Rosa Lewis (1867-1952).

pay for it, rather than to those who have consumed it but haven't got the blunt. Speaking of which, the fizz that is, whole crates of the stuff are downed on a single evening in the Elinor Glyn, a white and gold sitting room for the use of her guests in which there is a sofa so large that four people could (and often do) sleep on it at the same time. In fact, from the moment the sun goes down, it's party-time at the Cavendish. Court Balls and Coming-Out dances start and end here and, if you don't want to be woken in the small hours by Rosa and told to come and join in the fun, it's essential to keep your door firmly locked.

As Fahran and I stepped into the hotel on my first day here, Rosa shrieked at me though the open glass-panelled doors of her Parlour in her unique and bawdy Cockney:

"'allo, Crolonel, luv, what the bleedin' 'ell brings you to Lunnon? And 'ooze bloomin' idea was it that yer put up at my 'ouse?"[142]

"It was my man, Searcy's, suggestion," I called back to her.

"Good for fruckin' 'im. Well, stop pissin' around in the 'all, tell that well-'ung drarkie of yours to take yer brags up to number twenty-one – Dirty Scrott will show 'im the way - then come in 'ere, rest yer plates of meat, take a prull on this," she rattled a magnum in a large cooler bucket, "and tell me wot sheep yer've bin shaggin' in the wilds of Wales".

We'd drained the bottle by the time she let me go and I honestly don't remember much about the meal that was served to me later in my suite, beyond the fact that it included her famous quail pudding. What I do remember was being woken in the middle of the night by an insistent beating on my door. Before I could roll out of bed and grab my dressing gown, the oak burst open to reveal Rosa, glass of fizz in hand.

---

[142] Editor's Note: Rosa Lewis's Cockney was, in the words of Pauline Massingham who knew her well, 'of a kind that is rarely heard today. Although she scattered H's wherever she went, her great peculiarity was that she [frequently] introduced an R between a consonant and a vowel. So, she said... bralcony for balcony. When she called for Moon, the faithful white-haired porter, she often shouted "Mroon!"' *The Duchess of Jermyn Street* by Daphne Fielding, 1964, published by Eyre & Spottiswoode.

"Come on, Crolonel, dear. Stir yer bleedin' strumps. There's a bloomin' good prarty in the Eleanor Glyn and it ain't cromplete without ya."

Rubbing the sleep out of my eyes, I struggled into a smoking jacket, staggered down the stairs and joined the *jeunesse dorée*. The clock in the hall was striking two, and I'd consumed the best part of another magnum, when I finally managed to prise myself out of the sofa and staggered up to my room, which I was sure was number twenty-two and where I knew Fahran would be dozing whilst awaiting my arrival.

I pushed open the door and was a bit surprised to be assailed by the smell of cigar smoke and Eau de Portugal: had Fahran changed his cologne and been at my humidor I wondered? I was even more surprised when I saw in the dim light from a bedside lamp not Fahran asleep on my bed, but a naked bint, legs splayed and face-down on the pillow. Her well-rounded rump was pleasantly dimpled and the luxurious bush between her cheeks was inviting to say the least.

"That was quick, sir," she murmured into the feathers.

I didn't bother to enquire what she meant but assumed that she was one of Rosa's nice clean tarts off the 'dilly and thoughtfully provided for my after-hours entertainment. Now, I may be eighty-four (or thereabouts) and have consumed a skin-full of fizz but my bayonet still knows a well-oiled scabbard when it sees one. Without a word, I slipped off my togs and lowered my aging carcass onto her back. Then, as she let out a low groan of pleasure, I slid my principal asset between her legs and started happily humping away. We'd been at it for a couple of minutes when, to my irritation – for it quite put me off my stride – I distinctly heard a crapper being flushed in the bathroom. Damn, I thought, that must be Fahran, but old habits die hard and he'd seen worse so I carried on giving the bint of my best.

"What the bloody hell?" someone growled behind me.

It didn't sound like my valet, so I craned around to see who was there: to my horror, I saw the unmistakeable figure of the King-Emperor clad in nothing but a shirt and a cigar...

CHAPTER SIXTEEN: SEVERED HEADS & RICE PUDDING

What the hell do you say when your sovereign catches you *in flagrante delicto* with his mount of the moment: 'She's a fine romp, Your Majesty' - or - 'I thought I'd better break her in for you, Sir'- or - 'Hang on a moment would you, Bertie, whilst I finish…'? Clearly none of these would have done. Rendered momentarily speechless, I swiftly disengaged, grabbed my clothes, gave my former employer a deep bow and headed for the door.

"Not so fast, Speedicut!" he snarled. "What the devil do you think you arre doing in here?" I have always found that at times such as this only the truth will suffice.

"Going to bed, Your Majesty."

"But this is *my* room."

"Is it, Sir? I most distinctly thought it was mine. But I see that I have must have been mistaken… If there's nothin' else, Sir, may I bid you a goodnight?"

Bertie was too shocked at my *sang froid* to reply and, in any event, the girl on the bed intervened before either of us could say anymore.

"Look 'ere, gents, Ma Lewis 'as only paid me fer an 'our, so can you please make up your minds which of yer is going ter do the business? If you both want to, it'll be double."

I didn't linger a moment longer: the thought of sharing a tart with our monarch was more than even I could bear. Thank God Fahran found me wandering the corridors or I might have been searching for my room for the rest of the night.

…

6 Stratton Street, London W, May 1906 [extract]

Life's really not quite the same without dear old Searcy. I'm glad I was in London for the end and I'm pleased to be able to tell you that – like all old soldiers – he simply faded away. Ivan is, of course, quite distraught (as am I) and has said that he will change his name to Searcy by deed poll. He's also said that he is at my disposal to act as my private secretary. Let's hope that, if I ever need it, he's got Searcy's brain.

...

Hotel Reitenberger, Marienbad, Bohemia, August 1907

Over more years than I care to remember, I have learnt that when C-G gets an idea into her head there is no point in trying to deflect her: pissing against a hurricane would produce better results. This is why we have exchanged the comforts of Stratton Street for the dubious delights of a Bohemian spa town when we could quite easily, as I proposed over a breakfast towards the end of last month, have gone to Bath.

"I don't care what you say about the pleasures of the Pump Room, Jasper; if His Majesty thinks that Marienbad is the best place for a cure, then that is where we will go."

"But it's half-way across Europe," I protested feebly, "and if Bertie's there at the same time it will be absolute hell."

"That's as may be. Her Majesty was particularly insistent that we should go so that I can rep..." She stopped in mid-flow.

"Report what?" I demanded.

"Nothing, Jasper. Please pass the marmalade."

"Am I to understand, m'dear, that the real reason why we are goin' to traipse half-way across Europe in the heat of high summer is so that you can spy on Bertie for Alix?"

"Certainly not, Jasper. That's an absolutely disgraceful suggestion. I can't think why the thought ever entered your head. Now will you please pass the marmalade."

M'thinks, I said to myself, that the lady doth protest too much. But it could have been worse: if Bertie had followed in the footsteps of his forebear we would have ended up in that run-down dump, Brighton. As it is, Marienbad is actually a reasonably decent sort of a place with comfortable hotels, pleasant parks, delightful scenery, excellent food and a theatre. The latter puts on pretty good entertainment imported from Vienna and elsewhere, including a burlesque show featuring the nubile Canadian, Maud Allan, whose *Dance of the Seven Veils* leaves nothing to the imagination even before the last veil falls.[143]

Needless to say, the town is small and it's therefore difficult to avoid bumping into *incognito* overweight Kings and Emperors taking the air (and, if forced, the waters), particularly if your wife insists that you stay in the same hotel as the Duke of Lancaster, which is the incog that Bertie uses on the continent to ensure that he is recognised wherever he goes. There was, however, one person in Marienbad who did not know that the portly, bearded gent, permanently veiled in a cloud of cigar fumes and with a fox terrier trotting by his side, was His Majesty The King-Emperor. I was lounging in the hotel lobby one morning whilst waiting for C-G when Bertie appeared through the front door, cigar in hand, and headed for the lift at the same moment as a brash-looking Yankee, with a large stogie clamped between his teeth, emerged from the dining room. Instead of giving way to the ruler of the Empire-on-which-the-sun-never-sets, who he clearly hadn't recognised, the ex-colonist made to enter the lift first just as our sovereign had reached it. There was a collision, the Yank cannoned off the enormous royal paunch and lost his balance and his cigar.

"Pardon *me!*" said the discombobulated American, in that rather quaint and utterly common way that they do.

---

[143] Maud Allan (1873-1956).

"Cerrtainly," said Bertie, waving his Havana in a vague sort of benediction as the lift attendant swiftly closed the gates. It was much as I could do not to howl with laughter but I couldn't supress a guffaw.[144]

"What is so amusing?" I heard a voice say behind me. I turned in my chair and saw Fritz Ponsonby.

"Hello, Fritz. I was just watchin' a replay of the American War of Independence, although this time we won."

"I see," said the courtier gravely, "well, you're just the man."

"For what?" I asked suspiciously as, despite C-G's role as Sneak-in-Chief, I had no intention of being dragged back into Bertie's affairs even if I'd been welcome which, after the Cavendish affair in '05, was doubtful: royalty have long memories, y'know.

"To give me some advice on a rather tricky situation that has arisen with my employer."

"Providin' it's only advice you want, Fritz, tell me all."

"You know of His Majesty's love of the theatre?"

"Indeed."

"Have you heard of a show called *Die Hölle* that was playing at the local theatre?"

"Unfortunately, yes. M'wife thought it was goin' to be a new opera, which would have been bad enough, and insisted that we went: it turned out to be a Viennese vaudeville show full of un-funny jokes of a distinctly lavatorial nature."

---

[144] Editor's Note: Historians have previously ascribed this incident to a Parisian hotel during a visit by Edward VII to the ex-Express Eugénie. Perhaps it happened twice.

"That's the one."

"We walked out at half-time."

"So did The King."

"So, what's your problem: does he want a refund?"

"No, it's not that. The problem is that His Majesty's early exit was reported in the British press as an act of moral outrage and, ever since, we've been bombarded with letters, including one from the Bishop of Ripon, praising The King for walking out of 'an improper show which challenged the norms of decency and morality'."

"What's wrong with that?"

"The King feels that he's been made to look like a hypocrite. The reason he left the theatre was not because he was outraged but because he was bored. He's told me to write to the Bishop telling him the truth and stating that he has no wish to pose as a protector of morals, particularly when abroad."

"I'd have thought that he would have been pleased to be placed with the angels for once."

"Unfortunately not and, to make matters worse, he has now expressed a desire to watch Madame Allan's new production, *The Vision of Salomé*. I haven't seen it but, if it's anything like that bugger Wilde's play and The King's attendance is reported in the newspapers, all hell will break loose."

"I know the lady in question." Alright, I was stretching a point, but I had wagged her paw when we were introduced earlier in the week by C-G's chum, the ghastly Mrs Hall Walker. "I'm sure she'd be amenable to a private Command Performance."

"Where? We couldn't possibly accommodate the troupe in The King's suite and if he buys the entire theatre for one night it will be front page news in every paper from Valparaiso to Vladivostok."

"Why not arrange for Madame Allan to perform an extract or two – the *Dance of the Seven Veils* and that business with the head of John the Baptist, for example?"

"So, you've seen it?"

"Ye-es," I replied rather hesitantly, for I'd managed to see the show in rehearsal the previous day whilst C-G was playing bridge with a clutch of aged Archduchesses. I have to tell you that it was about the lewdest thing I'd ever seen, and that includes some very *risqué* shows in Atlanta and Pigalle: the most that Madame Adam's wore was two oyster shells and a small Austrian coin and they were discarded fairly early on – and what she did with the severed head of the Baptist is still giving me nightmares…

"So, is it suitable?" I thought for a moment, then took the plunge.

"For a private, all male audience – yes." Well, it was hardly my problem if Bertie saw the performance and burst open his inner tube.

"As you know the lady, Speed, do you think you could arrange it?" My God, I thought, it's the Matilde Kschessinska business all over again, even if Ignatiev's not involved. I was about to say 'absolutely not', when C-G appeared.

"Captain Ponsonby, how lovely to see you. I do hope Jasper isn't making a nuisance of himself."

"Not at all, Lady Charlotte-Georgina, in fact he has most generously offered to help me arrange a matter for The King."

"Really? And what might that be, Jasper?"

"Nothin' to bother yourself with, m'dear," I said, as I sensed C-G was already compiling notes for her next report to Alix. "Nothin' at all."

"Oh, don't be so modest," said Ponsonby, before I could kick his ankle. "Sir Jasper has most obligingly agreed to arrange for His Majesty a private performance of some extracts from…"

"*Götterdämmerung*," I interject hastily, naming the most boring opera I could think of at short notice.

"I didn't know it was playing here or that His Majesty liked Wagner," said C-G, who knows all too much about the works of Ludwig's Nemesis and Bertie's preferences when it comes to entertainment.

"It isn't. But, so Fritz says, The King has recently developed a taste for *The Ring*," I said quickly, whilst Ponsonby looked as though he'd unexpectedly stepped into the Fourth Dimension, "and thanks to my contacts at the Hofburg…"

C-G appeared to be satisfied by these lies and a short while later we bid our *adieus* to the still puzzled-looking courtier and went for a gentle promenade around the springs which litter the town centre, whilst I racked my brains as to how I was going to get Toronto's answer to Sarah Bernhardt to agree to wiggle her tits and crotch at my former employer.

In the end, it was easier than falling off a log. Whilst C-G took her mid-afternoon nap, I nipped off to the theatre where a sovereign to the lout on the Stage Door gained me admittance to Madame A's dressing room. She was reclining on a sofa, clad in a silk dressing gown and glowing with exertion, having just come off stage after her *matinée*.

"Madame Allan," I said, doffing my panama, "Jasper Speedicut. We have met."

"To what do I owe the pleasure," she said, sitting forward whilst her dressing gown slipped open to reveal the edge of the North American prairie.

"I am here to beg a favour of you."

She looked at me suspiciously, as though whatever was coming next would probably involve her having to reprise with me on her sofa the more vigorous moments of her dance.

"Yes?"

"His Majesty The King would be most obliged if you would…" I got no further.

"In the absence of Mrs Keppel, it would be my pleasure," she interrupted, with a glint in her eye that clearly said that, whilst shagging me was not on the cards, screwing the monarch of half-the-world would not be a problem.

"I think you may have misunderstood me," I said quickly. "His Majesty would be most obliged if you would dance for him after supper in his rooms."

It was her turn to look surprised.

"Is that all?" she drawled.

"As far as I know, ma'am." She thought for a moment.

"And my reward?"

I hadn't a clue but, at the very least, she would get a signed photograph in a silver frame and I said so. She appeared satisfied with this.

"I'm most obliged to you, ma'am – His Majesty's Private Secretary, Captain Ponsonby, will, I'm sure, be in touch about the precise arrangements."

An hour later I brought the glad tidings to the said man.

"I'm most obliged, Speed," he said. "And don't worry: all that will be required is the dancing."

"Really? I think that Madame Allan is expectin' – at least is prepared for – a bit more, if you follow my meanin'?"

"I do, but His Majesty's treatment tires him somewhat."

"What treatment?" I asked, assuming immediately that he was being treated for the pox.

"A course of radium for a persistent and unsightly lesion on his nose."

So, I was right on that score, then.

. . .

Editor's Note: The next letter, written from the Palais Lieven, St Petersburg, in April 1908, was sufficiently long for me to justify editing it and subsequent letters into narrative form.

. . .

Some time ago I recorded the fact that C-G had suggested to Minnie, the Dowager Empress of Russia, that the solution to the problems of the 'little bleeder', otherwise known as the Tsarevich Alexei, might be a faith healer. Well, it appeared that the Dowager Empress had mentioned it to Mitzi Montenegro,[145] a barking-mad gypsy Princess from a *mittel-Europa* backwater where they get rid of their rulers by chucking them out of top-floor windows. Anyway, Miss Defenestrater was married to one of the Tsar's cousins and, because of her fascination with the dark arts, was known in Petersburg as the 'black peril'. She had been very chummy with the Tsarina, whom she'd introduced some years back to a Frog charlatan called Philip.[146] Despite the fact that he was exposed as a fraud and banished from the Court, Mitzi – encouraged by C-G's advice to Minnie – last year introduced the haughty Hessian harpy, otherwise known as the credulous creature who wears the Russian Consort's crown,

[145] HIH Grand Duchess Militza Nikolaevna of Russia (1866 – 1951).
[146] Anthelme Nizier Philippe (1849-1905).

to some smelly and over-sexed *moujik* from Siberia who went by a name that sounded like 'rice pudding'.[147]

However, I soon learned that this Siberian was a stallion of a very different colour to the Froggy fruitcake and had actually managed to halt Alexei's bleeding when the quacks had wrung their hands in despair. This has led to his unofficial accreditation as Miracle-Worker-in-Chief to the loonies at Tsarskoe Selo. As a direct consequence of that, Rice Pudding became the toast of the town where he was not only feted by *le gratin* but, so Dimitri Lieven told me, was rogering the brains out of anyone of either sex foolish enough to fall under his spell (or should that be smell?), which seemed to be a broad cross-section of Petersburg Society. Anyway, we were bidden by Zenaïde Yusupova's younger boy, Felix, to meet the mountebank at the end of the month.[148] Young Felix, who was beautiful rather than handsome, had a reputation for dressing-up in his mother's frocks and rocks and picking up Guards officers in night clubs around the city… So, it promised to be an entertaining evening.

…

In the event, the *soirée* chez Yusupov exceeded even *my* expectations. It was held in Felix's rooms in the basement of the Yusupov Palace, which had been rigged out in a distinctly oriental style with low lighting and lots of Turkey rugs and divans. It would not have looked out of place in the Topkapi harem – except that, as a Mussulman institution, the Grand Turk's groin exchange didn't have bumpers of frozen vodka, gallons of the finest French fizz and gilded buckets full of Imperial Persian caviar on the sideboard.

We had been told to dress casually, so C-G wore a sort of corseted kaftan she'd bought at The Passage and I donned the Russian costume I'd been given by Felix's papa around the time Dorothea got hitched. The rest of the guests, who had also obeyed the joining instructions, comprised a brace of minor married Romanov fillies (minus their husbands) and my

---

[147] Gregory Yefimovich Rasputin (1869 –1916).
[148] Princess Zenaïde Yusupova (1861-1939) & Prince Felix Yusupov (1887-1967).

old chum Alexei Kirillovich Vronsky,[149] who gave up on the girls after his older and married mistress threw herself under a train and, in lieu, had a limp-wristed Guardee in tow. Felix was also in native attire, but not as it is worn in the hovels of the Urals: his outfit comprised soft boots, baggy velvet britches (under which he was clearly wearing no hose) and a closed-necked, gold-and-silver-embroidered silk shirt, nipped-in at the waist with a jewelled belt with a massive blue diamond clasp that would have paid our staff's wages for a century. The belt, however, was completely over-shadowed by a huge brooch-set white diamond which Felix had clipped above his left tit. To top it all, he'd disguised one of his rather odd-looking ears with an enormous pearl and I'm damned sure that the boy had put kohl around his eyes and rouge on his lips.[150] Had C-G not been with me, I would certainly have made a grab for him. As it was, he was not the main attraction. That was Gregory Rasputin who was the last to arrive. Shortly before he did so, Felix gave us a briefing on the *starets*:

"I must warn you that Father Gregory is very simple and direct in his manner, so please don't be offended if he asks you personal questions. He may also attempt to mesmerise you but don't worry, he's quite harmless and the sensation is really most enjoyable."

A moment or two later the man himself appeared. I'm not quite sure what I'd expected, but it was not a giant with long, lank hair parted in the middle and a long, straggly (and probably unwashed) beard that reached down to a heavy-looking gold cross. Like the rest of us he was dressed à la Russe although his clothes were not – as I'd assumed - made of coarse peasant cotton but shimmering silk and expensive leather. Up close he reeked of booze, sweat, garlic and a heavy scent. Of themselves, his size, smell and rig would have been remarkable enough – but the one feature which drew and held one's attention were his eyes.

---

[149] See *The Speedicut Papers: Book 2 (Love & Other Blood Sports)* et seq.
[150] Editor's Note: these jewels sound like the Sultan of Morocco blue diamond, a blue-grey stone weighing 35.27 carats, the even more famous Polar Star, a pure-white stone weighing 41.28 carats, and La Pelegrina, a pear-shaped natural pearl weighing 133 grains, all of which were in the Yusupov collection at the time.

Ricepudding paused rather theatrically at the top of the short flight of steps that led into the basement parlour and stared at us each in turn. For some reason, he made a bee-line for me. My Russian wasn't too bad at this time – although anyone who was anyone in Russia spoke French - but Rasputin talked in a sort of mangled Siberian dialect, which I won't attempt to reproduce and much of which Felix had to interpret for me.

"Gregory Yefimovich," said our host, as the great brute bore down on me, "may I introduce you to an English friend of my mother's, Colonel Sir Jasper Speedicut?"

"There is no need," he replied, as he grabbed my extended paw with both of his own extremely dirty ones. "I know this man."

"I'm not sure that I've ever had the pleasure," I said, as his shining steel-grey eyes seemed to stare through mine and I tried, unsuccessfully, to withdraw my hand which he'd started to fondle.

"We have not met, that is true, but thy soul is stained with the blood of Mother Russia - and the semen of her sons." Thank God C-G had been distracted by one of the Romanov bints and didn't hear that last bit, which anyway Felix had translated *sotto voce*. "We will speak later."

Not if I can help it, I thought. For in those brief moments, I had sensed that the brute had tried to take control of me, although for what reason was not clear. But it wasn't just me. Over the course of the evening, he tried it on with everyone: C-G was fascinated and repelled by him in equal measure; Vronsky seemed to be indifferent; but the two Grand Duchesses and Alexei's catamite were instantly seduced by the combination of smut and scripture which made-up the bulk of Ricepudding's coarse conversation. If the rest of us hadn't been present, I'm damned sure that he would have tupped all three of them - probably at the same time: quite what Russian aristos saw in the *moujik* was beyond me, other than being rogered nine-ways to Moscow by his doubtless enormous and rancid weapon. I said as much to Vronsky the following day, as we shared a steam bath in a Russian *hammam* on the Nevsky Prospekt.

"You are probably right," he replied, "although I have no personal experience, you understand?"

"Of course not – if I remember rightly, Alexei Kirillovich, your tastes are much more refined." He laughed at this oblique reference to myself in younger days.

"Take my advice, Speed, and stay well clear of Rasputin. He knows your wife is close to the Dowager Empress – that's why he got Felix to invite you both last evening – and he will have a purpose which he will pursue ruthlessly. Thinking about it, it's probably to persuade or, if that fails, to compromise you so that you will instruct Charlotte-Georgina to change the old Tsaritsa's mind: Maria Feodorovna hates him almost as much as she hates her German daughter-in-law, you know."

"He'll be barkin' up the wrong tree if he tries that; little does he know that Charlotte-Georgina hasn't listened to me in fifty years," I said, with considerable feeling.

"Anyway, you must take care. If he invites you to a meeting of the Khlysty you *must* refuse."

"The Khlysty, what's that?"

"It's a sect which believes that you can only reach God through prayer, chanting and mass sexual intercourse."

"Nothin' wrong with that," I said, at the delightful prospect.

"Except that it's illegal. Be careful, Jasper, that uncouth Siberian peasant has you in his sights and he's a danger to you as well as the Tsar and Tsarina, who foolishly listen to his homespun politics. Did you know that Rasputin addresses them as *batiushka* and *matushka*? Mark my words, if something isn't done about him it's going to end in tears, not just for them but for the rest of us as well."

Vronsky rambled on in a similar vein for quite a long time then eventually changed the subject onto the prospect for his race horses during the upcoming season. Meanwhile, I allowed my mind to wander and, in the steamy heat, I must have dozed off. I seem to remember hearing Alexei say that he had to be at some luncheon or other and not to stay too long in the steam or I'd become even more of a wrinkled old prune than I was already. But, whether he did or not, I started to dream about him in our younger days and the fun we'd had in another steam bath *en route* to Sevastopol…[151]

It's strange how easy it is to conjure in one's sleeping mind the sensations of yesteryear. As though it had only been fifty-five minutes rather than fifty-five years ago, I felt Vronsky's firm hands caress my head and neck, whilst he muttered what sounded like prayers. Russians are mystical folk when they are aroused, so I thought nothing of it. Then I felt his hands move down my chest, across my still reasonably firm stomach and onto that region from which all pleasure surges (or, in my case, now only dribbles). His voice changed and he muttered that it was only through sin that one could achieve holiness. Poor old Vronsky, still suffering from the guilt of the nursery, I thought. Nonetheless, in my dream his massage was as firm and as sensuous as it had once been and I felt myself rise to the occasion, but each time that I thought the end was going to occur he relaxed his grip and moved to another part of my anatomy, all the while intoning some nonsense that he wanted me to impart to *batiushka* and *matushka*, whoever they might be. Apart from this incessant drivel, it really was bliss. If only real life could still be like this dream, pleaded my unconscious as, after I don't know how long, the dream-Vronsky brought me to a shuddering conclusion and I awoke bathed in more than just the sweat generated by the *banya*. I opened my eyes and found myself staring not at the ceiling but at two phosphorescent beams of light melting into a great luminous ring: Rasputin's leering face was just inches above mine.

---

[151] See *The Speedicut Papers: Book 2 (Love & Other Blood Sports)*.

CHAPTER SEVENTEEN: CROWNS AT ANCHOR

I sat up abruptly at the shock of finding the foetid peasant's eyes boring into mine, my forehead connected painfully with his chin and, emitting a low groan, he slumped backwards. It was as neat a knock-out as Bob Fitzsimmons or 'Black Jack' Johnston could have delivered in the ring.[152] However, I didn't wait for any applause. Instead, I gathered up my towel and bolted first for the dressing room and then the Lievens' palace. C-G was waiting for me in the Malachite Saloon.

"Where have you been, Jasper? If we don't leave now we will be late for luncheon with Monsieur de Diaghilev and the Grand Duke will not be amused. Besides which, I am *so* looking forward to meeting the great Monsieur Chaliapin, who – if you hadn't dozed through the whole performance – you will remember we heard the other night on his return from Paris."[153]

"I don't give a damn about your pansy opera friends," I said hotly, "but I do care about our safety. As soon as we are back from luncheon you are goin' to tell the servants to pack and I will instruct Ivan to book us on the first train to civilisation."

"What are you talking about, Jasper; we are due to stay for at least another two weeks? And what on earth do you mean about our safety?"

"I'll tell you in the motor." Which I did - at least, I gave her a highly expurgated version of my encounter with Rasputin. "… In short, m'dear, this fellow has got it into his head that you have influence with Minnie and that you will be able to change her mind when it comes to him."

---

[152] Robert Fitzsimmons (1863-1917) & Jack Johnson (1878-1946); both were heavyweight boxers.
[153] Sergei Pavlovich Diaghilev (1872-1929) & Feodor Ivanovich Chaliapin (1873-1938).

"I believe that the Dowager Empress *does* listen to me," she said, as Dimitri's chauffeur pulled-up in front of the Hotel Europe where our host was holed up, "but not on *that* subject. Her opposition to the *starets* is implacable. However, I still don't see why we have to leave."

"Because Vronsky says that we must." C-G had always with good (but not for the right) reason been suspicious of Alexei Kirillovich and she started to protest as we headed across the hotel lobby to the lift, but I cut her short. "We're leavin' and that's that."

The meal that followed was not nearly as high-brow operatic as I'd feared or C-G had hoped. Diaghilev was a good host, albeit that he looked like a chubby and moustachioed badger, with a wide streak of silver hair bisecting his obviously dyed-black mop; and he lisped like a Uranian, which he undoubtedly was. Chaliapin was altogether more robust, with a deep sonorous voice and an imposing presence. The rest of the party were an assortment of prancers, none of whom opened their mouths although they all looked very decorative; a strange-looking composer called Stradivarius; and a stage artist called Leo Back, who was definitely a member of the Chosen Race.[154] It was a bohemian mix but by no means from the bottom drawer, as was so often the case in Paris or London, a fact emphasised by the presence of the Grand Duke Vladimir, who was married to the most bejewelled woman in Russia and was acting as Diaghilev's banker and chief negotiator with the Imperial authorities.[155] All the conversation was, of course, about opera and dance, although most of it focused on Diaghilev's revolutionary plan to take the Russian ballet to Paris the following year [1909].

"You have no idea of the problems I'm having with the management of the Imperial Ballet," he said, to the table in general. "It's not just that they

---

[154] Editor's Note: almost certainly Igor Fyodorovich Stravinsky (1882-1971) & Léon Samoilovich Bakst (1866-1924).

[155] HIH Grand Duke Vladimir Alexandrovich of Russia (1847-1909) & HIH Grand Duchess Maria Pavlovna, née HH Duchess Marie of Mecklenburg-Schwerin (1854-1920), who was known as 'the grandest of the Grand Duchesses' and whose collection of jewellery rivalled that of the Dowager Empress; her famous pearl drop tiara has, since the Russian Revolution, been in the British royal collection.

don't like the idea of my taking Russian ballet to the French but, following our recent triumph with *Boris Godunov* in Paris, I think they are jealous. Without their co-operation, it's going to be extremely difficult to raise the cash for what is going to be a not-inexpensive trip."

"My dear Sergei Pavlovich," said the Grand Duke soothingly, "how many times do I have to tell you that, with the support of His Imperial Majesty and the *galoshisty*,[156] I will find you the money and get you the necessary permits?"

Frankly, most of this stuff was of no interest to me, nor were a brace of flat-chested dancers - one called Puddleova and the other called Carstairs, I think - who the impresario had placed either side of me at the dining table.[157] There was a lot of batting of eyelashes at me on their part (these ballet-types actually *expect* to be kept by the likes of me and the Grand Duke) but neither of them uttered a word. I would far prefer to have been sat next to a Slavic-looking, high-cheek-boned boned boy called Vaslav something-or-other who Diaghilev kept close to him and who he said was going to be the next great dance sensation.[158]

"He has this extraordinary ability to appear to hover at the top of a *grand jeté*, don't you my dear?" said the bi-coloured Svengali, as the boy blushed. "His Slave in *Le Pavillon d'Armide* will amaze the Parisians."

Well, people like Diaghilev always said such things about their boyfriends, so I didn't pay much attention to his puff and, anyway, I didn't give a damn about what the boy could achieve on or above the boards. I would, however, have been delighted to watch him pirouette naked between my sheets...

---

[156] Editor's Note: *galoshisty* in Russian means the 'rubber gang' (a smutty *double entendre*) who were a group of multi-millionaire industrialists in the rubber industry led by Hendrik van Gilse van der Pals (1856-1928).
[157] Editor's Note: again, almost certainly Anna Pavlovna Pavlova (1881-1931) & Tamara Platonovna Karsavina (1885-1973)
[158] Vaslav Nijinsky (1890-1950).

By the time we left, my nightmare on the Nevsky Prospekt had receded somewhat, although I was still determined that we should put the Baltic and the North Seas between me and Rasputin as soon as possible. Ivan was waiting for me in the hall of the Lievens' palace with a cream coloured envelope on a salver. I flipped it over and saw that it was a letter from our Embassy. Without bothering to go to my rooms, I slit it open and read:

British Embassy
St Petersburg

His Britannic Majesty's Ambassador to the Court of His Imperial Majesty The Tsar of All the Russias presents his compliments to Colonel Sir Jasper Speedicut Bart and begs to inform him that he is Commanded by His Majesty The King to join His Majesty's Suite-in-Waiting on His Majesty's Yacht Victoria & Albert *during the forthcoming State Visit of His Majesty to His Imperial Majesty at Reval from 9th June. Lady Charlotte-Georgina Speedicut is also, by His Majesty's Command, appointed a Temporary Lady-in-Waiting to Her Majesty the Queen.*

"Shit and damnation!" I groaned.

"Jasper, *pas devant les domestiques* - anyway, what's the matter?" I handed her the letter.

"Good," was all she said when she'd finished reading it.

"What on earth do you mean by 'good'?" I demanded.

"Nothing, Jasper." At which point the kopek dropped.

"Is this your doin', m'dear?" I asked her, with more than a hint of menace in my voice.

"Err, I did suggest to Her Majesty in my last letter that His Majesty *might* find your knowledge of the Russian Court useful during Their Majesties' State Visit..."

"What knowledge?" I nearly screamed.

"Well, you know Stolypin and Isvolsky and some of the other Ministers - and you know heaps of Grand Dukes and Grand Duchesses."[159]

"To say hello to, or to pilot around a ballroom, but what I know about the political situation in this damned country could be written on the head of that Fabergé hat pin you bought the other day."

"And then, of course, you know Father Gregory."

"That is precisely why I want to be a thousand miles away from here, not stuck in Russia for another month having to dance attendance on royalty. Really, Charlotte-Georgina, there are times..." Without another word, I stomped off to my rooms telling my secretary to come with me.

"Look here, Ivan," I said, as I slumped into a chair in my bedroom and indicated that he should pull up another. "I've got a real problem and I need your help."

"How can I be of assistance, Your Excellency?"

Old habits die hard with Ivan. Anyway, I gave him an *un*expurgated account of my recent meeting with Rasputin and the reason why I thought our delayed return to London would not be conducive to my health.

"There could be a solution, Excellency, but I will need some hours to see what can be arranged. May I respectfully suggest that you do not leave the palace, nor receive visitors, until I have completed my enquiries?"

I nodded my agreement and told him to send Fahran to me with a decanter of brandy. It wasn't until much later that Ivan reappeared.

"May I have a word with you, Your Excellency?" he murmured into my ear, as C-G and I were taking coffee with Dorothea and Dimitri after

---

[159] Pyotr Arkadyevich Stolypin (1862-1911), Prime Minister & Minister of Internal Affairs; Count Alexander Petrovich Izvolsky (1856-1919), Imperial Foreign Minister.

dinner. I led him out into the garden, where it was still bright as day despite being nearly midnight. "You may recall, Excellency, that the late Mr Searcy was a member of an organisation known as the Nehemiah?"

"I do indeed," I said. "It's that club for butlers, valets and gentlemen's gentlemen."

"Correct, Excellency. Unfortunately, as a Russian, I did not qualify for full membership of the Nehemiah, but the late Mr Searcy arranged for me to be made an associate member with responsibility for the Nehemiah's sister organisation in St Petersburg: the *Obshchestvo Dvoretskikh*." I must have looked puzzled for he added, "it means the Society of Butlers."

"I see," I said, although I couldn't see exactly where this was leading.

"The *Obshchestvo Dvoretskikh* is, like the Nehemiah, not without influence and I have spoken to the *Glavnyy Dvoretskiy*, the head of the Society. He has assured me that he will arrange for Father Gregory to be recalled to his family home in western Siberia immediately. By the time the priest has discovered that he has been on a fool's errand and returns to St Petersburg, you and Her Ladyship will be safely back in London. I hope that is satisfactory, Your Excellency?"

Satisfactory? It was bloody marvellous news and I very nearly leaped up and kissed him. As it was, I told him that he was to accompany me to Fabergé the following day where he was to choose a cigarette case which I would have suitably engraved.

"Your Excellency is too generous."

"Not a bit of it, Ivan. I haven't had any reason to call on your special services since we lost Mr Searcy, but you have proved today that you are every bit as resourceful as he was." I saw tears start to well up in Ivan's eyes. "Yes, yes," I said soothingly, "we both miss him very much, but I'm sure he's smiling down – or up - on both of us as the result of your actions. Now be a good chap and tell Fahran that I'm going to need him to brush the moth out of my Dress uniform for this State Visit next week."

I won't trouble my readers over much with the events of the next few days, beyond telling you that there are worse ways of spending time bobbing around on the Baltic. The *V&A*, which we boarded on its arrival at Reval, was (as I already knew) a comfortable enough tub, but the Tsar's *Standart* and its sister ship the *Polar Star* were the last word in luxury and style. The royal and Imperial yachts were moored opposite one another and surrounded by British warships and those Russian ones which the Nips hadn't sunk (as I'd predicted) at Tsushima in '05. Contrary to protocol, but as a well-judged mark of respect by Nicky for his uncle, the Visit started off with the Tsar and his family coming aboard Bertie's boat. Whilst the two monarchs conversed in private, the politicos paced the deck and Alix – with C-G holding rolls of film for her - snapped picture after picture of the Tsar's nippers with her Box Brownie: the four girls really were very pretty and the young Tsarevich was a picture post card Prince, even if he has to be carried everywhere by a burly Russian matelot. Meanwhile, quite what was required of me was unclear until later on that first evening when I was summoned to attend upon Bertie. I wasn't sure what sort of a reception I would get for, as my readers may recall, the last time that I'd been with him – as opposed to being one of a crowd at a ball or a dinner - had been under rather testing circumstances.

"Ah, Speedicut – come in," he rumbled, as Ponsonby ushered me through the door of the After-Deck saloon. "I need yourr advice."

"How may I help Your Majesty?" I asked, as I suddenly noticed Jackie Fisher lurking in a corner.

"You know these Rrussians quite well, it seems."

"Better than most of my fellow countrymen, Sir. My daughter is, after all, married to one."

"Which is why you are standing beforre me now," he growled. "I want to give my nephew a present and I would like yourr advice as to what that should be. And don't suggest a signed photograph," which is exactly what I had been about to do, "or a cigarette case – or a snuff box."

Damn, what did that leave, I wondered? At that moment, I noticed that Fisher was tapping the gold rings on his uniform sleeve. Actually, he might have been brushing off fluff, but I was distinctly under the impression that he was trying to convey a message to me. This time it was a sovereign that dropped.

"You could offer to make him a British Admiral, Sir, to add to his Colonelcy of the Greys."

"Now why didn't I think of that?" barked the monarch at Ponsonby.

"Because, Sir, it would require the sanction of your government, who might not be willing..." In contrast to Fritz, who looked seriously concerned at my suggestion, Fisher was smiling: so, I'd clearly interpreted his gesture correctly, which was a considerable relief.

"Stuff and nonsense, Fritz. As Head of our Armed Forces, such appointments are mine and mine alone. There are damned few powers of the Rroyal Prerrogative rremaining, but crreating honorary Admirrals of the Fleet is certainly one of them. Now what's on the progrramme for tomorrow? Of course, there's the Guard of Honour on the *Standart* to be negotiated. I suppose I'll have to say something in Russian."

"Indeed, Sir," said Fritz.

"Speedicut, send that Russian valet of yours along to see Ponsonby so that he can translate whatever is appropriate." Realising that this was my cue to leave, I gave Bertie a head nod and reversed out of the cabin, followed by Fritz.

"You've really done it this time, Speed," said the courtier, still looking distressed. "Asquith is going to have a seizure when he hears about this Admiral business."[160]

---

[160] The Rt Hon Herbert Asquith (1852-1928), British Prime Minister 1908-1915. The British government was, indeed, very angered at the appointment without prior consultation of the Tsar as a British Admiral of the Fleet.

"Not my problem, I'm afraid, old boy," I called breezily over my shoulder as I sauntered back to my bunk and he returned to the overweight lion's lair. C-G was waiting for me.

"Jasper, I need your advice."

"*Et tu, Brute?*"

"What's that?"

"*Et tu, Brute?*" I repeated in my best Greek.

"That's no way to refer to His Majesty," said C-G, who hadn't had the benefit of a classical education. "Now tell me: have you been of service to him?"

"I hope so," I replied. "Now what's *your* problem?"

"You know there is to be a banquet on the *Standart* tomorrow night?"

"Yes."

"Well, Her Majesty wants to know if she should cede precedence to her sister, the Dowager Empress, when she's taken in to dinner."

"Surely, she'll go in on the arm of the Tsar and The King will take in the Dowager Empress."

"Indeed, but Her Majesty understands that, if that happens, the Tsarina may have one of her headaches and not attend at all. And that would be a great insult which could well destabilise the whole Visit."

"I see," I said and this time I did, for the Hessian horror was absurdly prickly when it came to protocol and bitterly resented her mother-in-law's precedence over her. I gave the knotty problem a moment or two's thought. Then on the bulkhead wall I noticed a photograph of Bertie's boy Georgie,[161] in yachting rig, arm-in-arm with Nicky who was similarly attired; they looked like identical twins. "Got it!"

"You've got what, Jasper?" said C-G, sounding peevish.

"The answer. It's simple. Tell Alix to tell Bertie that he should take *both* Empresses in together – one on each arm. Is there anythin' else? I'm clearly on a roll in the problem department, so fire away."

"As a matter of fact, there is. The Dowager Empress has arranged a surprise for her guests."

"Is that wise?"

"Oh, it's really quite a harmless surprise. She's engaged a Ladies Chorus to sing English sea shanties during the banquet."

"What's the problem with that?"

"The Russian Secret Service. You know how scared they are of anarchists and they won't let the Ladies Chorus any closer than fifty yards from the *Standart* – and at that distance no one will hear them."

"What about if they were thoroughly searched before they came aboard?"

"Well, I suppose that could be arranged. I'll tell Her Imperial Majesty."

The following day we all clambered into a steam pinnace which puffed its way over to the *Standart*. Bertie and Alix were first up the companionway ladder to be confronted by a full naval Guard of Honour.

"Good morning, my children," said Bertie in Russian to the muscled and grizzled matelots arrayed before him. This was the traditional greeting that Ivan had translated for him, at least I hoped to God that *was* what he had translated.

---

[161] HRH The Prince of Wales, later King George V (1865-1936).

"God Save the King!" they shouted back, as I realised with relief that The King hadn't said 'I want to suck your pricks' or something equally inappropriate. Ivan, it seemed, was more reliable that Khazi when it came to translations.

The honours over, the Suite-in-Waiting were dragged off by our Russian counterparts to an open-air buffet where we were served kirsch, which I liked but Fritz complained tasted of boot polish, and a mountain of caviar sandwiches. Meanwhile, the Heads of State did whatever they do in those circumstances: awarding each other Orders, decorations and high military and naval rank, I supposed, and, in Bertie's case, doubtless rustling up business for Ernest Cassel in the shape of an Imperial Russian Loan or two.[162]

After an excellent luncheon, we returned to the *V&A* for (in my case) a much needed rest, but by six we were once again back with the Ruskies. The State Dinner exceeded the luncheon in every respect, until – that is - we got to the recital by the Ladies Chorus of Reval. It was hardly my fault that the Okhrana had stripped searched – and I mean stripped stark naked – the poor bints before they were admitted to the dining room. It was even less my fault that C-G, who'd been deputed by Minnie to look after the Choir, was included in the search. I can't bring myself to record what she said to me later... Anyway, it was little wonder that the Chorus' subsequent rendition of some of our more popular nautical music sounded more like a Gregorian chant - or that C-G looked as though she'd been ravished but an entire Squadron of Cossacks and *not* enjoyed it.

Fortunately, none of the royals seemed to notice that anything or anyone was awry and it wasn't too long before the Choir had been pitched overboard. Then the band struck up the *Merry Widow* (in honour of Minnie?) and Jackie Fisher, who fancied himself on the dance floor, was soon waltzing away with the Tsar's sister, Olga,[163] not to be confused with Nicky's daughter of the same name. Poor sister (as opposed to daughter) Olga was married to some Oldenburg Prince who's was queer as Dick's hatband and rarely left his palace on Sergievskaya Street, where

---

[162] Sir Ernest Cassel, GCB, GCMG, GCVO (1852 – 1921).
[163] HIH Grand Duchess Olga Alexandrovna of Russia (1882-1960).

he was surrounded by handsome footmen.[164] Needless to say they had no children, so who could blame her for taking a turn or two with a British Admiral with a roving eye and a rolling gait, albeit that he also had a paunch and bad breath?

...

Editor's Note: There is a gap in The Speedicut Papers which recommence in 1910.

---

[164] HIH Duke Peter Alexandrovich of Oldenburg (1868-1924).

CHAPTER EIGHTEEN: THE END OF AN ERA

It's the damnedest thing, but there are times when the truth is quite simply stranger than fiction. Now, I've always recorded the truth but the events of 6th May 1910 were so bizarre that I'm going to set them down exactly as they happened. If, dear reader, you don't believe them, well that's your look out.

The gutter press had been full of Bertie's illness for days before and they went into a positive frenzy of excitement when it got out that Alix had hobbled back as fast as she could from Greece to be at the old boy's bedside. Although, and this was a fact that I'd gleaned from Fritz, our cussed old bugger of a King had actually refused to be laid horizontal and was sat firmly in a chair, with a large cigar dangling from his paw. This was despite the fact that he didn't have the energy to raise the Havana to his lips and, if he had been able, one puff would certainly have finished off what was left of his lungs.[165]

C-G and I had come up to Town from Wrexham as I was fairly sure that I would have a role in the inevitable State Funeral, assuming of course that the grim reaper didn't claim me first. We were taking tea on our first afternoon back at Stratton Street, when Ivan appeared with a salver on which was another of those ill-omened cream-coloured envelopes. I saw at once that it was from the Lords and had been hand delivered, but I couldn't think why anyone would be writing to me from there. I tore it open to find a note from Brother Esher asking me if I could meet him in his rooms 'at your earliest convenience, and certainly no later than 6pm, to discuss a matter of the utmost urgency'.

Now, my readers already know what I thought of that slimy courtier and I was minded to chuck the letter on the fire and forget it, for no good had ever come of dancing to his fiddling. But C-G spotted what I was up to

---

[165] Editor's Note: Speedicut is correct. It was only after the King had suffered a series of heart attacks and was unconscious that he was put to bed.

and, afore I could reach the fender (as my readers know, she can spot a coat-of-arms at twenty paces) she had prised it from my fingers and read it.

"Jasper, I will ring for the motor immediately. You *will* answer Lord Esher's summons, as it is sure to concern His Majesty."

Then she rang the bell and, before I knew it, I'd been bundled into my cape, virtually pushed down the front steps into the new Daimler with Atash at the wheel and was halfway to Westminster before I'd caught my breath.

A good looking young page met me in the Central Lobby and took me off to Brother Esher's lair deep in that frightful building that Albert the Kraut had foisted upon an unsuspecting nation: for that alone he deserved the equally ghastly memorial that fouled the edge of Kensington Gardens. Brother Esher rose from behind his desk, made me a polite bow and offered me a pew next to the fire.

"A glass of something, Brother Jasper? Never too early, eh? Brandy and soda's your drink, I seem to remember."

With that the page, who seemed to be doubling as his butler (and God alone knew what else besides, although I had a good idea and wouldn't have minded trading places with Brother E at that moment) poured me a fishbowl full.

"As you may know, Brother Speedicut," Esher continued, "Her Majesty has recently returned from Corfu to be with His Majesty. I saw her earlier this afternoon and, although most distressed at the condition of The King, she is composed and, I believe, ready for the worst. As you also know, Her Majesty is the most considerate of ladies and she has entrusted me with a task with which I crave, as a loyal member of the Brotherhood, your assistance."

I nodded, to show that I was still awake.

"Before I go on, Brother Speedicut, the Great Boanerges has empowered me to tell you that what I have to say next is covered by your Oath. Do I have that agreement?" I nodded again and he seemed to be satisfied, for he then exploded his mine.

"Her Majesty believes that His Majesty would die more peacefully if he was to be given the opportunity of seeing a certain lady – I am certain you know to whom I refer – before he dies. But, whilst this is Her Majesty's most compassionate Command, it can never be known to have happened for it would be sure to be misinterpreted."

Damn right it would, I thought, and rightly so: old Alix pimping for her own husband on his death bed? I'd never heard anything like it. Perhaps she hoped that the sight of La Keppel's vast arse would finally push Bertie into the arms of the Virgin Mary. Now that was a thought that had clearly not occurred to Brother Esher sitting opposite me. To cover my surprise, I took a long pull on the brandy and nearly choked, for the cherub in the corner had failed to include the soda. Once I had recovered from a coughing fit that nearly sent me ahead of Bertie, I finally spoke.

"And how, Brother Esher, may I be of assistance? I hardly know the lady in question."

"That is not a problem, Brother Speedicut, for she certainly knows of you."

Damned right she does, I thought, for I had given her well-upholstered rump an exploratory squeeze in the box at Doncaster races in '96, after Bertie's horse pulled off the Derby-St Leger double and they were all too pissed to notice what I was up to.[166] But Alice K did - and had never spoken to me since, even when I was herding her into the royal cattle pen at the Coronation. However, there was nothing to be achieved by confessing to this, as Esher was clearly not to be gainsaid, so I let him go on.

"If you will agree, Brother Speedicut, Her Majesty would be most grateful if you could collect Mrs Keppel from Mrs Ronnie Greville's house in

---

[166] The horse was *Persimmon*.

Charles Street at ten o'clock tomorrow morning and take her in a closed carriage to the Mews entrance. I will meet you there and escort you both to the private apartments."

Well, I thought, that promised to be something to tell the grandchildren when I next saw them in Russia and so, with a suitable show of reluctance, I agreed.

The following morning, in our best town coach with the blinds down, Atash drove me the short distance from Stratton Street to Charles Street, bundled La Keppel, who was smothered in a completely opaque lace veil that reached her ankles, into the seat opposite and we set off for BP.[167] Aside from the half-stifled sobs that were emanating from behind the lace, she uttered not a word. Once at the Mews it took us nearly half-an-hour to get to the door to Bertie's bedroom, involving miles of musty corridors and a rickety lift that should have been in a museum but managed to get us to the second floor.

Standing in front of the royal oak was Alix, looking composed and for all the world as though she had just had her wig dressed, for there was not a strand out of place. La Keppel dropped her a deep curtsey, drew back her veil and, at Alix's silent direction, slid into the room. Over her shoulder I could see the old boy slumped in a chair with his eyes closed. You've left it too late, I thought, but Alix shut the door behind the old trollop's elephantine rear and then stared between Esher and myself at the far wall, saying not a word.

A couple of minutes later, or it could've been half-an-hour - it was difficult to tell – the door flew open and La Keppel lurched out, tucking a stray lock of hair behind her ear. She staggered into a deep curtsey to Alix, overbalanced and collapsed in my arms. She was the weight of a young rhino and I near as dammit toppled onto the floor under her. Had it not been for Esher, who steadied us both, I think we would have all ended up on the floor in a scrimmage that would have done at Rugby but not in the palace. Fortunately, Alix had seen none of this for, as La Keppel had left

[167] Buckingham Palace.

the room and thrown her curtsey, the Viking Queen was already halfway through the door which she had pulled firmly behind her.

"Let's get her out of here," whispered Esher; together we practically dragged the old bag to the far side of the landing. At this point she appeared to recover somewhat, for she drew herself up, pushed away our arms and made for the stairs. But she had hardly taken three steps before she collapsed in a heap, wailing like a banshee.

"I never did *any* harm," she shrieked. "There was *nothing* wrong between us. What is to *become* of me?" This was followed by sobs and wails that should have woken the dead.

Esher looked simply appalled and, if he could have got away with it, I'm damned sure he would have knocked her out. But by this time, she was having what C-G would call a 'turn' and my sawbones would call a 'neurotic attack'. Anyway, whatever it was called, there was no reasoning with her and so Esher summoned a pair of strapping young footmen to pick her up. He then swept a heavy cloth off the nearest table, threw it over her head and practically pushed the three of them down the stairs. At this point, even I was in shock and it took some persuading on Esher's part to get me to follow him on the route march back to the Mews.

By the time we got to the carriage, La Keppel, who had had to be practically thrown in there by the footmen, was somewhat more composed. Nonetheless, I begged Esher to accompany me on the trip back, to which (to do him justice) he readily agreed. Perhaps he was worried that I would cart the old baggage off to Printing House Square with the whole story.[168]

. . .

---

[168] Editor's Note: This story, including the words uttered by Mrs Keppel and her general demeanour - although not all the details nor the involvement of Lord Esher - was common gossip in Society after King Edward's death. However, the source of the story has always been thought to be Mrs Keppel herself, for she was well known for her self-promotion.

The following day, I heard about Bertie's final moments from Fritz at the Verulam. It appeared that, later that same afternoon, Georgie had informed his papa that the royal nag, *Witch of the Air*, had won its race at Kempton Park.

"I am very glad," responded The King.

"They were his last words," said Fritz. "His Majesty died at 11.45 pm last evening."

"Not an inappropriate end to the reign," I hazarded.

"Indeed not, Speed," said Fritz. "You know that the newspapers are already calling it 'the Edwardian era'. It's only been a nine-year period in our history but will undoubtedly be remembered with nostalgia, in stark contrast to that of Queen Victoria."

"You're probably right, Fritz," I replied, "although whether the new King will be happy for his papa's time on the throne to be remembered for its roisterin', licentiousness and conspicuous consumption remains to be seen."

"Hmm," said Fritz, who I think feared being given the Order of the Boot for his services to Bertie, "I suspect that the new reign will be an altogether different and more sober affair."

Speaking of affairs, old ones that is, whilst Bertie was *en route* to his Maker, Sibella had been in touch: it emerged that she wanted to send the boy to her brother's old school, namby-pamby Marlborough, where 'he'll get a good education'. I wanted him to go to Rugby, where he'd be thrashed regularly and get a proper grounding in the carnal arts. And what was the outcome of this dispute? The little sod was to go to Eton where he'd learn nothing and – with his looks – probably be buggered senseless by the members of Pop.

...

Following Bertie's demise - and despite a lifetime of service to the old scoundrel - I was not involved in the late poodlefaker's funeral. Fritz Ponsonby, who I tackled about it at Pratt's a few nights before we left for Wrexham, was quite frank.

"You have to realise, Speed, that King George is determined to clear from his Court all of those people whom he considers have been inappropriate adornments to his father's reign – and that includes you and numerous members of, ahem, the banking fraternity."

"Cassel, Rothschild and the assorted Sassoons?"

"Precisely. Although they will not be dismissed without some public recognition."

"So, can I expect a peerage?" I asked hopefully.

"I think not," he said firmly.

That notwithstanding, a liveried Palace flunkey delivered a parcel to me just before we left London inside which was a smart red leather box containing a KCVO and a note from Fritz saying that it was for 'services to The Queen Mother': for that read 'dealing with Mrs Keppel'. Mean sods, I thought, they might have run to a G. Anyway, this looked suspiciously to me like a 'thank you (i.e. bugger off) and never darken our doorstep again' from Georgie. So, as I was clearly not welcome at the Court of King George, I decided that after a few weeks at the Dower House, we would hoof off to Russia to visit Dorothea and the Ruskie grandnippers.

Meanwhile, according to Brother Esher who I saw at Brooks' the night before we left for north Wales, a stiffness had already returned to the Court which had been happily absent for the previous nine years.

"His Majesty," said Esher, who was a terrible old gossip like so many of his kind, "hates going out in Society, preferring – can you believe it - to spend his evenings pouring over his stamp collection."

"What about little Miss May?"

"If by that you mean Her Majesty the Queen Consort," Esher sniffed, "Her Majesty has abrogated to herself a role that is totally subservient to, and supportive of, her husband's wishes: so, she doesn't go out either."

"And Alix?"

"Her Majesty the Queen Mother," said Esher pompously, "has withdrawn into secluded widowhood at Sandringham."

"That ugly dump?"

"The very same."

"So, if they don't go out and about in Society, what do the royal pair get up to of an evenin'?"

"The King and Queen dine every night in full evening dress, whether they have company or not – and, other than the family, that is usually not."

"God, how dull."

"Well, it does at least give Her Majesty the opportunity to wear her growing collection of diamond jewellery.[169] Even if there is no one else present to appreciate it," he added, rather bitchily.

"So, with what else does she occupy her time?"

"When not in pursuit of more diamonds, she's dedicated herself to a mission, which she's pursuing with ruthless vigour and determination, to return to the royal collection - on a free of charge basis, naturally - as many

---

[169] Editor's Note: In addition to wearing the massive Cullinan I and II diamonds as a brooch on her formidable bust, Queen Mary had the almost as massive Cullinan III & IV stones set as a brooch or a necklace pendant. The Cullinan I & II are now in the sceptre and the Imperial State Crown, although they could still be worn as a brooch as the settings have not been removed.

items of furniture and fine art that she can identify as having escaped from the royal palaces over the preceding centuries. Her regular visits to the antique showrooms of the West End, not to mention assorted country houses and stately homes, are sending their owners into paroxysms of despair at the prospect of having to *give* her some of their choicest pieces."

And, so Esher went on to inform me, whilst Miss May dedicated herself to robbing from the rich, Georgie was having to deal with a constitutional crisis, bequeathed to him by his sainted pater: it looked, so Esher said, as though the new King would have to flood the Lords with hundreds of new Liberal peers. It was a pity that I was a Tory, as I might have had a chance of being advanced to the ermine, which would have kept C-G off my back, for she had yet to get over her disappointment in that department when the Parisian cup was snatched from my lips.

. . .

Editor's Note: There were no letters in The Speedicut Papers covering Speedicut's next trip to Russia, although there is a passing reference to it in the next section of the extant text.

. . .

No sooner had we got back from Russia, safe and well (no thanks to that fucker Rasputin), than we were plunged into mourning and found ourselves staggering backwards and forwards from St Paul's for the entombment of C-G's relations. It started with the GB who drowned in a yachting accident on the Solent; quite why he went boating with Charles Hadfield on a blustery October day was a mystery. Anyway, we had to inter an empty coffin as his body was never recovered and was probably feeding the mackerel off Southampton. We'd hardly slammed the door of the family tomb on the GB's box when Hadfield's employer or, more correctly, his business partner, who hadn't been well for years, awoke from a coma, heard that he'd acceded to the Dukedom as the 9th Duke (the Dowager Duchess Maud never did foal) and promptly had a terminal stroke. So, Charles Hadfield, Sibella Holland's undoubted lover and the son of C-G's elder sister, Charlotte-Elizabeth Hadfield,[170] become – *faut de mieux* and to C-G's fury - the 10th Duke of Whitehall whilst Esher and Co squabbled over who should be the next GB.

Whilst on that subject, it looked at one moment as though the compromise candidate might be the new Duke of Whitehall. The fact that he wasn't in the Brotherhood didn't seem to matter to some of our number. However, shortly after he acceded, he'd found himself embroiled in a spot of bother with the authorities having been charged with the murder of the ghastly Lionel Holland. Sentenced to hang, he was reprieved following the eleventh-hour and fifty-ninth minute discovery by Sibella of a suicide note. Personally, I think he was guilty as charged (and I wouldn't be at all surprised to learn that he'd also killed a few other FitzCharles on the way to the strawberry-leafed coronet) but I must also record that his escape from the gallows was to my considerable relief. This was not because I liked the murderous bounder, but because to have spent my declining years married to a Duchess-in-her-own-right would have been totally intolerable.[171] However, the acquittal notwithstanding, Whitehall had quite sensibly withdrawn from Society to live quietly with his childless wife at Whitehall Towers. That, of course, left unresolved the question as to who was to be the next Great Boanerges.

And whilst on the subject of the gallows and the Brotherhood, I read in *The Times* over breakfast one morning that Hawley Crippen had swung for the murder of his wife. If I remembered rightly, I mused to myself whilst buttering a crumpet, Crippen had for a time been an offshore member of the Brotherhood responsible for our business in North America. Indeed, I once saw him creeping out of Whitehall House around the time of the royal tarts saga.[172] Curiously, a few months before he died, the late GB mentioned to me that Crippen was living in London and had been around to see him on some business or other. Well, he certainly wasn't *in* the Brotherhood at that time, or I would have seen him at meetings, but perhaps he was trying

---

[170] See *The Speedicut Papers: Book 3 (Uncivil Wars)*.

[171] Editor's Note: Had Whitehall been executed, the Dukedom would have passed to Lady Charlotte-Georgina Speedicut.

[172] See *The Speedicut Papers: Book 7 (Royal Scandals)*.

to grease his way back in or was after something. Although there didn't seem to be much doubt about Crippen's guilt, it was an uncanny coincidence that he was caught as a result of being recognised by Brother Kendall,[173] who used his ship's wireless to alert the police. The Brotherhood has always been effective at silencing people – as the Wilde business proved – but what could Crippen have been up to if we had a hand in his long walk to the short drop? Was he trying to blackmail the Brotherhood about the death of Clarence,[174] the Whitechapel tarts or both? Well, there was probably nothing in it: just my over-active imagination, which some years ago took over from my previously over-active middle leg.[175]

...

May 1911 found us at Dalhousie Castle, a draughty keep north of Hadrian's safety barrier, surrounded by slavering Picts in ill-fitting tartan frocks – and that was just the men. Why were we there? The answer was because C-G, who had been reading a book about the Virgin Queen, had decided to emulate the parsimonious royal spinster. So, instead of incurring the expense of opening Stratton Street prior to the start of the 1911 London Season, she announced that we were to make a 'progress' to the frozen north via a clutch of her distant ducal and other coroneted relatives.

Our first stop was Belvoir, where Henry Rutland kept a pretty decent table,[176] which made up for the horrors of his draughty castle. From there we progressed to the Fitzwilliams at Wentworth Woodhouse. God only knew how Billy would be able to afford the upkeep of the ridiculous house,[177] which was said to have the longest façade in Europe, if it wasn't

---

[173] Captain Henry Kendall (1874-1965) was Captain of the SS *Montrose* on which Crippen and his mistress, Ethel Le Neve, were attempting to escape to Canada.

[174] HRH Prince Albert Victor, Duke of Clarence & Avondale (1864-1892).

[175] Editor's Note: What is interesting about this letter is that, recently, there has been considerable evidence that Crippen did not in fact kill his wife and that the remains found under the floor of his house were not hers. This raises the possibility that Crippen was – like Oscar Wilde - framed by the Brotherhood, perhaps because he was – as Speedicut speculates - trying to blackmail the Great Boanerges about the Ripper victims and their connection with the Duke of Clarence.

[176] Henry Manners, 8th Duke of Rutland (1852-1925).

[177] William Wentworth-Fitzwilliam, 7th Earl Fitzwilliam (1872-1943).

for the fact that it was sitting on one of his more productive coal mines. Next stop was the Percys at Alnwick. Henry Northumberland was at one time Treasurer of the Household,[178] which probably accounted for why his cellar was almost as spectacular as the ridiculously ornate interiors of his castle. Finally, we took our lives in our hands, crossed the great divide and ended up at Dalhousie, which the eponymous Arthur had been trying to let again in order to keep the lead on the roof.[179] Unfortunately for him, he didn't have a coal mine on the property, hence the need for a tenant.

None of this would really be worth recording were it not necessary to explain how we came to be a bare eight miles from the scene of a quite extraordinary event. The story began on the evening of our arrival when we were subjected to a disgusting meal of Scotch specialities 'to welcome you north of the border' as Mary Dalhousie announced as we sat down: you'd have thought that a Heathcote-Drummond-Willoughby would have known better than to serve a thin mutton gruel laced with bullet-hard barley, followed by haggis, neeps and tatties (whatever they might be), all washed down with whisky. As my readers must by now know, I can only tolerate *that* drink *in extremis*, which is what I suppose it was.

"I do hope you won't mind," twittered our hostess, as bowls of something called cranachan – a sickly mess made up of whisky, honey, raspberries and whipped cream - were placed in front of us, "but we've invited The Great Lafayette to luncheon tomorrow."[180]

"Who?" I couldn't help asking, whilst I toyed with the muck in front of me.

"Surely, you've heard of The Great Lafayette, Sir Jasper?" replied her husband. I said that I hadn't. "He's reputed to be the world's greatest illusionist and he's brought his show to Edinburgh. He's been enormously successful, you know."

"He's said to earn simply thousands," chipped in Mary D.

---

[178] Henry Percy, 7th Duke of Northumberland (1846-1918).

[179] Arthur Ramsay, 14th Earl of Dalhousie (1878-1928).

[180] Sigmund Neuberger (1871-1911). Neuberger was reputed to earn, at current values, circa £8 million per annum.

"And it appears that he plans to settle down here," Arthur went on, "and we're rather hoping he'll take the castle off our hands..."

"What makes you think he'll do that?" I asked in astonishment.

"Last week his dog died." I mumbled 'so what?' but he didn't hear me. "He had it embalmed and then buried in Piershill Cemetery," he went on, with what seemed to me to be a complete *non-sequitur* and, being me, I said as much.

"I understand that the dog, a mongrel terrier called Beauty which was given to him by the great Houdini,[181] was the apple of The Great Lafayette's eye," Arthur continued. "It had a diamond-studded collar and its own suite of rooms in his London flat and his private railway carriage, both of which were equipped with the dog's own special bathtub; his Rolls-Royce motor's mascot was replaced with a bronze of the dog; and his specially printed cheques bear an image of Beauty between two bags of gold with the legend 'my two best friends'."

"It sounds to me," I said in astonishment, "that the master's as barkin' as his late pooch. But, that aside, how do you know he wants to settle around here?"

"In order to get permission for Beauty to be buried at Piershill," said our hostess, "The Great Lafayette had to agree to be buried there himself. So, it stands to reason that he wants to live here - and where better than in this house, which is so convenient for the Empire Palace Theatre where he's performing."

"I see," I said, as C-G gave me a warning look, "so we've all got to be terribly nice to him so that he'll get out the doggy cheque book?"

"That's the idea," said our host and then changed the subject.

---

[181] Harry Houdini, born Erik Weisz (1874-1926).

The following noon we gathered in the draughty hall, along with a brace of plaid-bedecked local lairds and their raw-faced wives, for yet more whisky and to await the arrival of The Great Lafayette for luncheon. After a disgusting breakfast of thick porridge and inedible kippers, I'd taken some time in Dalhousie's library to try and find out more about the luncheon-guest-cum-prospective-tenant. The little-used room was stocked mostly with the unreadable works of Scott and the late Queen. However, after a rather dusty search, I found an article in a bound volume of old copies of *The Times*, which informed me that The Great Lafayette was actually a Bavarian member of the Chosen Race called Sigmund Neuberger, who'd been brought up in Canada from the age of sixteen, and that he was, indeed, as financially successful as our hosts had claimed. Richer, in fact.

A short while later, the great man's car swept up to the front door. I observed through a side window that the mascot on the bonnet was bound in black crêpe, as was the man himself who was of medium height, clean shaven and with hair parted down the middle. On his distinctly un-Semitic nose perched a pair of rimless pince-nez, which gave him the air of a bank clerk. In a word, he was completely unremarkable. However, when - over a meal which I can't bring myself to record - he was asked to hold forth on his show, this insignificant man clad in deepest mourning became completely mesmerising. I don't know how he did it, but he transported us with his descriptions to another world in which he performed incredibly imaginative and daring acts including conjuring large animals and people out of thin air. But it was when he got to describe his Finale – entitled 'The Lion's Bride' - that he really got our attention with the assertion that he fed a beautiful maiden to a ravening beast.

"Oh, surely not, Mr, err, Lafayette," I exclaimed in disbelief. "There must be some sort of substitution at the last minute – or the lion is mechanical."

"You do not believe me, Sir Speedicut?"

"Well, frankly, no - I don't." Both C-G and our hostess gave me very dirty looks.

"In that case come and see for yourself. In fact, I invite all of you to come to the theatre this evening for the second house; you will watch the show from my private box. And you," he said, leaning towards me, "Sir Doubting Thomas, may watch the performance from the wings where – if there are, as you believe, any tricks or sleights of hand – you will be able to see them. What do you all say?"

Needless to say, the invitation was quickly accepted by everyone around the table and, by nine o'clock on Tuesday 9th May, I had a seat behind the velvet arras whilst the Dalhousies, C-G, the lairds and their 'ladies' were perched in the stage box. During the two hours that followed, I have to admit that I was very hard put to see how most of the illusions were performed. I was, in consequence, determined to uncover the secret of 'The Lion's Bride', particularly as I was positioned only a few yards from the cage of the smelly brute and it was most definitely *not* mechanical.

The curtain rose on the grand Finale to reveal an Englishman's idea of an oriental harem, as depicted in *One Thousand & One Nights*, full of busty, skimpily-clad bints, jugglers, exotic dancers, fire-eaters (one of whom kindly lit my cigar as he was passing) and dusky-skinned toughs in bulging loincloths. To the music of that frightful Kraut revolutionary thundering out from the pit, the performers pranced in front of the lion's cage in which the King of the Jungle prowled, farted and made grunting sounds, whilst a real horse and a pack of dogs looked distinctly nervous on the opposite side of the stage.

Suddenly, the music changed from the *Ride of the Lesbians* to that frightful Wedding March from *Lowergrim*, or whatever the absurd piece is called and, from the wings opposite my position, under a very strong spotlight which threw the rest of the stage into semi-darkness, a beautiful girl is an elaborate wedding gown was dragged-on by a brace of virtually-naked African slaves. Then, and I almost couldn't believe my eyes, the lion's cage door was opened and she was flung in. Old Leo, who had in the interim stopped pacing, looked as though Christmas had arrived early and started licking his chops. Everything then seemed to happen at once: the lion let out a terrifying roar, the girl screamed and the King of the Jungle pounced – except that, as it did so, its skin fell away to reveal The Great Lafayette. It was a truly spectacular trick that I still haven't worked out.[182]

Along with the packed audience, I jumped (actually, I rose rather creakily) to my feet and started to applaud. Unfortunately, I forgot that I had a lit cigar in my hand, it flew from between my fingers and collided with a piece of scenery. Even more unfortunately, this was draped with some painted material and, before anyone knew what was happening, the flames were licking up the flat. To judge from the audience's reaction, they must have thought that this was part of the act, for they started cheering wildly. I knew better and beat a hasty retreat. As to what happened next, I have to rely on C-G's eye witness account:

"It was only when the orchestra broke into the *National Anthem* and the Safety Curtain started to descend that we knew that something must be amiss," she recalled afterwards. "But still no one moved. Then, for some reason, the Safety Curtain came to a juddering halt about two feet above the stage and this must have created a draft, which fanned the flames behind it into an inferno. Clouds of thick acrid smoke started to billow into the pit from under the gap and we all decided it was time to get out."

In the days that followed, the newspapers reported that The Great Lafayette had been burnt to a cinder trying to save first the lion and then the horse, along with ten other performers including midgets and his body-double who, at first, was thought to be Mr Neuberger himself and whose ashes were damned nearly buried - after a funeral procession watched by quarter of a million Jocks - between Beauty's stuffed paws. It was the sort of tragedy-turned-cock-up that you couldn't invent. I will, however, leave the last word to Arthur Dalhousie, who was wholly unaware of my inadvertent role in the affair:

"Damn – now I've got to find another tenant. This house wouldn't suit you would it, Sir Jasper?"

---

[182] Editor's Note: The 'switch' of the lion and The Great Lafayette was carried out whilst the audience were distracted at the spot-lit entrance of the lion's victim.

...

Editor's Note: The Speedicut Papers again stop for a period, although I found a brief note to Flashman congratulating him on his appointment as Great Boanerges of the Brotherhood of the Sons of Thunder. This letter also mentioned the lifting of the sixty-year-old threat of prosecution for Flashman's attempted rape of Miss Prism and Flashman's return from Paris to live on his modest estate at Ashby-de-la-Zouch[183]. This may be a timely moment to remind readers that the editing of these letters has had as its dual objectives not only to bring Speedicut's story to the attention of the public but also to solve the riddle of the Ashby find as recounted in The Speedicut Papers: Book 1 (Flashman's Secret).

The narrative resumes with another extract from a Speedicut letter to Flashman:

...

8 Stratton Street, London W, April 1912 [Extract]

Fahran's got my traps packed and we're catching the boat train this afternoon. I'm quite looking forward to this trip, which is a belated 90th birthday present from Charlotte-Georgina, as I haven't been to New York in years and the White Star's new liner is said to be the *nec plus ultra* in luxury. Brother Ismay has reserved for me an outside cabin on the exclusive C Deck (worth £200 each way, would you believe?)[184] and told me that I'll be on the Captain's table along with the ghastly Duff-Gordons and himself.[185] It's a great pity that C-G has unexpectedly been laid low with gout, and so is unable to travel with me, but she insisted that I go anyway. Free of her control, I intend to get up late, play cards for the highest stakes on board and consume as much of Ismay's free booze as my liver will stand. I'll write again from New York once the *Titanic* has docked.

...

---

[183] See *The Speedicut Papers: Book 1 (Flashman's Secret)*.

[184] Editor's Note: £8,000 for the round trip at today's approximate values.

[185] Joseph Bruce Ismay (1862 – 1937), Chairman & Managing Director of the White Star Line; Sir Cosmo Duff-Gordon, 5th Baronet (1862 – 20 April 1931) & Lucy, Lady Duff-Gordon (1863 – 1935)

CHAPTER NINETEEN: A TITANIC ICEBERG

As everyone in the world must know, four days out from Southampton on the night of the 15th-16th April 1912 the dratted *Titanic* struck a 'berg, sank like a stone and took two-thirds of her passengers and crew with her including, in a very bizarre coincidence, an elderly filly sired by that damned scribbler Hughes. He was the blighter who had tried to wreck mine and Flashy's reputations with his wretched book about Rugby in the old days.[186]

Worse than the loss of Lillian Hughes, which was of no consequence to me, was my passport, most of my cash and all of my wardrobe. Together with my moolah, plenty of other money went to the bottom including an Astor,[187] a Guggenheim,[188] and a Mr and Mrs Strauss,[189] all extremely well-heeled members of the Chosen Race. Along with the front row of the synagogue on Fifth Avenue, hoards of the equally heathen Irish also perished, trapped as they were below deck in Steerage, poor blighters.[190]

Well, at least Fahran and I survived, along with rather less than half of the First Class passengers. These included Brother Ismay, the owner of the *Titanic*, who slipped into a half-full lifeboat and, on landing in New York, hid in the Ritz Carlton refusing to see anyone; and the Duff-Gordons, who had cut me the whole time we were on board, which was a damned cheek: he may have been the fifth Baronet but she was just a jumped-up

---

[186] *Tom Brown's School Days* by Thomas Hughes (1822 –1896).

[187] Colonel John Jacob Astor, (1864-1912) a millionaire property developer was the wealthiest passenger aboard.

[188] Benjamin Guggenheim, (1865-1912) although by no means the richest of his successful mine-owning family, was travelling, to the horror of his family, with his French mistress, her German maid and his French valet/secretary and chauffeur. The women survived but the men did not.

[189] Isidor Strauss (1845-1912) was co-owner of Macy's department store in New York. He and his wife Ida, pleading age and not wishing to be separated, refused to go into a lifeboat. They sat in deck chairs holding hands until they were washed overboard. Isidore's body was later recovered, Ida's was not.

[190] There were 120 Irish passengers in 3rd Class. Most did not survive.

divorcée seamstress. It took me a few weeks but, as you will read, I got my revenge on them in the end.

But I've just realised that I haven't told my readers what *actually* happened on that terrible night. I blame this oversight on encroaching senility brought about by a lifetime's indulgence in the *vieux fine*. Anyway, I'll put that – the oversight that is - right straight away, particularly as even today there's still a lot of damned twaddle being reported in the gutter press (and talked about in the clubs) concerning what actually happened on board the *Titanic* after she struck the 'berg. Needless to say, most of the more sensational (and highly inaccurate) stories were put about by Ismay, to cover his tracks and to protect what little was left of the White Star's reputation and share price. What *I'm* going to recount now is my own first-hand experience and it doesn't include a lot of dramatic, second-hand balls about men dressed as women and the rest of the crap that's been in the rags. I'm only going to relate what I saw or was told at the time. That said, as I was already in bed when we collided with Neptune's ice cube, for the early bits I have to rely on what Second Officer Lightoller later told me over a dinner I gave him by way of a 'thank-you' at the Union Club in New York:[191]

"I was on my way from my quarters to the bridge when we struck," he said. "I heard First Officer Murdoch,[192] the senior officer on watch, order the Quartermaster to go 'hard-a-starboard' and telegraph for the engines to go Full Astern. But here's the problem, and as it's a bit technical so you'll have to bear with me: Murdoch gave a Rudder Order but the Quartermaster, who had spent most of his service on sailing boats, took it as a Tiller Order, and swung the helm over so that the ship steered into, not away from, the 'berg.

"That of itself would have been enough of a bloody disaster, but when he realised the ship had stopped, Mr Ismay ordered Captain Smith to carry on sailing,[193] thereby increasing the water pressure below the water line

---

[191] Charles Herbert Lightoller (1874 –1952)
[192] William Murdoch (1873 –1912).
[193] Captain Edward Smith (1850 – 1912).

and causing the *Titanic* to sink far faster than should ever have been the case. In addition to all of which, there'd been a fire raging in one of the coal holds since we'd left Southampton and that might have compromised at least one of the watertight compartments...".[194]

Quite why Lightoller didn't tell the subsequent Enquiries this appalling saga of cock-ups was, and remains, a mystery to me; I suspect he only imparted it to me under the influence of the Union's best brandy.

Anyway, back on the ill-fated liner: some of the passengers have since claimed that they felt a judder when we struck, but I didn't - although that too may have been the fault of the Emperor. Indeed, the first I knew that anything was wrong was when Fahran came to my cabin.

"Huzoor, you must get dressed and go on deck. And you must take your life jacket with you."

"Why ever should I do that? It's fifty degrees below out there." I said sleepily.

"Because, huzoor, we have struck an iceberg."

"Who told you that rubbish, Fahran?"

"Your cabin steward, huzoor."

"Well, there's no rush. The ship's unsinkable and, even if she does founder, there are more than enough lifeboats."

---

[194] Editor's Note: This is a claim has been recently made by Lightoller's grand-daughter, Lady Patten. The confusion, if such it was, occurred during a period when shipping communications were in transition from sail to steam. Two different systems were in operation at the time, 'Rudder Orders' (used for steam ships) and 'Tiller Orders' (used for sailing ships). Crucially, the two steering systems were the complete opposite of one another, so a command to turn 'hard a-starboard' meant turn the wheel right under one system and left under the other. The fire in the coal hold was a fact; its possible impact on the watertight compartments either side of it was another contributing factor to the disaster that was not considered at the subsequent Enquiries.

"That's what I said to the steward, but he said that he wouldn't rely on either of those facts, huzoor. So please get up, allow me to dress you and then we can both get in a queue for one of the boats."

I was about to argue the toss, but I noticed a determined set to Fahran's jaw. So, I did as he'd instructed and fifteen minutes later we were both on deck. It was organised chaos: Lightoller and his fellow officers were bellowing that only women and children would be allowed into the boats.

"It's pointless freezin' our balls off out here," I said to Fahran. "Let's go to the smokin' saloon and have a glass or two whilst they get the bints and nippers off. I'm sure we'll be told when it's our turn."

"Am I allowed into First Class as your guest rather than as your servant, huzoor?"

"I'd like to see anyone try and stop you," I said, as I led the way back inside past the dance band which was thumping out *Alexander's Ragtime Rubbish*: it was infernal music, but I assumed they'd been told to play it to stop the passengers panicking. We bimbled into the smoking room, which was pretty well empty save for a group of four hardened card sharps, who I'd been avoiding for the past couple of days, who were playing poker.

"Come and join us, Sir Jasper," one of them called over to me.

"No thanks," I said. "If what I've been told is true, we're in deep enough water as it is without my getting' in any deeper. And this lifebelt," I said holding up the cork-filled canvas, "will be no bloody help to me if I agree to play with you."

They all laughed as the room started to tilt, which shows you how damned serious the situation was fast becoming: if the room had been level, and New York in view, at least one of them might have called me out for the implied insult. As it was, they doubled the stakes, which were high anyway, and carried on playing as the tilt gradually got worse.

I'm not sure for how long Fahran and I waited to be called whilst they loaded the women and children, but I do remember that all the waiters seemed to have legged it, so we didn't get a drink. I was about to suggest to Fahran that we should stagger off to the dining room when Andrews,[195] the ship's architect, entered with a very serious look on his phiz.

"What's the score, Andrews?" I said to him, as he passed my chair.

"An iceberg has stopped play," he replied, in a feeble attempt at a joke.

"So I believe, but that's surely not the end of the innin's?"

"As a matter of fact," he said, looking grimmer by the second, "I fear that it is."

"But how can that be so? The ship's unsinkable."

"Unfortunately, instead of colliding head-on with the iceberg, which would have been bad enough but she would have survived, it seems that we have scraped along the side of the 'berg and there is now a long gash below the waterline with which neither the pumps nor the watertight bulkheads can cope.[196] It's a mathematical certainty that the *Titanic* is going to sink and, by my calculation," he got out his fob watch, "she'll do so in less than an hour."

"What?"

"If you take my advice, you'll go back on deck and try and find a lifeboat."

---

[195] Thomas Andrews (1873 – 1912).

[196] Editor's Note: Andrew's statement is at odds with the Lightoller's claims mentioned earlier by Speedicut, although it remains a fact that, had *Titanic* struck the iceberg head-on, the ship would not have sunk and might even have been able to limp into New York harbour. It is now generally accepted that, by scraping alongside the iceberg, a large number of the ship's steel plates were ripped, or buckled under the pressure, and too many of the watertight compartments were thereby compromised for *Titanic* to remain afloat.

"But there's no rush, surely? There's more than enough capacity in the boats for everyone, even if we were fully loaded which I know we're not."

"Actually, Sir Jasper, although we are carrying more boats than is required by the Board of Trade regulations, even if every lifeboat gets away fully loaded there will still be half the ship's company left on board when she founders."

"Good grief!" I gasped. "What idiot ever agreed to short-changing the lifeboats?"

"It's not idiotic but logical, Sir Jasper. The most effective lifeboat is the ship herself – the lifeboats themselves are designed only to tranship the passengers and crew to a rescue ship. Unfortunately, neither the Board of Trade, nor I, foresaw an accident of this nature..."

"But there must be a vessel near us which at this moment is steamin' to the rescue, surely?" I asked, hopefully.

"I'm afraid not. There is a ship within sight, but she's static and not responding either to our radio calls or to the distress rockets. The next closest is the *Carpathia*: she has responded and is on her way, but she can't possibly get here before dawn."[197]

"My God, so what are we to do?"

"If you stay on board you will drown. You might try for one of the collapsibles. They will be the last to be launched and may well be overlooked by most passengers. If you do, make sure you've wrapped up warm. It will be very cold in the boats." He paused for a moment. "But whatever you do, if you decide to try and get off, *don't* jump overboard wearing that life vest: it will break your neck when you hit the surface. But then the freezing water will kill you in a couple of minutes, anyway, so it might be a better way to go if you can't get into a lifeboat..."

---

[197] Editor's Note: SS *Californian* was about 10 miles from the *Titanic* and was still there the following morning; RMS *Carpathia* arrived on the scene at 0400hrs, two hours after the *Titanic* had sunk.

"And what are you goin' to do?"

"Me? Oh, I think I'll have a whisky…" he said, pulling out a hip flask.

So that was it: death by drowning, if one stayed on board, or death by freezing or a broken neck if we jumped for it. Fuck it, I thought, if this is the end then let's make a party of it. So, I settled m'self deeper into the chair and asked Fahran, who hadn't left my side, to find us a bottle of brandy and two glasses. He returned a couple of minutes later.

"I've found these, huzoor," he said, holding up a brace of bottles of Mr Delamain's best. God knows where he'd got them, but I wasn't about to ask. "But there weren't any glasses."

"Then let's take a bottle a'piece and make do without the niceties." He handed me one, I stripped off the seal, pulled out the cork stopper and held up the flask. "Here's to your very good health, Fahran! I think we should ensure that when we meet your father and Mr Searcy we should both be – as they say in Bow Street – 'in no fit state'."

"Cheers, huzoor!"

Half-way through my bottle, two men in full evening dress appeared in the doorway, which was odd as gentlemen don't dress for dinner on the first night out or a Sunday, which it was. It may have been the Frog firewater, but I had the distinct impression that both were finding it hard to remain upright. Perhaps they'd also hit the Delamain, I thought. As they drew closer I saw that it was Ben Guggenheim and his man, who had a plaid rug draped over one arm.

"On your way to a party, Guggenheim?" I asked, "and why aren't you wearin' your life jacket?"

"We are dressed in our best," he said pompously, "and are prepared to go down like gentlemen. As to the life jacket, it is very uncomfortable."

"So, where's your girlfriend?"

He looked outraged at this reference to his mistress, with whom he was travelling, and completely ignored my question. Instead he said:

"Should you get off, Speedicut, I'd be obliged if you would tell *my wife* that I played the game out straight to the end."

Whatever that might mean, I thought, as he took a chair by the fireplace and his valet took post behind him. You know, that's the problem with the *nouveaux riches*: they always want to be seen to be doing what they think others believe is the way a gentleman would behave. It never is, of course, as I was about to prove.

Whilst Guggenheim prepared for his stately progress to Eternity, the angle of the tilt increased still further and the furniture that wasn't screwed to the deck started to slide downhill. When my nearly-empty bottle of Delamain slipped off the table and crashed to the floor, I changed my mind about our options and decided to take Andrew's advice. Well, unless you're a pompous multi-millionaire in an unhappy marriage, hope springs eternal even in your nineties.

"Time to try our luck with the collapsibles, Fahran."

"Lead on, huzoor," he said, with a rather forced smile.

No sooner had I hauled on my life jacket and stumbled, with Fahran's help, out onto the deck than I caught sight of Lightoller and a bunch of tars.

"Ship ahoy, Lightoller," I called out to him.

"Sadly not, Sir Jasper," he called back, "but if you follow me, I'm going to try and get the collapsibles away. If you can both give me a hand, there will be room for you."

"You can't expect much help from me, Lightoller, but my man Fahran's still fit. If that qualifies us both for a place, lead on."

...

It was no easy job to prise the canvas and plywood emergency lifeboats loose from their fastenings whilst the water surged all around and the *Titanic's* rear end rose higher and higher out of the water. The first boat crashed over the side and floated away, but Lightoller and his bravos got the second one free. However, just as they were turning it over to get it set-up, Neptune decided otherwise and we were all swept off, clinging for dear life to the trailing lines. God, it was cold in the water but, of course, both Fahran and I were insulated by alcohol and were eventually pulled onto the upturned boat by Lightoller. If we hadn't both had a skin-full of Ismay's brandy I'm damned sure we would have frozen to death. The Master Baker, who was also on our collapsible, was roaring drunk on gin and that too saved his life.

And that's really all there is to tell. It was certainly a night to remember, although one that I would prefer to forget. The sight of the aft section rising to forty-five degrees, rotating on its axis, then settling back to the horizontal before again pitching forward and then disappearing from view, along with over a thousand souls, will stay with me for the rest of my days, as will the cries of those in the water. However, I can't close this awful story without debunking some of the myths, which I can do from my personal experiences or those related to me later by reliable fellow survivors on the *Carpathia*.

As you may have read, Captain Smith – like Andrews - did the decent thing and went down with his ship, although whether or not he stood on the bridge until the last (as some have claimed) or jumped into the freezing briny (as others have said) I don't know as I didn't see him. I've already told you about Ismay, who should have shot himself instead of feebly offering his resignation, which he knew wouldn't be accepted as he controlled the White Star's board. Perhaps relatives of the bogtrotters who drowned in the freezing briny, or were dragged down inside the hull, will get him yet: I hope so.

There was actually some shooting, as Smith had issued his officers with pistols when it was clear that the situation had gone from dire to disastrous. Lightoller told me that he had to fire a few rounds in the air to stop a lifeboat being swamped, as did Fifth Officer Lowe,[198] but it was First Officer Murdoch who had to use his Webley in earnest and I saw it with my own eyes. Like Lightoller, once all the rigid life boats had been launched – many only half-full - Murdoch tried to launch a collapsible. He'd got one afloat when it was rushed by a crowd of men who would undoubtedly have sunk it. Murdoch shot two of them, put the gun to his own head, saluted with his free hand, said: "Gentleman, every man for himself, goodbye," and pulled the trigger.

And the stories about the life boats not returning to try and pick-up the floaters are also true – but they had been told to keep well away from the sinking ship, lest they be sucked down. Anyway, by the time they could have rowed back, most of those in the water had frozen to death as we could tell from the eerie silence all around us. As for the tales of men dressed up as women, and the band playing *Nearer my God to Thee* as the briny washed over them, neither I nor any of those I spoke to could be sure. But I do know about the Duff-Gordons. For those of my readers who have never heard of Sir Cosmo Duff-Gordon and his wife, Lucile, read on.

Cosmo was an arrogant Scotch laird who walked around as though he has a Ducal (rather than a Baronet's) poker stuffed up his arse and a pile of rusty coronets in the bank. In reality, he had his hands as deep in the booze trade in Spain as they were in sheep shit in his Scottish glens. His great uncle was a whoring partner of my Papa back in the Regency, who bought a Baronetcy off Prinny when the old fool finally staggered onto the throne in the earlies of the last century. As for Miss Lucy, or Lady Duff-Gordon as she liked to be known, she was a prime piece of flesh to whom I would have applied an exploratory squeeze had she not frozen me to ice the first time I sat next to her on Smith's table. However, to be fair, in the guise of 'Lucile - Couturier to the Nobility & Gentry', Miss Lucy has done old lechers like me a real service by loosening corsets, slitting skirts and generally promoting a display of more flesh than had been seen on bints of all ages since those French tarts threw-off all their clothes during the first Frog Revolution.

---

[198] Harold Lowe (1882 – 1944).

That said, like all self-made madams intent on climbing the slippery pole of Society, she took a damned high line with anyone whom she considered was not superior to her, including everyone except the Royal Family and a few old-money aristos. Actually, I'm not even sure about the Royal Family, although I was certain Miss Lucy gave them a discount to keep their custom and so ensure her trade with the rich arse-lickers who creep around in the wake of royalty. Apparently, so I've been told, Miss Lucy also started the fashion for 'dress shows' and mannequins. If you ask me, she was running a stable of loose-hipped fillies for the bucks to plunge. And my proof? Well, her sister was the bodice-ripping novelist, Elinor Glyn, who kept Curzon warm at night - and these things run in families...[199] But I digress.

In sum, the Duff-Gordons were the greatest pair of snobbish, self-regarding ninnies one was likely ever to meet and, thanks to Ismay, I was stuck with them on the heaving foam. Well, as my readers should know by now, I don't take kindly to noses in the air. However, despite liking them slightly less than the pox, from what I saw of them during the sinking (and what I heard afterwards), the D-Gs actually behaved no differently to anyone else. Truth to tell – and it sticks in my craw to say it – they maintained what the Frogs call *sang froid*: sheer bloody stupidity in the face of appalling danger more like. And they certainly didn't take advantage of what I'm sure they would have asserted was 'their position', unlike the despicable Ismay who barged women and children overboard in his rush to climb into one of the few boats near him not full to overflowing. Nor did the sainted Cosmo pull-on dear Lucy's shawl, cover his whiskers and pretend to be her maid, which certain others are alleged to have done, probably because she would have cracked him around his phiz for leaving her 'vulnerable to chills in an open boat'.

Anyway, putting the D-Gs to one side for a moment, after the *Titanic* had headed for Davy Jones' locker, those of us who had managed to get off her spent some hellish and damned cold hours in open boats before we were picked up by a rust bucket called the *Carpathia* and landed in New

---

[199] Elinor Glyn (1864-1943); George Nathaniel Curzon, the Rt Hon the Earl Curzon of Kedleston GCSI GCIE PC, later 1st Marquess Curzon of Kedleston (1859-1925).

York. A fat lot of help was offered to us by the White Star johnnies on the quayside, so I made my way to the Union Club where I telegraphed to London for some funds.

Two weeks later, by which time I had just about recovered and was thinking of heading back across the pond, there was a Benefit Concert at the Metropolitan Opera in aid of the families of the crew who were lost, which was most of them. As I'd nothing better to do (and the White Star had – disgracefully - stopped paying the wages of the *Titanic*'s crew from the moment that she foundered), I stumped up the sub, plus quite a bit more on top, and tooled around to the opera house with Fahran.

The evening, which we were told at the start had raised twelve thousand Dollars, was under the patronage of the US President – a complete nonentity called Daft - and the Connaughts, who had come down from Canada for the occasion.[200] As a consequence of the royal presence, or perhaps because it was the only thing suitable in the Met orchestra's repertoire, the concert started with some unbelievably dreary Kraut funeral music. Worse was to come and the first half ended with *Nearer my God to Thee*, which the programme said had been played as the unsinkable tub sank like a stone: as I've already noted, I'm pretty sure it wasn't. Nonetheless, the whole audience dissolved into floods from the first note of the mawkish hymn.

The concert picked up a bit in the second half with sentimental songs by the full-titted Scotch songbird, Mary Garden. Then a fat Eytie tenor waddled on and belted out a load of gut-wrenching arias that had most of the audience back in sobs: Fahran howled along with the rest of New York Society and I'll confess that I, too, had to reach for my snot rag when the Wop sang Fanny Ronald's favourite Sullivan piece, *The Lost Vocal Chord*.

[200] William Taft (1857-1930) and TRH The Duke and Duchess of Connaught & Strathearn; Prince Arthur (1850-1942) was the seventh child of Queen Victoria and was married to Princess Louise of Prussia (1860-1917).

I must, I thought at the time, be getting old if I react so easily to such bourgeois tripe.[201]

So how, I hear my readers ask, did I get my revenge on the Duff-Gordons for their placing me in Outer Mongolia on that bit of the voyage when we were still afloat? Well, when I got back to London there was a rumour doing the rounds that the D-Gs, who had enemies a'plenty around Town, had bribed their way into a half-empty boat, insisted that it be launched without further delay or unnecessary additional baggage – human or otherwise – and had then stated firmly that smoking was DEFINITELY not permitted by the tars manning the oars. It was also being said that they had refused to allow the matelots to row back to pick-up survivors, but my readers now know the score with regard to *that* accusation. To cap it all, the D-Gs had promised to tip the tars £5 each when they reached dry land.[202] This was, of course, prime territory for a campaign of revenge and when, as was inevitable, I was asked if I knew anything about their alleged behaviour during the sinking I simply looked at the ceiling, cleared my throat, shuffled my feet and lit another cigar. Caligula couldn't have done it better and the D-Gs were damned from thereon. I'm told they don't go out in Society anymore and Cosmo can't read a newspaper without being physically sick. Good. Pity I couldn't wreck the bitch's frock business too, but then I do forgive her - at least a bit - for letting an old *roué* like me have a better view of a bulging cleavage. I may be over ninety but the fire's still alight - just.

---

[201] On 29th April 1912, the Metropolitan Opera staged a Benefit Concert in aid of all the victims' families (not just the crew) which opened with excerpts from Brahms' *German Requiem*. The second half included sentimental songs sung by, amongst others, Mary Garden (1874-1967); Enrico Caruso (1873-1921) sang only one piece, *The Lost Chord* by Sir Arthur Sullivan (1842-1900), which had been much performed until her death by Sullivan's mistress, Fanny Ronalds (1939-1916), who was buried with its score clutched between her hands.

[202] In 1912 £5 was worth approximately £1,000 today. It was a significant sum of money for a sailor whose wages were probably not more than £50 a year.

CHAPTER TWENTY: SHANGHAI LILY

But, yet again, I anticipate: before I could fix the Duff-Gordons' fate, I had to get back to London. Fahran and I achieved this by taking berths on one of the Hamburg-America Line tubs headed east.

During the crossing, which was in all other respects completely uneventful, I found myself at the same table in the dining saloon as a rather cool Prussian military type by the name of Major Ulrich von Stumm. He was suitably impressed to hear of my encounters with the late Chancellor Otto von Bismarck,[203] and other assorted (and highly edited) tales concerning his fellow countrymen.

Fresh off the boat train from Southampton, along with Fahran, a small valise containing two ready-made suits that I'd bought in New York and not much else, I took von Stumm for luncheon at the Verulam where I'd decided to stay as Stratton Street was shut up. Once fed and watered, and I'd seen von S off the premises, I then headed in the direction of Mr Anderson's new premises in Old Burlington Street where I dealt swiftly with the fact that most of my wardrobe was feeding the fishes: I told Anderson to send what promised to be a large bill to Ismay.

The following morning at breakfast, the club's hall porter brought me a stiff envelope with an embassy crest on the reverse. I put it to one side whilst I munched my way through the first decent plate of bacon and eggs I'd enjoyed since the 14th April: Americans seemed to think that a pile of pancakes drowned in a sickly syrup sets you up for the day and the Germans had even more barbarous ideas as to what constituted a good breakfast. Breakfast done, I strolled into the ante room with the envelope clutched in my paw along with a copy of *The Times*, which was still full of nonsense about the sinking.

Easing my ageing bones into a suitably comfortable chair in front of the fire I must have nodded off. The next thing that I remember was a club

---

[203] Prince Otto von Bismarck (1815-1898).

servant making a devil of a racket by knocking over my empty coffee cup as he struggled to rescue *The Times* from the fire, where it was burning merrily: the best fate for the damned rag in my view. Thinking that I'd better read the letter before I set the club alight, I slit the envelope with my pocket knife (one of the few things that I hadn't lost when I went overboard) and saw to my surprise that it was from von Stumm inviting me to a reception at the German Embassy that night, Orders & decorations etc to be worn.

Clearly, my new togs from Anderson would not be ready for a week or two, so I tooled round to Stratton Street, got Fahran to open up the house with his spare key (mine was at the bottom of the North Atlantic) and recovered my spare evening clothes.

...

Several hours later I was decanted out of a hansom into the candlelit magnificence of His Imperial Germanic Majesty's Embassy in Carlton House Terrace, held together by my second-best set of tails and as much tin-ware as my ageing shoulders could support: I knew from long experience that you have to impress these Embassy types or you get shunted into a corner with an elderly and moustachioed bint who looks like the Witch of Endor and doesn't speak any language known to man. However, a gleaming chest encrusted with the evidence of a lifetime of undetected crime and a gaudy ribbon across the shirt front (on this occasion the Order of the Black Eagle - well, why not?), usually guaranteed one at least some time with the Ambassador's son or daughter, which made these embassy events half-bearable, particularly if you managed a fumble with one of them behind the potted palms in the conservatory later in the evening.

However, on this occasion the young of both sexes were in short supply and the party seemed to be mostly composed of military brass hats and a Kraut royal being fêted in the corner by a bunch of stuffed-shirted diplomatics. Hum, I thought, this is going to be a merry affair: time to punish the fizz, which, to do the Krauts credit, seemed to be in abundant supply. No sooner had I positioned myself in the direct line of a footman with a magnum of the Frogs' best, than I felt a firm grip clasp my upper arm and the scarred face of von Stumm swung into my line of sight.

"Ah, Sir Jasper, how good of you to come. We are honoured you could accept this invitation at such short notice, as His Imperial Highness The Crown Prince is most anxious to hear at first hand of your experiences on the *Titanic*.[204] May I present you?"

Before waiting for a reply, he propelled me over to the group gathered around the tightly uniformed figure of the royal I'd spotted earlier. As Dorothea once told me when I was with her in Russia, all these foreign royals wore corsets, which allowed their tailors to stitch them into their absurdly tight parade uniforms and hang more gongs on them than you would think the tailoring could stand. Most un-English, but half of 'em are confirmed shirt-lifters anyway.

This princeling was no different to his Russian cousins, with a tunic so tight that it was a wonder he could breathe; his array of Orders put my display to shame. For some reason, when I had gassed with von Stumm on the boat, I had not mentioned my fluency in German or that I had the Order of the Black Shite Hawk. So, he was slightly surprised, although he tried not to show it, at the gaudy orange ribbon across my waistcoat and the twinkling Star on my left tit. He was even more impressed when I launched into my finest *Hochdeutsch* in response to HIH's enquiry after my health.

My readers can guess what happened next. Royalty, having given my various decorations the once-over (for some reasons they always do it), asked me politely to recount the horrors of the recent past and yours truly did his best to make it even more dramatic than it had been.

But, as always happens – it must be to do with the thinness of the blood royal – after the first five minutes I could see from the dulling of his eye behind the gleaming monocle that I was losing his attention. When he interjected "*Sehr interessant!*" into my monologue for the third time, I took

---

[204] HIH Crown Prince Wilhelm of Prussia (1882-1951).

the cue and wrapped up sharpish, but not before the gleaming fish eye had started to scan the room over my shoulder. Von Stumm also got the hint and steered me away from the royal presence, after much clicking of heels and notional tugging of feudal forelocks by the *pickelhaubes* and a curt neck bow from myself.

My host then propelled me towards a great side board on which were arrayed copious quantities of the fizzing white restorative and piles of chopped sausage and pickled cucumbers, which embassies all around the world seem to think is a reasonable substitute for a proper six-course meal.

"I wonder, dear Sir Jasper," he said, breaking back into English, "if you would do me the great honour of partaking of luncheon tomorrow?"

Having nothing better to do, I agreed to meet him at Ritz's establishment on Piccadilly,[205] which boasted a *table d'hôte* menu that would have satisfied Gargantua. Actually, I would have preferred to go to the Cavendish, as Rosa Lewis might not supply better vittels but there was always the option of a roll in the hay with one of her tame tarts after luncheon. But von Stumm was paying and so it was to the Ritz that I repaired the following day, where the pride of the German Army was waiting for me. At first, he was guarded. He talked around a number of military and political topics that were the stuff of gossip in the Grub Street gutters, but then he moved on to less public subjects.

"I believe, Sir Jasper, that you spent some time as the guest of The Mahdi?[206] *Das ist richtig, nicht whar?*"

I had no idea how he knew about all that but he was right – and damned uncomfortable it was to be reminded of it too.[207] But I smiled and said that he seemed to know a lot about me.

"That is correct, Sir Jasper."

---

[205] César Ritz (1850-1918). Ritz was known as the 'king of hoteliers and hotelier to kings'. The Ritz Hotel on Piccadilly opened in 1906.
[206] Muhammad Ahmad bin Abd Allah, otherwise known as The Mahdi (1844 – 1885).
[207] See *The Speedicut Papers: Book 7 (Royal Scandals)*.

"So why do you want to know about that arse-scratchin', flea-ridden lunatic who emerged out of nowhere in the '80s, brandishin' the Koran in one hand, a bloody sword in the other and declarin' Holy War on the world?"

"I have, shall we say, an interest," he replied, with Germanic smugness. Well, that was the surest admission he was another bloody Kraut secret squirrel. So, a bottle of Rothschild's best notwithstanding, I was instantly on my guard.

"What do you want to know?" I parried, with what I hoped was disarming charm. Von Stumm paused, considered me for a moment and then sprang a question right out of deep cover.

"When you were the guest of The Mahdi, Sir Jasper, did you ever hear of the legend of Kasredin?"

"No, I don't think so," I said, dredging back through what was left of my memory.

"Then let me remind you, Sir Jasper. The legend of Kasredin is a Turkish folk tale which states that a great leader, known as 'the Emerald' or 'Greenmantle', will rise out of the desert and lead the faithful in a holy war to drive the infidel from the face of the earth. It's a not dissimilar conviction to that of the Jews' belief in a Messiah."

"Or to the fantasies with which The Mahdi adorned himself."

"Precisely, Sir Jasper."

"You know, come to think of it, I seem to remember that the bugger – or it might have been one of his followers – did tell me that he would declare himself to be the Grand Mufti or the Giant Panjandrum or some such, once he got to the steps of Hagia Sofia in Constantinople. Barkin' mad, of course, but the swivel-eyed shit and his followers really believed it. If you ask me," I went on, as von S poured me another glass of claret, "it was religious moonshine, no more and no less. Of course, there have been plenty of false prophets claimin' to be the Chosen One – possibly even the Emerald – and doubtless there will be more in the future. But it's all, as you would say, *blödsinn* – rubbish."

"*Ja*, I agree. But the peasants believe it, *nicht wahr?*"

"Certainly," I replied, "but they also believe that the earth is flat, that bankin', 'baccy and booze are a sin and that women are neither to be seen nor heard – well they may be right on that one – and they mutilate themselves in ways that I don't care to dwell on. And they do it all in the name of religion."

"That is certainly correct, but the power of that religion, if it could be harnessed by educated men, might be used to great effect in the affairs of the world, could it not?"

"If you *could* harness it – and I have seen at first hand its power – that might be so. But, in my experience, you would have a damned sight easier job herdin' cats away from a bowl of cream or getting' the Irish to wash."

Von Stumm paused for a moment and then abruptly changed the subject.

"This has been a most enjoyable and informative luncheon, Sir Jasper, I thank you for giving up your time to answer my questions. Perhaps we will do it again."

Then he signed to the waiter, paid the bill and made his farewell with a heel click like the crack of a pistol, which made the two old trots at the table door table nearly swallow their pearls.

I thought that would be the last I would see or hear of my beer-swilling travelling companion, but a couple of days later I received a second letter embossed with the emaciated and coroneted chicken that the Krauts use as their national symbol; at least it doesn't have two heads like the Austrian and Russian shite hawks. Again, it was a letter from von Stumm, this time inviting me to meet a colleague of his, a certain Hilda von Einem. From the sound of her name, which was for some reason chillingly familiar, she was likely to be a beefy matron, with a flat chest, thick woollen stockings and a 'keep off the grass' sign in her piggy eyes, which would, of course, be hidden behind thick horn-rimmed specs. If she wasn't that, then she would be a full-titted, bass-voiced Valkyrie. Either way, not very appealing. You see, I knew my German *mädchen*: only one in fifty was worthy of a glance and one in the Secret Service, for if she was a 'colleague' of von Stumm that she certainly was, would definitely be numbered among the forty-nine. However, as I was still in London and not yet planning to return to Wales and C-G's chilly embrace, I accepted.

This time the rendezvous was at a dark, smoky restaurant in a Soho basement, kitted out like a Munich beer hall and run by one of the forty-niners, a beefy woman in a *dirndl* with long plaits (you can be sure her name was Heidi) who barged her way around the place heaving armfuls of *steins* overflowing with light, frothy beer which - in my limited experience – was undrinkable muck. But, again, I digress, for there in a corner, only half-visible through the smoke haze was von Stumm... and Shanghai Lily, who my readers may recall – and I certainly did – from my last visit to Shanghai. She was older now, of course, but quite unmistakable.

Quite how Lily the 'coaster', who I'd last seen cavorting half-naked around a bordello-cum-palace-of-varieties on the Bund pursued by a priapic but ill-equipped Yankee Major of Marines, had turned into Hilda von Einem of the Prussian Secret Service, I couldn't fathom. So convinced had I been that she would be a strapping and moustachioed product of the Fatherland that I was, momentarily, completely winded. From their behaviour, both von Stumm and Hilda-Lily appeared to put this down to my nonagenarian exertions involved in getting down the steps into the cellar, rather than to my surprise at seeing her: age had to have its benefits from time-to-time.

Anyway, whilst I recovered my breath with a pint of what was supposed to pass for beer, I took a long look at Fraulein von E: a quick glance had shown me that her hands were still bare of the dreaded ring-that-binds. Although seated, she was obviously tall, with a nipped-in waist and tits that, whilst not exactly bursting out of the top of her dress, were certainly willing to do so at a moment's notice, and an upholstered rump that was elegantly positioned half-over the end of the bench on which she was perched. The lamplight above her cast a curious butterfly-shaped shadow below her nose and, when she spoke, it was in a baritone purr that was utterly lacking in the letter 'r'.

Discretely but fashionably dressed in a well-cut outfit, that could and probably did come from the ghastly Lucile's frock shop, she was all woman, probably somewhere in her mid-thirties and about as prime a piece of temptation as had ever crossed my path. In a lifetime of debauchery and unrestrained lechery, I have long since come to recognise women who are, without question, ready for a serious bout of mattress gymnastics. More often than not they are *not* your firm-hipped, wasp-waisted, full-busted classical beauties with a pouting lower lip but, rather, there is a certain cast of face that seems to signal, without anything being said: 'come and get me – and be prepared for the consequences'. Lady Randy was a prime example of the type and Lily was another. But, just like Lady Randy, she also exuded danger and this put me on my guard.

After the introductions, during which Lily affected not to recognise me but admitted on my enquiry that 'Fruity' Fritz was her uncle – I was delighted to learn that he was (appropriately) beneath the sod - we made some small talk although it was clear that von Stumm had an agenda. Before long he steered the chat back to our earlier conversation about my time in the Soudan as the guest of the Mohammedan's answer to William Gladstone.[208] At this point, von E sat forward and her finely chiselled nose started to quiver like a pointer. Ah ha, thinks I, we're getting to the point, but we didn't.

Having established the circumstances of my stay with the lunatic goat herd, the talk moved-on to a discussion of the Berlin-to-Baghdad railway, which the sausage-eaters had been building since 1903 and were no nearer to completing than when I had first heard about it on a European brothel hopping tour - for that read diplomatic mission - with Bertie of late-lamented memory.

---

[208] William Ewart Gladstone (1809-1989), Liberal Prime Minister and self-appointed rescuer of 'fallen women'.

After a deal more talk about the decline and imminent collapse of the Ottoman Empire, an event that wiseacres had been confidently predicting since the First Crusade, the party broke up and I returned to the Verulam alone – for, despite the look in her eye, there was no invitation to a late-night libation at von E's hotel - and I was none the wiser as to what the whole evening had been about.

The following morning over luncheon at the club I found myself sitting next to young Brother Buchan on an otherwise empty club table.[209] As he was a leery cove with a Secret Service background, I tried him out on the previous night's events, minus my lecherous thoughts concerning Miss Lily. He listened with great care but could offer me no clues.

"I don't see, Brother Jasper, how it would advance the Germans' railway project if the whole Middle East went up in flames, although it would of course be highly detrimental to our interests in Egypt, our control of the Suez Canal and our tenure of India. But there's no talk in the bazaars of a new Emerald knocking around in the desert, and if there was, I'm sure that my department in the Foreign Office would know about it."

After luncheon, I loafed into the library to down a *burra peg* of brandy and check on events in the outside world courtesy of the gutter press: *The Times* informed me that the American Inquiry into the *Titanic* cock-up had concluded that White Star, Ismay & Captain Smith were to blame, so no surprises there. There was also a story about how our German cousins had just launched the *Imperator* in Hamburg, with that moustachioed buffoon they call the Emperor announcing it to be the 'biggest liner ever built'. According to 'Our Man in Glasgow', Cunard's new tub the *Aquitania* under construction on the Clyde should have been a foot longer but, according to 'Our Man in Hamburg', not to be outdone the Krauts had stuck a large shite hawk on the prow of *Imperator* making her a short beak longer than *Aquitania*. Is that the way that grown-ups were supposed to behave, I thought? When nations descend to the 'my prick's bigger than yours' school of diplomacy you can be sure there's trouble in the wind.

---

[209] Editor's Note: This was, presumably, John Buchan (1875-1940), diplomat, novelist and later Governor of Canada and 1st Baron Tweedsmuir.

Just as I was settling into a second *peg*, a club servant said that there was a lady asking for me in the hall.

For one mad moment, I thought that Charlotte-Georgina had come up to Town to check on me. But no, the figure standing by the porter's lodge, although her head was draped with a veil, was none other than Shanghai Lily, otherwise known as Fraulein Hilda von Einem. Her top hamper alone, upholstered in what was doubtless another of Madame Lucile's expensive rigs, was quite unmistakable.

"Good mawning, Sir Jathper," she lisped, in her delightful Kraut accent, "I do so apologise faw dithtubbing you, but I have to talk to you. Could you join me in my cawwige faw a few minutes?"

Well, even at ninety-odd you don't turn down an invitation like that, so I barked at the hall porter for my ulster and hobbled out after her delightfully swaying rump, on which, if memory served me right, she had a birthmark on the right cheek — at least it looked like a birthmark from where I was lying at the time, although to be fair she was on t'other side of the steam room and my vision was being interrupted by the rhythmic swaying of a pair of small oriental bristols...

Once inside the carriage, which was closed and with the blinds down, she ordered the coachman to head for the Row, slipped back her veil and gave me a deeply penetrating look from under her abundantly long lashes (even at my age you notice these things, you know) and got straight to the point.

"Sir Jathper, you hold my weputation in yaw hand...."

Actually, I was planning to hold something rather more substantial than that the next time the coach swayed around a corner.

"I said nutting last night," she went on, "but I knew you wemembered where we last met - and I voz zo afwaid that you vould zay something. Von Stumm, of course, knows nothing of my time in ze East."

Without warning, she slid her gloved hand between the folds of my great coat and headed for the sentry box. Now, the guard on duty there may have been dozing more often than not for the past decade, but he immediately sprang to attention.

"But you did not... and I vanted to say, dank you."

Without more ado, she went face-down onto my by now bulging crotch and proceeded, without so much as a by-your-leave, to open my flies, call out the duty sentry and, using her lips, encourage him to discharge his weapon.

Well, I thought, that's one less volley they'll be firing over my coffin. Now, I'm a fast mover but Miss Lily-Hilda had carried out an act that, if the blinds had been up and a Peeler peering in, would have seen her in Holloway with a nod (and a note of her address) from M'Lud with a speed that would have shamed an Apache squaw with a scalping knife. Most women don't, in my experience - which is (as my readers know if they've read this far) extensive - perform that particular drill with any great skill, but Lily-Hilda was an expert having doubtless learned her craft in the knocking shops out East; I've always found that boys do it better. Anyway, the cry of pleasure I let out when she detonated the charge was loud enough to startle the horses, causing the carriage to lurch alarmingly and my seductress almost tumbled into the foot well; thank God, she'd already disengaged. A moment later she was back on the seat next to me, gently dabbing her lips with the corner of a lace-edged handkerchief.

"Now, Sir Jathper, to business." I only just stopped myself from saying that I thought what we had just done was her business. "You see, ve can both do each uzza a fawor."

Ah, so it wasn't my grey whiskers or fearsome, if somewhat historical, reputation that had brought on this sudden urge on her part to get in a practice bout at my expense.

"I need some infawmation."

Hmm, I thought, what's coming next? But all she did was to tell the driver to whip up and return to her hotel. Imagine my surprise when the door of the carriage was opened and I found myself staring at the familiar portico of the Cavendish Hotel. Well, if Ma Lewis let her in the house, Miss Lily was either a *very* high-class tart or she was paying well. Rosa was nowhere to be seen as we went through the hall and up the stairs to madam's room on the first floor, but I knew our arrival would not pass unremarked. Throwing her muff into a corner and removing her hat and veil, Lily adjusted her hair in a mirror and turned to me.

"Sir Jathper, I said in ze cab that ve could help each uzzer, and so ve can. But first, I have been asked by von Stumm to give you this." From inside her bag she pulled out an envelope which looked and sounded as though it was stuffed with cash. "He has asked me to say that this a small dank-you for yaw time to date."

Before I could protest, she'd stuffed the envelope into my breast pocket with no further explanation. Well, thought I, there goes the problem with the Stratton Street drains: I can sort out von Stumm's demand later.

"Second, I vant you to meet a fwiend of mine who is staying in London with His Impewial Highness. You may alweady have seen her and, if not, you will know her. Her name is Magawetha Zelle." I stared blankly back at her for, as far as I knew, I had never heard of the woman. "No? You do not know her? Well, pewaps ze name Mata Hawi means something to you?"[210]

---

[210] Mata Hari (1876-1917).

CHAPTER TWENTY-ONE:
TRICKS OF THE TRADE

Now you're talking, I thought. For the name Mata Hari certainly did mean something to me: she'd been the talk of the clubs for months and not because of her pretty blue eyes neither. She was an 'exotic dancer', whose oriental gyrations and poses would have put the lead back in the pencil of a Turkish harem eunuch. In fact, it was a miracle that she'd not been arrested for indecent exposure and the corruption of public morals; but then I suspect that the Commissioners of Police, in whichever town she was performing, were enthusiastic patrons of Miss Hari either on or off the stage.

What little I knew about her, for I'd not seen her act, had been told to me by Fritz Ponsonby and Johnny Dawson, who had both seen her earlier in the year [1912] in Paris.

"Apparently," said Fritz, "she was born in Holland but, after her father went bust, her parents spilt and she found herself headed for Skid Row. So, at eighteen, she answered a marriage advertisement, shipped herself out East and married a drunken Dutch colonial twice her age. Almost needless to say, the marriage was not a success but, in between bouts of being beaten-up, she learned to wiggle and gyrate oriental-style. Returning to Paris she quickly got herself an agent and a whole posse of paying admirers."

What Fritz didn't say, but I heard later from Johnny Dawson, was that Mata Hari's act was as fake as the Spanish posturing of that whip wielding houri, Mrs Rosanna James of the Monto (better known as Lola Montez or the Countess of Landsfeld).[211]

"But that's neither here nor there," said Johnny, with a wistful look in his eye, "as her rounded rump and bouncing boobies on-stage, and her trick

---

[211] Lola Montez (1821-1861). See *The Speedicut Papers: Book 1 (Flashman's Secret)* et seq.

pelvis off, make up in spades for any lack of authenticity on the boards. She's in Town with her cheque-book-of-the-moment," he went on, "who is none other than The Crown Prince of Germany."

This was the monocled Prussian Princeling I'd met at the Embassy. Punctuality may be the politeness of Princes but, in my experience, so too is the prerogative to poke the best bit of skirt in town. Anyway, so Johnny said, her act had been temporarily suspended, except for purely private performances for HIH, and she was busy spending her way through the Prussian Privy Purse with a style that put all of Bertie's popsies to shame.

"As you may know, Magawetha is in London with His Impewial Highness and she is keen to meet you," Lily continued. "In fact, if it is not inconvenient for you, she will be here shortly."

A few minutes later there was a tap on the door and Rosa poked her head in.

"Som'un to see you, drearie," and, giving me a lewd wink, Rosa ushered in a heavily veiled figure and vanished. She was always discreet, was darling Rosa, but I suspected that she would have her ear to the keyhole for the next few minutes.

"Sir Jathper," growled Miss Lily, "may I intwoduce you to Mrs MacLeod, who you may know better as Mata Hawi?"

The veiled figure extended an expensively gloved and heavily perfumed hand, which I stooped to kiss. Then, with one sweeping movement that was like the beat of an exotic bird's wings, she removed veil, hat and coat and stood there, panting very gently, her hour-glass figure silhouetted against the window and a gleam in her dark eyes that lit up her round face. Momentarily lost for words, for she exuded an aura of naked carnality that I hadn't encountered since I'd first met Lady Randy, I shuffled by feet and tried to take my eyes off her monumental assets.

"Sir Jasper, His Imperial Highness has told me of your terrible ordeal on the *Titanic* and I so wanted to meet you to hear at first hand of that awful night. So many good friends lost… You travelled with dear Benjamin Guggenheim, I believe? Is it true he made sure that his lady travelling companion and her maid were safe and then went and changed into evening dress?"

Well, I could soon confirm that that was indeed what the ridiculous fool had done - and much good it had done him or his valet, who had been obliged to share in the late millionaire's pantomime heroics. We chatted on in a similar vein for half-an-hour or so, whilst Lily hovered in the background. Then, just as I was telling Miss Hari (or should that be houri?) how I had saved myself, Lily cleared her throat.

"I have to go out. Are you happy to be left on your own?"

"That's a damn silly question," I said with gusto. As Lily left, she blew me a kiss and said she would ask Rosa to send up some champagne, which duly arrived.

In Lily's absence we gossiped on, exchanging stories about people we had both known out East and, eventually, Margaretha said she had to be going as the Crown Prince was expecting her at the Savoy and hated to be kept waiting.

"Is there any chance that we could continue our conversation tomorrow night?" she asked. "I have so enjoyed talking to you and there is still so much we have not spoken about."

Needless to say, we agreed to meet back at the Cavendish at six in the evening the next day and, once she was safely out of the door, I tottered down the stairs to Rosa's parlour, as I knew the nosey old trot would expect a report.

"Well, you're in a league abrove your usual, Jasper!" were Rosa's opening words, as she reached for a magnum of fizz and poured me a beaker full. "Quite what you thrink you're bleedin' doin' at your age mixin' with two of the most 'spensive bits of tit-and-arse in London is well breyond me. So, sprit it out afore you get too prissed to remember."

So, I told her, including – since this was Rosa Lewis – Lily's delightful if exhausting attack on me in the carriage, the money and my rendezvous with Miss Hari scheduled for the following evening in her establishment.

"Hmm," said Rosa. "Well, I'd heard from Tom Ribblesdale that that Lily trollop gives great 'ead,[212] but what you're doing with that prainted tart oo calls 'erself Mata Aree, I'm buggered if I can frathom. I would've thought that she was way too 'spensive for you, you old skinflint. Anyway, she's well orf limits now that she's shracked up with that stuffed sausage what calls 'imself a Crown Prince."

"Frankly, Rosa, I've no idea what either of them see in me, except that they all seem keen to hear about my time on the *Titanic* - and who wouldn't?"

"Nah, dearie, there's more to it than that, so you be a good boy and stay on your guard. I know you, with a tit in y'r face and y'r dick in a pussy y'r brains will head straight to your wrinkled old bralls - and gawd only knows what trouble you'll then be in. I suggest you be sensible for a change, forget that Dutch tart and trot off back to Charlotte-Georgina in Wrexham. She may be as cold as a marble statue's cunt, but she'll keep you outta trouble."

She rambled on for a bit longer, but I finally tired of her well-intentioned lecture and staggered out to the pavement to find a hansom, with Rosa's shrill warnings following me into the street.

The next evening, togged up in a new dinner suit that Anderson had said were now all the rage - as if I cared at my age - I tooled over to the Cavendish. As I walked to the rickety lift, which was to take me to the second floor where the Dutch bint had booked a suite, I got a very leery look from Rosa who was lurking, as usual, in her parlour.

---

[212] Thomas Lister, 4th Baron Ribblesdale (1854-1925) was a Liberal politician who was famously painted in 1890 by John Singer Sargent (now in the National Portrait Gallery). He was a rather tragic figure, whose two sons were both killed in battle. He spent a lot of time at the Cavendish Hotel, keeping a permanent room there, and may at some time have been Rosa Lewis's lover. His first wife died in 1911 and he then married in 1919 the widow of Colonel Jacob Astor who had died on RMS *Titanic*.

A minute or two later – for the lift was damnably slow - I tapped on Margaretha's door. She let me in, dressed in a low-cut evening gown that showed her assets off to perfection. Dinner had been laid on a small table in front of a blazing fire and a bottle of fizz was chilling on the sideboard. Even without Rosa's warning, I would have been on my guard as I knew full well that I was about to launch the good ship Speedicut into iceberg strewn waters, and I knew what that could lead to. However, to my surprise the ocean remained calm, the only icebergs to be seen were conjured up by me as I once again retold my tale of disaster, and dinner passed off with all the propriety of a ladies' literary luncheon. But, dear reader, know me. Even at ninety-odd I had another thought on my mind and it wasn't a floating block of ice but something altogether warmer and wetter.

Dinner done, Margaretha rang for it to be cleared away and the brandy brought up. Now, I thought, it was going to be only a short hobble to the finishing line and so it should have been. But, just as Margaretha went around turning down the lamps – no new-fangled electricity for Rosa – and I was unbuttoning my weskit, there was a sharp rap on the door and Rosa stuck her head into the room, puffing like a blown racehorse.

"You better be sharpish, you two; 'is nibs is on the way up in the lift. I tried to 'old 'im, but 'is pecker's up and 'e came over all royal, so I legged it up the strairs to warn you."

She then disappeared and the door closed. Now this, as my readers well know, was not a new experience for me; but at ninety you're not so nimble and window ledges are definitely not to be considered.

"There's a way out to the back stairs through the bathroom," Margaretha hissed, "but you'd better be quick. Go!"

I moved as fast as I could into the connecting bedroom. However, instead of exiting via the bathroom, for some reason I decided that it would be fun to hear Margaretha get out of this fix and so I hid behind the sitting room door, which I left slightly ajar. Chancy, I know, but I wanted to hear how the lissom Dutch bint would cover the situation.

A moment later the oak into the suite opened and I heard her run to it. Judging from the sound of slurping and munching, she had instantly fixed herself like a limpet onto the Prince's face to stifle any outraged remarks that he might have made. What happened next was no surprise, as Miss Margaretha was a professional and knew her business: I heard the unmistakable sounds of buttons popping and shortly thereafter the sounds of royal ecstasy. The job done, and he didn't take long, the Prince fell to prosing in his clipped German, which I had no trouble understanding.

"So, who were you dining with, my dear?" The voice was tense.

"Oh, just that old Englishman who was on the *Titanic*... I wanted to hear more about what happened..." She sounded as though her mouth was full again.

"Interesting." The voice had relaxed somewhat. "Well, you know, von Stumm has been trying to get an altogether different tale out of him, but to no avail... Aah, that is good... Von Einen also tried and, although she has given him some money, she too thinks she will fail as the old man is obviously on his guard. I wonder. I wonder... Please just stop for a moment... Do you think he might be susceptible to your charms, my dear?"

There were more sounds of sucking, some further exhausted sighs from the by-now spent princeling and then Margaretha spoke:

"He's very old." Damned cheek! "But Hilda said that he still has *some* life in him." I should think so too: at least nine occasionally stiff inches.

"Really? Well, I think you should arrange to see him again, for we believe he has a piece of information that is vital to the future of our beloved Fatherland." The sucking stopped.

"And what might that be?"

And to my surprise he proceeded to tell her the story of my time as a guest of the mad mullah, the legend of Greenmantle and the bollocks about the coming of the Emerald to raise the stinking masses in a great Jihad.

"We have reason to believe," he went on, "that The Mahdi had a son and we think that this Englishman not only knows this but also knows where he is hiding." What? That was complete bollocks. I knew no such thing. "If we can but find him, we have our Emerald and we can pursue our plan to raise the Mohammedans in a great holy war that will drive the British from Egypt, the Canal and India, whilst we secure control of Europe." God, I thought, will those damned Krauts never give up their ambition to be *Deutschland über Alles*? "You must use all your charms, my dear, and I mean *all* your charms, to get this information from him. Can you bring yourself to do that?"

I did not wait to hear her response, but quietly slipped out of the Cavendish via the bathroom and the backstairs, into a hansom cab and back to the Verulam. The following morning saw me and Fahran on the train to Wrexham and Charlotte-Georgina's safe but chilly embrace. I knew trouble when I heard it and, as I have stated often enough before, I have done more than my bit for King, Country and the Brotherhood and I had no intention in my twilight years of doing one jot more; even if the reward would be a spectacular evening or two sampling Mata Hari's undoubted skills. So, I wrote to Flashy in his new role as GB, and told him to find another Brother to track down this threat to our national security. Meanwhile, I was back in the warm and secure embrace of my study in Wales – and that's where I intended to stay.

. . .

Editor's Note: Judging from the contents of the last few letters in the Ashby find, which recommence two years later in 1914, it would seem that Flashman, in his role as the Great Boanerges, did indeed allow Speedicut to give up his pursuit of the threat posed to the British Empire by Hilda von Einem, Major von Stumm and their search for the Emerald, for there is no further mention of them in the remaining letters. My research has uncovered the fact that the task was, instead, assigned to the Hon Sandy Arbuthnot who, one presumes, was also a member of the Brotherhood.[213]

---

[213] See *Greenmantle* by John Buchan.

262 |

However, Speedicut was not to be allowed to see out the remainder of his days in complete tranquillity for, once again, the hydra heads connected to the death of the Duke of Clarence re-grew. As readers of The Speedicut Papers *will know, earlier letters have established that the Brotherhood was prepared to go to considerable lengths to keep the true facts of the death of The Duke of Clarence out of the public domain, including manipulating the legal system to silence peripheral or associated witnesses such as Oscar Wilde. One witness, however, would appear to have escaped the immediate attention of the Brotherhood: Nurse Edith Cavell.[214] The narrative resumes in June 1914.*

...

C-G was determined to attend a Court, so we were down in London for a few weeks where, shortly after our arrival, I received a rather unexpected letter from Flashy in his role as GB which had been forwarded to Stratton Street from Wrexham. A bit late in the day, I responded to him saying that, of course, I remembered the Cavell gal and who could ever forget Madame Margaretha Zelle – the curvaceous Mata Hari of the trick pelvis and bouncing boobies, to say nothing of her other charms and accomplishments. But, as I wrote back, I was not at all clear at the connection he'd made between the two of them. Yes, he'd stated plainly enough that the Dutch bint was thought by our intelligence boys to be working (presumably flat on her back) for the sausage-eaters. He'd also spelled out, in words of one syllable, that Miss Cavell was now a fully paid-up member of our Secret Service and had been 'placed' in Brussels as a British 'sleeper' in the event that the Krauts ever did precisely what the

---

[214] Nurse Edith Cavell (1865 – 1915). Speedicut's letters covering the death of the Duke of Clarence hint that Nurse Cavell, who had been sent to Sandringham on the orders of the Great Boanerges and remained there at the request of Dr Broadbent (a member of the Brotherhood), had played a role in the Prince's death. This proposition takes on greater significance when one realises that Nurse Cavell did not actually start training as a medical nurse until 1905-6. Prior to that, she had been a children's nurse or governess to a succession of families, including the Whitehalls for whom she probably started working in 1888 or 1889. Following the death of The Duke of Clarence in 1892, Nurse Cavell resumed working as a governess and from 1900-1905 lived in Brussels, where she worked for a Belgian family. In 1905, she returned to England where she studied to be a nurse. On completion of her training, she returned to Brussels and remained there until her execution in 1915.

Schlieffen Plan envisaged and took out Belgium on their way to Paris.[215] What I couldn't get my ancient head to comprehend was the connection between the two and what precisely it was that the Brotherhood wanted from me.

Whilst I waited for a reply, I read in *The Times* that poor old Franz-Ferdinand of Austria and his Hungarian mistress had been shot in Sarajevo by a Serb anarchist.[216] As I said to Charlotte-Georgina, I wouldn't have put it past the *schnitzels* to invade Serbia as a reprisal. Thank God, I added to myself, it was all happening on the other side of Europe or, before you could say Edward Grey,[217] we'd all be embroiled in the *fracas* and that would have really upset the Season and turned the breakfast butter rancid.

...

A couple of weeks later, as the dogs of war in central Europe started barking, I received a reply from Flashy. It appeared that darling Margaretha was playing *both* sides of the political blanket - whilst, at the same time, making an unspecified demand on the Brotherhood - and that Miss Cavell, she of the steely eye and the 'keep your hands to yourself my lad' manner, was her Secret Service controller. Well, that was a marriage of opposites if ever I'd seen one, but then common sense never was the Foreign Office's strong suit. Anyway, because I was one of the few people still standing who knew both of them, Flashy ordered me to meet up with Miss Margaretha in Paris, check that she was playing us straight and find out what it was that she wanted from the Brotherhood. So, I told him that if he was able to lay-on an all-expenses, First Class round-trip to gay Paree I'd be willing to do my duty to King, Country and – of course – the

---

[215] The Schlieffen Plan was the strategic plan for the German invasion of France via the Low Countries. It was formulated by Count Alfred von Schlieffen in 1905 and subsequently modified by the German General Staff. The existence of the plan was known to British intelligence.

[216] HIH Archduke Franz-Ferdinand of Austria (1863-1914) and his morganatic wife, the Duchess of Hohenberg (*née* Countess Sophie Chotek) (1868-1914), were assassinated on 28th June 1914.

[217] Sir Edward Grey (later 1st Viscount Grey of Fallodon) Bt KG PC FZL DL (1862 –1933).

264|

Brotherhood and try and find out what the loose-hipped Dutch trot had got on her mind.

Meanwhile, as I'd predicted to C-G, it looked as though the Austrians were going to have a bash at Serbia, although a Russian mobilisation might, of course, have made them think twice.[218] In my considered view at the time, it was a lot of fuss over nothing: Franz-Josef had another perfectly serviceable heir, unencumbered with a morganatic wife,[219] and, anyway, he (F-J, that is) wouldn't have known what to do with Serbia even if he could have annexed it without Nicky unleashing his Cossacks.

On the last day of July [1914] a man from Thomas Cook's delivered to Stratton Street a package containing two tickets for the next day's Boat Train and a reservation at the Ritz.

---

[218] On 23rd July 1914, Austro-Hungary delivered a deliberately unacceptable ultimatum to Serbia. On 24th July, Russia ordered a mobilization in the Odessa region and on 25th July Serbia mobilized despite accepting all but one of the terms of the Austro-Hungarian ultimatum the following day. Austro-Hungary broke off diplomatic relations with Serbia on 26th July and declared war on Serbia on 28th July. Editor's Note: As Speedicut's letter does not mention Russia's mobilization against Austria-Hungary on 29th July and on the 30th against Germany it must have been written just before the events which made the First World War inevitable.
[219] HIM The Emperor Franz-Josef of Austria-Hungary (1830-1916); HIH The Archduke Karl (later HIM The Emperor Karl I of Austria-Hungary) (1887-1922).

CHAPTER TWENTY-TWO: ONCE MORE UNTO THE BREACH...

Editor's Note: It seems appropriate in this, the final chapter, for me to leave Speedicut's account in its original format.

...

Ritz Hotel, Paris, France, November 1914

I have done as you [Flashman] directed and met up with Mata H. Despite this damned silly and utterly unnecessary war, she has had no trouble crossing frontiers as she is a neutral – at least that's what her passport says – and, after a fairly intense discussion with her, during which we both kept our feet on the floor, I'm reasonably sure that she is playing us, rather than the Germans, straight.

Of course, since the Kraut juggernaut rolled through Belgium, I have been unable to get to see Miss Cavell, but Margaretha tells me that she is safe and secure in her hospital in Brussels from where she is already running an escape route for our boys via Holland. There is a possibility that MH, who thinks that I am here on Secret Service business, may be able to get me across the border as part of a diplomatic mission, but don't hold your breath.

I have not yet tested the water with Margaretha on the other task you have given me as it would compromise my ostensible reason for being in Paris. I think that should wait until I have returned from seeing Miss Cavell. Anyway, MH is currently out-of-town, so I'm just going to have to go on spending the Brotherhood's money on foie gras and fizz until she gets back, whenever that might be.

...

Les Trois Rois, Basel, Switzerland, January 1915

Don't ever think to accuse me of prizing my own hide over that of the interest of the Country or the Brotherhood. For I have just spent the past two weeks behind enemy lines and I am lucky to be able to tell you the tale.

In my last letter, I said that MH had an idea to sneak me into Belgium as part of a diplomatic mission. Whilst that might have been possible when the front line was fluid, before I could make my move both sides had settled down to a stalemate with uniformed Brits, Frogs and Krauts digging trenches like demented moles. So, the chances of getting across the opposing front lines in one piece went from slim to zero.

Margaretha said that, despite this, there were still two routes open - by boat from neutral Bilbao to Ostend or by train via Switzerland. In the interests of speed, no pun intended, I decided to brave the sea route and the submarines. Thanks to Brother Bertie,[220] our Embassy obtained false papers for me for the outward-bound journey in the name of Hercule Velo, an ancient Belgy, and the cover story was that I was travelling back to Belgium with my daughter (MH, who else?) in order to end my days in the land of my birth. The return leg would see me posing as a decrepit Dutchman with a business in Bern. Unfortunately, for my comfort and security, the Embassy wallahs drew the line at forging papers for Fahran, so he was left to guard my kit in Paris.

MH and I set off from Paris by train in tolerable comfort as, thanks to the diplomatic pansies in the Faubourg Saint-Honoré, we had a double berth on a *wagons lits* reserved for us (the trains are all standing room only since war broke out) and we duly trundled from Paris to the Spanish border without incident, beyond – that is - Margaretha's demand to share the lower bunk with me on the pretext that it was cold. Quite what the steward would have thought if he had walked in on us, God only knows, but Margaretha insisted that we had unfinished business and would brook no argument (well, mild protest) from me. How she managed to get (and keep) me at Attention I'm not sure, but she did. Of course, she's a professional: whether my heart would stand the strain was another matter

---

[220] Sir Francis Bertie (1844-1919), later 1st Viscount Bertie of Thame, was the British Ambassador in Paris from 1905 to 1918.

altogether. However, as she undid my braces and slid down my bags, I decided it would make no difference to my time in Eternity if I were to meet St Peter, or the other chap, with a grin on my face; I was still smirking when the train pulled into Bilbao. One of these days some clever chemist will invent a pill to get and keep us old soldiers at the Salute: then the gals will have to lock up their knickers. Meanwhile, I suppose we will have to continue to take ground pearl and suffer the appalling indigestion that goes with it.

Anyway, the fact that I hardly had the energy to walk after MH's carnal ministrations was no problem, as we had decided that my cover would be enhanced if I was to adopt a semi-comatose wheelchair-bound state. For once in my life this did not require any degree of pretence, for the hour spent alternately with MH's boobs and bum in my face had left me in a state of semi-collapse!

There's not much to Bilbao, as the railway only got there towards the end of the last century of sacred memory, and it certainly had no hotels to match even the worst in Bognor, but we found a tolerably clean *pensione* on the edge of a strange, English-style park that looked absurdly out of place in the town.[221]

We didn't have long to wait before being able to join a Spanish coaster that was running olive oil from Spain into the Low Countries, on which we travelled as supercargo. MH had managed to get us on board by the simple expedient of promising the greasy dago Captain that she would show him the best time he had ever known if he gave us passage.

By the time we landed in Ostend, *El Capitano* was a shadow of his former self and I'd had sufficient time to recover my energy levels, having had the cabin largely to m'self. MH got a rousing cheer from the crew when she wheeled me down the gangplank, so I wouldn't be at all surprised if

---

[221] Editor's Note: The Doña Casilda Iturrizar Park is located in the district of Abando, near the city centre and covers an area of 21 acres. It is an English-style garden designed by Ricardo Bastida and was opened to the public in 1907. It was named after a local benefactress who donated the grounds to the city

she had shown some of them a good time too. As we were sailing under a neutral flag we had no problems with our boys in dark blue, who seemed to have command of the Channel. The problems only started when we landed.

You know my views on the Krauts, so I won't repeat them; all I can tell you is that war has not improved our corseted cousins. The form-filling, pass-checking and general officiousness was endless. I think it must have taken us the best part of the day to get through the checks and even the sight of MH's plunging and perfumed cleavage, which she had been careful to put on prominent display, seemed to make no difference. However, to cut a long and extremely tedious story short, we finally got to *la gare* and were able to squeeze me, the wheel chair and MH into a Third Class carriage on a train bound for Brussels that was full to bursting with stinking Belgies; personal hygiene has never been the Belgians' strong suit and the stink was made worse by the excess of garlic and cheap cigarettes on which they seem to exist. After several hours, during which the train travelled at a snail's pace and we were nearly asphyxiated, we pulled into Brussels, grabbed a broken-down horse-drawn cab that was almost as bad as the train, and checked into a half-decent hotel just off the Grand Place, observing on our way there that half the Kraut Army seems to be stationed in the city.

Later that evening Miss Cavell, to whom MH had sent a message, joined us in our suite. Being, technically at least, an 'enemy alien' she has to be very careful with whom she is seen and so had sneaked-in through the staff entrance and up the back stairs. She seemed well, although her ice maiden air was, if anything, more pronounced and she gave a very obvious sniff at the sight of the double bed in the adjoining room: I assume she is still *virgo intacta*, at least as far as our sex is concerned.

I had agreed with MH that she would give Miss C and me some time on our own together 'to discuss Foreign Office business' and so, after a few minutes, MH made an excuse that she needed to see the manager and swept out of the room. I decided that, as time was short, I should get straight to the point.

"Edith, m'dear," I said, "I'm *not* here on government business but on behalf of an organisation that is well-known to you."

She stiffened somewhat, if that was possible within her excessively starched nurse's outfit, but said nothing.

"I am tasked by this organisation with askin' you a simple question."

She still said nowt but I could see she was on her guard.

"I am not goin' to beat about the bush, m'dear. Is it true that you have expressed certain views to our friend Miss Zelle relatin' to the untimely demise of the late Duke of Clarence, views that would seem to implicate in his death the organisation I have made my way here at considerable danger to represent?"

Still she said nothing, so I ploughed on.

"If it is true, then I'm sure that I don't need to tell you that such views are entirely misplaced, should never again be repeated and, indeed, you should take the earliest opportunity to correct them with the person to whom they were vouchsafed. To do otherwise might make your position here in Brussels, shall we say, difficult? Is that clear?"

Cavell nodded but again said nothing, although I could see that the message had sunk home for what little colour there had been in her angular cheeks had drained away and she started to fiddle nervously with the edge of her apron. It was a damned awkward situation, but at last she cleared her throat.

"Sir Jasper, what you assert is indeed true – but there is an explanation. I am, as you know, resident here in Brussels at the express wish of His Majesty's government. Not only have I established an effective escape route for those of our boys who manage to find their way to my hospital, but I am also, as you know, 'running' Miss Zelle.

"What you may not know is that Miss Zelle was actually fully committed to the enemy and it took considerable persuasion on my part to turn her – and money played a major role in that exercise."

She did not say what other levers she had pulled, but I had my suspicions that the contents of MH's knickers may have played their part.

"The government funds that were available to me were extremely limited," she continued, "and were wholly inadequate for the task I had been given, so I decided to put the interests of my country before those of your organisation…"

"And?" I asked.

"And I readily admit that I gave Miss Zelle certain very limited information that I knew she would be able to convert into financial reward. It was a question of the greater good. I did not lightly disclose these confidences but only after much thought about what was in the best interests of my country. If I did wrong, then I will stand the consequences – but my *duty* has always been clear to me and my conscience is clear."

With that she got up, gave me a very steely look, smoothed down her apron and reached for her cloak. Well, she's got balls, I'll say that for her. She couldn't have made a cleaner confession and, as the damage had been done, there was really nothing more that I could say or do. We bade each other a fairly frosty goodnight and she left the room. Sometime later MH returned. I told her that I had concluded my business with Miss C and all that remained was to get me back to Paris in one piece. We had already agreed that I would return to Fahran and the City of Sin via the overland route through Switzerland, whilst she was going-on to Berlin before making her way back to Paris.

So, the following morning, after further endless checks at *la gare*, I boarded a train bound for Bern via the border crossing at Basel. This time I managed to get m'self a First Class compartment, but I had the 'joy' of sharing it with five members of the Prussian High Command. Unfortunately, as you may recall from an unfortunate incident on my way to Bokhara when the world was a damned sight younger,[222] I'm prone to talking in my sleep and, at my advanced age, I seem to be spending a fair amount of time dozing. However, surrounded by the Fatherland's finest, I was determined to stay awake. But the swaying of the carriage combined with the heat of the train and the Krauts' cigars pushed me, despite my best efforts, into the arms of Morpheus... I was rudely awakened to find myself looking into the cold face of an Austrian Colonel with a shaven head, duelling scar and monocle.

"Permit me to introduce myself," he said in perfect, but somewhat clipped English, "my name is Colonel Graf von Harath of His Imperial Majesty's General Staff attached to the German Legation in Brussels.[223] And you, sir, are?"

As I was unaware of what I had been dreaming, I had no idea what I had said, although it seemed reasonable to assume that I had spoken in English: I may be ninety-odd, but there's nothing wrong with my wits even if the rest of me has slowed to a greater or lesser extent in the last couple of years. With sickening clarity, I realised that I was going to have to bluff for all I was worth as my life clearly depended on it.

"I am a Dutch citizen, Herr Oberst," I replied in my best German, "returning to my family in Bern where we have a business."

"Show me your papers!" he demanded.

I passed them to him and, after a minute or two, he appeared to be satisfied. However, after practically throwing them back at me, he strutted out of the compartment.

"Keep a close eye on this gentleman," he instructed his colleagues as he left.

Some minutes later von Harath returned with an elderly civilian who, it emerged, was with the railway police. Von Harath addressed him in

[222] See *The Speedicut Papers: Book 1 (Flashman's Secret)*.
[223] Editor's Note: There is no record of an Austrian family by the name of von Harath; the nearest I could find is the ancient Bohemian family of von Harrach.

German with the usual sneering tone of an officer to a mere policeman that implied the Peeler wasn't fit to even lick the Colonel's boots.

"Herr Schicklgruber,[224] this gentleman claims to be a Dutch citizen on his way back to his family and his business in Switzerland, but my colleagues and I distinctly heard him muttering in English in his sleep. His papers seem to me to be in order, but…"

The Austrian signed for me to give the policeman my Dutch passport, the *laissez passer* that MH had wheedled out of the sausage eaters' Legation and my rail ticket. He glanced over them and then told von Harath that he needed to consult with his colleague. I spent the next hour in a frenzy of fear and foreboding, which was not improved when Schicklgruber returned.

"You will, please, to follow me," he said in German.

I dutifully shuffled down the corridor after him and, several carriages later, found myself in a compartment that had been turned into an office. There was a desk, with a powerful desk lamp and two chairs, one each side, on one of which was seated the most sinister cove I have seen this side of the Hindu Kush. Youngish, squat and with slicked-back black hair he had a pencil shaped moustache and wore a pair of steel rimmed *pince nez* clamped to his nose, behind which his dead black shark-like eyes flicked over my papers. To say that he exuded menace and danger would be a very considerable understatement. Without looking up, he signed to me to sit whilst he continued to riffle through my passport. Then, without warning, he flipped the shade of the lamp so that I was temporarily blinded by its glare. I protested, but he curtly told me to shut up. After what seemed like an hour, but it was probably only minutes, he started to question me.

"Herr de Leeuw – if, indeed, that is your name - whilst your papers appear to be in order, there remains the curious matter of your sleep-talking. Are you familiar with the English language?"

---

[224] Editor's Note: It is tempting to speculate that this was Alöis Schicklgruber, the father of Adolf Hitler, who was a customs official – but, unfortunately for historical symmetry - he died in 1903.

I replied that, like most of my fellow countrymen, I was fluent in several European languages including English, French and German. I ventured by way of explanation the old joke that, after all, who the hell spoke Dutch? It didn't elicit even a glimmer of a smile from my interrogator.

"It is my view," he continued in his clipped German, "that you are not a Dutchman – but an English spy. Whilst you may be fluent in many languages, it is a fact that people dream in their native tongue. It seems to me that you are damned out of your own mouth." He paused. "I have neither the time nor the resources to examine you further on this train, but when we arrive at the border, which will be very soon, you will be taken to a place where I will have, shall we say, the 'facilities' to persuade you to tell me the truth. Unless, of course, you wish to save me the trouble and confess your true identity now so that we can be shot of you – and I mean that quite literally – as soon as possible. The eventual outcome will be the same, but you will spare yourself a great deal of unnecessary pain in the meantime if you co-operate now."

Although my ancient innards were dissolving, I decided that I had no option but to continue my bluff and I informed him, with the greatest control I could muster, that I refused to say another word until I had seen the nearest Dutch Consul. He shrugged his shoulders and told Schicklgruber to take me to the next-door compartment and hold me there until we reached the border at Basel. As I left the compartment, he called out in English:

"Good luck!"

Well, I may be an old codger, but that is one trick for which I was prepared: it is, as you may not know, the oldest device in the interrogator's book. I turned slowly and said in my best German:

"Your English is excellent, sir. Perhaps it is you who should be subjected to interrogation."

Before he could recover, I was out of the compartment and back in the care of Herr Schicklgruber. I spent the next half-hour with my mind in turmoil, for there seemed no escape. Just as I was starting to despair, the train suddenly lurched, the lights dimmed and I heard the shrill scream of the brakes. The train juddered to a halt, the lights flickered back-on again and my companion left my temporary prison to find out what was going on. There were shouts now from all around and, whilst I couldn't make out what was going on, I realised that no one was watching me. So, I slipped out of the door, glanced into my interrogator's lair which was empty, save for my papers which were still lying on the desk. I grabbed them and headed for the nearest carriage door.

A quick glance up the track showed me that the train's progress had been halted by a cow, lit by the engine's headlights, serenely grazing between the rails. Beyond her were the bright lights of Basel station. I didn't hesitate for a second, but forced my old pins to get me down onto the track, into the cover of darkness and thence to the station.

Whilst in the shadows I passed the head of the train and saw that the *pikelhaubes* were arguing about how to move the cow. One of them, losing patience, got out his pistol and shot the poor beast in the head. Of course, it collapsed on the tracks and then friend Kraut had to work out how to move half-a-ton of dead milker off the track. And they call themselves the Master Race.

However, the pointless execution of a poor, innocent cow and the ensuing confusion gave me the time to make my way slowly into the station marshalling yard, all the Kraut guards having been ordered to the train to help move the bovine blockade. From there I got onto the platform, mingled with the crowd and slowly made my way through passport and military control on both sides of the border.

Although I was now safe on Swiss soil, I had nothing more than my papers, some cash and the clothes I stood up in. I was, however, free. I decided that my first stop should be a stiff drink, followed by a bath and bed, so I hailed a cab and told him to take me to the best hotel in town. This turned out to be this great mausoleum of a place. Anyway, I secured a room, ordered a very large brandy and sent a telegram to Brother Bertie in Paris telling him to instruct our consulate in Basel to look after me, which he and they duly did.

...

Ritz Hotel, Paris, France, February 1915

I overheard something quite extraordinary at the bar of this hotel last evening: it seems that our esteemed (not by me) First Lord of the Admiralty, otherwise known as Lady Randy's eldest pup or The Rt Hon Mr Winston Leonard Spencer Churchill, has a grandiose plan to use the Mediterranean Fleet to force the Hellespont, land a load of colonials on the beaches at Gallipoli, storm Constantinople and knock Johnny Turk out of the military equation. This will be followed by an advance through Eastern Europe to take Berlin in the rear (something the late Baron 'Fruity' von Einem knew all about) and so end the war. It's an absurd idea and can't possibly work: if I know about it so will the Grand Mufti, who will deploy thousands of bollock-less Janissaries to drive Britannia's boys back into the briny before then can get a grip on *terra firma*. There will, however, be a silver lining to this appalling folly: when it fails, as it is bound to, Churchill will have to fall upon his sword and will never be heard of again.

We may also be about to see the demise of another of my least favourite officers: that stuck up deviant, Kitchener.[225] Johnny Dawson who, despite his age and arthritis, keeps his ear as close to the ground as he can from a bath chair, has written to tell me that French is plotting to have K of K discredited and dismissed from his comfortable armchair in the War House.[226] Of course, French has loathed Kitchener since the Boer business and has been looking for an opportunity to discredit the bugger ever since K was made Secretary of State for War. The means to topple the brute is the apparent lack of shells on the Western Front, the production of which - along with recruiting - is his political responsibility. Apparently, so Johnny wrote, French has passed a load of highly sensitive information on the subject to some fellow on *The Times* and, for good measure, to that

---

[225] Field Marshal the Earl Kitchener KG, KP, GCB, OM, GCSI, GCMG, GCIE, ADC, PC (1850-1916), Secretary of State for War (1914-1916).
[226] Field Marshal Sir John French KP GCB OM GCVO KCMG ADC PC (1852 – 1925), later Viscount then Earl of Ypres, C-in-C British Expeditionary Force (1914-1915).

socialist leak-eating politico and Churchill's best friend, Lloyd George,[227] plus a brace of Tory grandees. It would appear that the documents place the blame for the drop-shorts having nothing to fire at the Krauts firmly in the lap of Herbert K. French clearly wants to exchange his cushy billet in France for an even cushier one in Whitehall.[228] Well, I hope he succeeds - the fall of my two least favourite Cabinet Ministers would make for a very jolly start to the Spring Offensive, otherwise known as the London Season.

From the opening bars of this letter you will gather that, after the horrors of my recent journey around the Continent, I'm back in the warm embrace of Mr Ritz's establishment in the Place Vendome and the tender care of Fahran, although he will have to return to London ahead of me as I have received a telegram from C-G informing that old Prissy Khazi, his mother, is dying.

A couple of days ago, I also heard – this time from the excellent Hall Porter here, who knows everything that's going on in your former place of exile - that Miss Margaretha was back in town and I saw her yesterday. I had already decided that the time was right to broach the subject of my real mission and this I duly did.

Unfortunately, I don't bring you good news: she has a price for her silence on the subject of the demise of the late and unlamented PAV. There is, however, a reason for this: the last couple of years have not been very kind

---

[227] The Rt Hon David Lloyd-George MP (1863-1945), Chancellor of the Exchequer and, from May 1915, Minister of Munitions then Secretary of State for War (1916) and later that year, Prime Minister.

[228] Editor's Note: This affair was known as the 'Shells Scandal'. Speedicut's analysis of it may be correct but, in any event, it was undoubtedly a conspiracy by French, Lieutenant Colonel Charles Repington of *The Times* and several politicians to discredit Kitchener or even have him sacked. It led to the removal of munitions production from the War Office to a new Ministry run by Lloyd-George, an effective demotion for Kitchener, and contributed to the fall of Asquith's Liberal government later in the year. It did not, however, advance French's career; he was removed as C-in-C of the BEF at the end of 1915 and appointed C-in-C Home Forces, a substantial demotion for which he was compensated with a Viscountcy.

to Miss MH. Her stage act has, of late, had very few takers and the rather battered state of her nether regions, as I know from first-hand experience, means that her premium in the flesh market has been dropping faster than her knickers. Consequently, she no longer has a queue of Crown Princes dancing attendance upon her or lining up for her favours. Instead, she is having to share the sheets with middle-ranking officers on both sides of the line, to say nothing of ageing ex-courtiers and the Captains of tugboats. Like many of her fellow *grandes horizontales*, who have spent like a sailor in port rather than saved as they should (La Belle Otero being the notable exception) Miss MH has suddenly woken up to the fact that, with her currency in a nose dive, she is unlikely to be able to maintain her life style beyond the date when her customers will opt for less well-aged meat. And she has no intention of taking the veil as Liane de Pougy is always threatening.[229]

Now, however, she finds herself in, as she sees it, a most 'advantageous position' thanks to Edith C's indiscretions: to spell it out, she wants no less than one hundred thousand gold sovs to keep her mouth shut. Of course, she thinks that in me she is dealing with the Keeper of the Bullion at the Bank of England rather than the aged emissary of the Brotherhood and, at the moment, I have not disabused her. But there will come a time when I will have to tell her and then who knows what will happen. I would welcome your instructions.

...

Editor's Note: The letter that follows is the last in the ninth bundle of The Speedicut Papers.

...

Ritz Hotel, Paris, France, March 1915

---

[229] Carolina Otero (1868-1965), known as La Belle Otero, accumulated millions and retired in style, but she became addicted to gambling and died in poverty. Liane de Pougy (1869-1950), later Princess Ghika, became a nun after the death of her son in the First World War.

My dear Flashy

Or should I say Great Boanerges, for the tone of your last letter hardly reflected our eighty-odd years of friendship? Well, perhaps the time for honest speaking has come at last. In plain words, I have to inform you that I have no intention of disposing, as you so delicately put it, of Miss MH nor do I have any intention, at my advanced age, of again risking the run into Kraut-occupied Belgium to silence Miss Cavell.

Let me tell you why.

In the first instance, even if she is getting a bit long in the tooth and her principal attractions have lost their former elasticity, MH is still – as I know full well - a prime piece of womanhood and a valuable asset to the Allied cause. Her removal would not only be unjust, it would also be unpatriotic and a damned waste of a great lay.

As to Miss Cavell, as far as I know her knees have never been parted so I can't use that defence on her behalf, but she has been a loyal tool of the Brotherhood and the fact that she felt obliged for, as she put it: 'the greater good', to disclose old facts that we would rather keep buried is insufficient reason to send her on an unjust and untimely journey to the great beyond. Besides which, I know that the escape route that she is running is highly effective and that she is in considerable personal danger as its coordinator. I may not have warmed to her, but La Cavell is not only a brave woman but a patriot and I'm not risking my aged carcass to eliminate her on behalf of the Brotherhood when she is doing such a fine job for her Country.

It also seems to me that what you propose is at odds with the penultimate clause of our Oath which, may I remind you, is to seek out and destroy the enemies of our Sovereign not to eliminate some of the Country's prime assets, particularly during a time of war. So, if you are still convinced that the termination of both ladies is desirable and necessary you are going to have to find someone else to do your dirty work.

As for me, I'm returning on the first boat train I can get on. It is my intention to travel to London where I'm planning to have luncheon with

Sibella Holland and (although he doesn't know he is) my young son, Charles Holland, who will be down from Eton for the Easter holidays. I will dine later with my nephew, Brother Whitehall who, I hope, will then pour me onto a train headed for Wrexham, where I intend to sit out the rest of the war (and however much of my life remains to me) with a barrel of the Emperor's finest, C-G, Fahran, Atash and Ivan – and Dorothea, Dimitri and my grandchildren if only I can persuade them to see sense and leave Russia.

One last thing: I hereby resign from the Brotherhood.

Sincerely

Speed

...

EPILOGUE
by the Editor

What happened next can only be a matter of conjecture. However, based on my knowledge of all the parties involved, I'm led to certain conclusions, which may also provide answers to the mystery of the bones and other artefacts unearthed at Ashby-de-la-Zouch with which this whole saga started.[230]

My first conclusion is that Charles Hadfield, 10th Duke of Whitehall, had at some point after acceding to the title been inducted into the Brotherhood by Flashman because he knew of the 10th Duke's murderous capabilities. In this regard, my researches have uncovered the fact that a memoir, written in prison by the 10th Duke prior to his (later annulled) execution, went mysteriously missing from his effects at the time of his release. It is possible that the prison's governor, Colonel Horniman, was a member of the Brotherhood and later passed it to Flashman in his new role as the Great Boanerges. It is also possible that Colonel Horniman was related to the author, Roy Horniman (1874-1930), and alerted him to the contents of the memoir as the FitzCharles saga bears some resemblance to the plot of *Israel Rank: The Autobiography of a Murderer* by Roy Horniman, published in 1907.

If I am right in this conclusion then my second conclusion is even more credible, which is that over dinner in London the Duke of Whitehall persuaded Speedicut to break his journey at Flashman's house in Leicestershire. There, on the instructions of Flashman, the Duke bound and murdered Speedicut, probably knocking him out with the Brotherhood's ceremonial mace, then cutting his throat with a dagger and burying him along with all the incriminating evidence. It is also possible that it was Flashman who committed the murder but, as he was by then in his nineties, I think that is unlikely.

---

[230] See *The Speedicut Papers: Book 1 (Flashman's Secret)*.

I am less sure about my third conclusion, which is that the presence in the grave of the dagger and the broken ceremonial mace indicates that, with this elimination of such a long-serving member, Flashman decided to end the Brotherhood. I think it more likely, given later events, that if the mace and the dagger were the instruments of execution and, with the mace broken by the violent blow which incapacitated or eliminated the ageing Speedicut, Flashman and Whitehall decided to bury them along with the other incriminating evidence – and the Brotherhood continues in existence.

My next conclusion is pure speculation. However, given what I have learned about the reach of the Brotherhood, it is virtually evidence based. It is this: that the execution of both Mata Hari and Nurse Edith Cavell were encompassed by the Brotherhood. The arrest of Edith Cavell on 3rd August 1915 on a charge of treason (the actual offence was smuggling Allied soldiers out of Belgium) was clearly the result of a tip-off to the German authorities and, once charged, her execution was a foregone conclusion. When the First Secretary of the US Legation in Brussels protested to the German Minister in Brussels, Baron von der Lancken, that the execution of Nurse Cavell would cause an outcry in the United States a colleague, Lieutenant Colonel Count Franz von Harrach (this may have been the officer who accosted Speedicut on the train to Basel and who Speedicut identified as von Harath), allegedly said that his only regret was that there were not 'three or four English old women to shoot'. Von Harrach was formerly Equerry to the Archduke Franz-Ferdinand and was with him when the Archduke and his morganatic wife were assassinated. This, perhaps, explains the Count's hard-line attitude. It has also recently emerged, and is confirmed in *The Speedicut Papers*, that Nurse Cavell was a Secret Intelligence Service operative, although whether or not the Germans knew this remains a mystery.

What is not a mystery, and is indeed now also on the public record, is that Mata Hari's arrest and trial by the French in 1917 was on the basis of trumped-up charges of spying for the Germans; she was found guilty and shot by firing squad on 15th October 1917. These two executions would have been a very tidy method of silencing the two women in a way that could not have incriminated the Brotherhood.

Finally, there is the question of an explanation for the disappearance of Speedicut. Clearly, not even in wartime does a prominent nonagenarian Baronet go missing without comment. Flashman, possibly aided by Whitehall, must have organised a cover-up that would at the very least satisfy the Speedicut family; I decided to search the public records for 1915 to see if there was any evidence for this. The answer lay in a recently released document in the Public Records Office archives in the shape of a memorandum written by Lord Bertie, the British Ambassador in Paris, to the Foreign Secretary, Sir Edward Grey. It was the cover-up that I was looking for – and it had all the hallmarks, particularly in the sign-off, of the Brotherhood of the Sons of Thunder:

TOP SECRET

British Embassy
Paris

5th April 1915

Sir

It is with great regret that I have to report the death of Colonel Sir Jasper Speedicut, Bart, KCVO etc.

As you know, although of a great age, Sir Jasper had agreed to come to Paris to assist with the exposure of a suspected foreign agent, Madame Margaretha MacLeod, known to the public as Mata Hari. Sir Jasper ingratiated himself with Mme MacLeod and, we believe, was in the process of procuring valuable information from her at the time of his death. Unfortunately, the exertions involved in this task proved too much for Sir Jasper and he was discovered on 1st inst. by a chambermaid in the bedroom of Mme MacLeod at the Ritz Hotel, Mme MacLeod having left the hotel the previous evening for Madrid.

The Embassy surgeon, with the agreement of the French authorities, has performed a post mortem examination and declared that Sir Jasper's death was from natural causes and probably occurred at around 7pm the previous evening. From the condition in which he was found, it would appear that he was pursuing his mission at the time of his death, although in the interests of propriety and national security, I believe that the precise circumstances should be withheld from Lady Charlotte-Georgina Speedicut, his family and the public.

I am arranging for Sir Jasper's body to be interred in a recently opened war graves site outside Paris. I trust that the Foreign Office will inform Lady Charlotte-Georgina that the return of Sir Jasper's body in wartime was not possible.

With sincere Brotherly feelings
I am, Sir,
Your Obedient Servant

Bertie of Thame
GCB GCMG GCVO
His Britannic Majesty's Ambassador to France

Of course, this stratagem would have failed if Speedicut had had luncheon with Sibella and Charles Holland as he had planned, because at least two people he knew would have seen him in London. So Flashman must have arranged for the luncheon not to take place, although how this was done remains a mystery. Anyway, whatever happened to Speedicut after he left Paris, it would seem that the family accepted the official line. This, at least, is confirmed by a plaque on the wall of St Giles Church, Wrexham:

To the Sacred Memory
of
Colonel Sir Jasper Speedicut, Baronet

Late of His Majesty's Tenth Royal Hussars (Prince of Wales's Own)
Knight Commander of the Royal Victorian Order, Grand Officer of the Legion of Honour, Knight of the Order of the Black Eagle, Knight Grand Cross of the Order of the Red Eagle, Commander of the Imperial Order of Our Lady of Guadeloupe, Commander of the Order of Franz Josef, Commander of the Order of the Redeemer, Servant of the Order of the Immaculate Conception of Vila

Viçosa, Commander of the Order of Medjidie, Hereditary Three-Tail Pasha of the Ottoman Empire and holder of many other Foreign Orders & Decorations
Soldier & Courtier
Who, during his life, carried out countless selfless deeds of Bravery on behalf of his Sovereign
and
Who gave his Life in the Service of his Country at her Darkest Hour
20th December 1821-1st April 1915
His body is interred near Paris
Dulce et Decorum Est Pro Patria Mori

So ended my quest to solve the riddle of the Ashby find through the editing of Speedicut's letters. On the journey, I have uncovered some fascinating insights into events of the nineteenth- and early-twentieth-centuries that have overturned - to the dismay of many - much received historical wisdom.

But the story does not end with the death of Speedicut, for I have recently been sent by Olga Lieven-Flyte, Duchess of Whitehall and Speedicut's great granddaughter, the unpublished memoirs of Charles Speedicut (né Holland) which cover the period 1915-1979. It will be interesting to see what scandalous revelations relating to the twentieth-century are contained within its covers...

CHRISTOPHER JOLL
www.jasperspeedicut.com

APPENDIX A: DICTIONARY OF
BRITISH BIOGRAPHIES

(This extract first published in the 2016 edition)

Speedicut, Sir Jasper Jeffreys, Baronet of the United Kingdom, KCVO (1821-1915), soldier & courtier, was born on 20th December 1821 at The Dower House, Acton Park, Wrexham, the eldest son of Algernon Jeffreys Speedicut and his wife Honoria. The Speedicut family claimed descent from George, 1st Baron Jeffreys, the seventeenth-century Lord Chancellor also known as 'The Hanging Judge', and enjoyed the status of minor gentry from the 18th century onwards.

Education, 10th Hussars & Central Asia

Jasper Speedicut was educated at Rugby School (1834-1839) where he was befriended by Harry Flashman (*ibidem*). In mid-1839, Speedicut's father purchased him a commission in the 10th (Prince of Wales's Own) Royal Hussars and he initially served with the regiment at Hounslow, Northampton and Dublin. In October 1841, following an incident with the Irish Nationalist group, the Young Irelanders, Speedicut was posted to India where he joined the staff of General George Pollock for the relief of Jalalabad. Later the same year, he was part of the force led by Captain Sir Richmond Shakespear formed to rescue the survivors of the retreat from Kabul held in Bamian. Speedicut was then tasked with assessing the fate of Lieutenant Colonel Charles Stoddart and Captain Arthur Conolly, who were being held by the Emir of Bokhara and was himself imprisoned by the Emir.

Early military career – India, Crimea, China & USA – and marriages

Following his escape from Bokhara, Speedicut spent time in continental Europe before re-joining his regiment in late-1844 prior to its posting to India in 1845. From 1845 to 1846 Speedicut was involved in the Sutlej campaign. On the death of his father, he took leave of absence from his regiment and went onto half-pay. He returned to Europe for the period 1847-1848 and assisted Prince Albert with the planning of the Great Exhibition (1851). In 1849, whilst in America on Great Exhibition business, he eloped with and married Lady Mary Steyne, only daughter of the 3rd Marquess of Steyne, and in late 1853 he joined Lord Cardigan's staff for the Crimean War. Whilst he was away in the Crimea, his wife died in childbirth along with the child she was carrying. After involvement in the Anglo-Persian War of 1856, by 1857 Speedicut was back in India where he became embroiled in the Mutiny. In 1860, he served with Captain Charles Gordon in the Second Opium War in China, returned to London in 1861 and married Lady Charlotte-Georgina FitzCharles, younger daughter of the 7th Duke of Whitehall. From late-1861 to 1863 Speedicut was in North America, where he fought on both sides of the Civil War. He was again in the United States in 1865, the year of the birth of his only child, Dorothea, and was present at the assassination of President Lincoln.

Overseas royal service – Mexico, France & Germany

In 1866, Speedicut was seconded by the British government to act as Equerry to the Emperor of Mexico and was involved in the downfall of the Mexican Empire and the execution of the Emperor Maximilian. He was appointed a Commander of the Imperial Order of Guadaloupe for his services to the Mexican Imperial Family. In the period 1870-1871 Speedicut served as an official government observer of the Franco-Prussian War and, somewhat unusually, received honours from both governments (Commander of the Legion of Honour and Knight of the Order of the Black Eagle). With the fall of the French Second Empire, Speedicut was instrumental in effecting the escape of the Imperial Family to England.

Further royal service – India and the Zulu War

Returning to regimental duty with the 10th Hussars in 1871, Speedicut came to the attention of the Prince of Wales, the regiment's Colonel, and was invited to join the Prince's staff for his tour of India in 1875. In 1879, Speedicut served in South Africa on Lord Chelmsford's staff and was present at the battles of Isandlwana and Rorke's Drift. He also witnessed the death of the Prince Imperial, son of Emperor Napoleon III.

Ongoing military career - Egypt & Sudan

From 1882 to 1885, with a brief interlude in Austria in 1883, Speedicut was for the most part in north Africa where he took part in the suppression of the Egyptian Revolt and witnessed the rise of the Mahdists in Sudan. In 1884, he was seconded to the staff of Major General Charles Gordon, with whom he had served in China, for the evacuation of Khartoum and spent a brief time in captivity as the sole survivor of Lieutenant Colonel John Stewart's party, which attempted to break through the besieging Mahdist forces. Speedicut managed to escape from the Mahdists and joined the relief force under the command of General Sir Garnet Wolseley.

Prince Albert Victor of Wales

On his return to England, Speedicut was appointed an Extra Equerry to HRH Prince Albert Victor of Wales (later HRH The Duke of Clarence & Avondale), eldest son of the future King Edward VII, with whom he served until the Prince's death in 1892. During this period, Speedicut's daughter married Prince Dimitri Lieven in Saint Petersburg. Speedicut was briefly in Bavaria in 1886 and in Austria in 1889 on detachment to the Austrian Imperial Family, service for which he was appointed a Commander of the Order of Franz Josef. From October 1889 to April 1890 Speedicut was "in waiting" to Prince Albert Victor during the latter's tour of India, before temporarily leaving royal service on the Prince's death in 1892.

South Africa, India and Sudan

In the period 1895 to 1896 Speedicut, initially on half-pay and then as an official War Correspondent, spent time in South Africa and was involved in the Jameson Raid and the 2nd Matabele War. From 1897 to 1899 he was once again in uniform as a War Correspondent for the Malakand campaign on the Indian North-West Frontier, then for the campaigns in Egypt and the Sudan, during which he was involved in the battle of Omdurman, and again in South Africa where he was captured by the Boers and escaped with his fellow captive, Winston Churchill (*ibidem*).

Boxer Rebellion & the siege of Peking

On his return to England in early 1900, Speedicut resigned his commission and, whilst on private business in China, became caught up in the Boxer Rebellion and was besieged in Peking. He returned to England in time for the death of Queen Victoria, re-joined royal service and had a minor but crucial role in the Queen's funeral and the Coronation of King Edward VII, for which he was appointed a Baronet of the United Kingdom. In 1903, he accompanied the King on his State Visit to Paris and, following the death of the King in 1910, he finally left royal service and was appointed a Knight Commander of the Royal Victorian Order by King George V in recognition of his past service.

Death

The closing years of Speedicut's life were not without incident as, on a visit to his daughter in Russia in 1908, he had an unfortunate entanglement with Rasputin, and in 1912 he survived the sinking of RMS *Titanic*. Colonel Sir Jasper Speedicut died at the Ritz Hotel in Paris on 1st April 1915; there is some evidence that he was there on government business.

Recent information

In 2011, written evidence emerged that Speedicut had been a lifelong member of a quasi-masonic group called The Brotherhood of the Sons of Thunder, an organisation operating at the heart of the British establishment, and that many of his exploits listed above were connected to this organisation. Known collectively as *The Speedicut Papers*, these documents also allege that Brig Gen Sir Harry Flashman VC was a fraud.

Printed in the United States
By Bookmasters